You Must Be from the North

You Must Be From the North

Southern White Women in the Memphis Civil Rights Movement

Kimberly K. Little

University Press of Mississippi
Jackson

www.upress.state.ms.us

The University Press of Mississippi is a member of the Association of American University Presses.

Copyright © 2009 by University Press of Mississippi
All rights reserved
Manufactured in the United States of America

First printing 2009

∞

Library of Congress Cataloging-in-Publication Data

Little, Kimberly K.
You must be from the North : Southern white women in the Memphis civil rights movement / Kimberly K. Little.
p. cm.
Includes bibliographical references and index.
ISBN 978-1-60473-228-3 (cloth : alk. paper) 1. Women, White—Tennessee—Memphis—Political activity—History—20th century. 2. Civil rights workers—Tennessee—Memphis—History—20th century. 3. Women, White—Tennessee—Memphis—Biography. 4. Civil rights workers—Tennessee—Memphis—Biography. 5. African Americans—Civil rights—Tennessee—Memphis—History—20th century. 6. Civil rights movements—Tennessee—Memphis—History—20th century. 7. Community life—Tennessee—Memphis—History—20th century. 8. Memphis (Tenn.)—Race relations—History—20th century. I. Title.

F444.M59A26 2009
323.092'2—dc22   2008044232

British Library Cataloging-in-Publication Data available

Contents

Acknowledgments vii

Introduction
TRASHING JIM CROW
The Sanitation Workers' Strike, 1968   3

Chapter 1
"YOU MUST BE FROM THE NORTH." "YES, NORTH MISSISSIPPI"
Women and Direct Action Protests, 1955–1964   11

Chapter 2
"ALL ARE WORTHY"
"Woman's Work" as a Catalyst for Civil Rights Reform   29

Chapter 3
"THE MESSAGE CAME ON A BEAM OF LIGHT"
Women in Religious Groups   50

Chapter 4
RAISING A GENERATION THAT DOES NOT HATE
The 1968 Sanitation Strike and the Radicalizing of Memphis Activists   64

Chapter 5
"LITTLE OLD LADIES WITH TENNIS SHOES"
The Relationship Between White Women and Racial Reform in a Post-King Memphis   87

Chapter 6
"BE THANKFUL IT WAS ONLY SAND"
Community Reaction to White Women in a
Movement for Black Civil Rights   110

Chapter 7
"I AM NOT YOUR SOCIAL CONSCIENCE"
Busing in the Memphis City Schools   128

Epilogue   145

Appendix   155

Notes   157

Bibliography   189

Index   215

Acknowledgments

I am grateful to a number of institutions and individuals who helped me through this long and difficult process. The staff and personnel of several archival collections deserve my thanks for assisting me in this project. Jim Cole and Ed Frank at the Mississippi Valley Collection of the University of Memphis McWherter Library, Wayne Dowdy in the History Department of the Memphis Public Library and Information Center, and all of the employees at the City of Memphis Archives not only helped me navigate box after box of source material, but also provided guidance and helpful suggestions throughout the research process.

I also owe an enormous debt to those women who shared their experiences and life stories with me in the course of my research. These women were patient and generous in their conversations with me, and they never failed in providing me with the name of an individual or organization that I had overlooked.

Several members of the Department of History at Ohio University deserve special mention for their assistance and encouragement throughout this endeavor. Sherry Gillogly provided assistance in maneuvering through the graduate program over the course of seven years while becoming a cherished friend in the process. My colleagues in the Women's Studies Program at Ohio University facilitated the manuscript revision process, fueling my late nights with plenty of laughter and kind words of support. I owe a tremendous debt of gratitude to Judith Grant, Jen Kanke, Lynette Peck, and Risa Whitson. Marvin Fletcher and Paul Milazzo also provided insightful comments on how to improve this work. In addition, Susan Burgess of the Women's Studies Program at Ohio University deserves special mention.

The community of friends who endured my alternating periods of jubilation and despair deserve many thanks for providing emotional sustenance throughout this process. Special thanks go to Cody Simpson Caldwell, Paul Chastko, Rick Dodgson, Jamie Fries, Brent and Renee Geary, Bonnie Hagerman, Korcaighe Hale, Sherry Hill, Bill Kamil, Henrik Laursen, Alex Liosatos, Keenon McCloy, Scott Martin, Anne Molineu, Elisa Spear Nabors, Mark Nabors, Tom Priggel, Trevor Ramsey, Kathryn Simpson, Erin Stanley, and Kirk Tyvela.

My family remains the true source of all my support and success. My sister and brother-in-law, Sherrie and Harvey Stafford, have encouraged and assisted me throughout this process; their children, Hunt and Halle, have enriched my life in ways I never thought possible. My "sister-in-law" Barbara Stafford and my uncle Cliff Lynch provided important social diversions in my numerous trips to Memphis and the Mississippi Delta, while Uncle Cliff also donned the hat of research assistant on several occasions. My father-in-law and mother-in-law, Blaine and Frances Beekman, and my stepson, Miller, also deserve special mention for their encouragement and support.

My greatest debt, however, is owed to four people: my colleague, Katherine Jellison, my parents, Glenda and Bud Little, and my spouse, Scott Beekman. Throughout our thirteen-year relationship, Katherine Jellison has inspired and encouraged me. Whether she suggested that I turn in my hat as a delivery driver and continue my graduate studies or forced me to write and rewrite the manuscript until it lived up to her "tough love" standards, "Dr. J." has earned my heartfelt thanks and respect. I can honestly call her my "academic mother." My parents, each in his or her own unique way, contributed to the writing of this book. Dad provided reliable transportation that could withstand countless journeys through Kentucky and Tennessee. However, the puzzled facial expressions and knitted brows he displayed when I informed him that the book was not yet done proved to be a most effective catalyst to completion of the work. My mother, especially, deserves an enormous amount of gratitude, not only for her suggestion that I focus my research on Memphis women, but also for her patience, words of encouragement, and "self-esteem workshops" when the road ahead looked too long. She remains my strongest ally and source of strength. My final and deepest thanks go to Scott Beekman, whose ability to muster up sarcastic comments in the margins of each chapter led to a much better book in the end. However, Beekman's role as my husband and closest friend is even more invaluable to me than his role as editor. Diversionary trips to the Bigfoot Conference and local wrestling events throughout southeastern Ohio were as important to the work as the research itself. I am eternally grateful to him for his sense of humor, love, and encouragement; I could not have written this book without him.

You Must Be from the North

Introduction

TRASHING JIM CROW
The Sanitation Workers' Strike, 1968

Echol Cole and Robert Walker died in a freak accident on 30 January 1968 while working for the City of Memphis Sanitation Department. Trapped inside one of the city's numerous archaic and dilapidated garbage packers, these men died a grisly death from injuries sustained while operating the machinery. Their fellow workers staged a walkout in protest of abysmal working conditions thirteen days later. Striking sanitation workers believed that a walkout would prove to be their only bargaining tool in an ongoing struggle between the public works employees and their employer, the city of Memphis, over issues surrounding better wages and the improvement of working conditions.

Mayor Henry Loeb refused to negotiate with the striking workers, due to his belief that the strike was an illegal one. A local court decision buttressed Loeb's belief in the illegality of the strike. According to a bill presented to the Chancery Court of Memphis, the strikers violated an injunction of 26 August 1966 that prohibited "employees of the Public Works Department of the City of Memphis . . . [from] striking against the City of Memphis." The ruling also applied to those "influencing, advising, coercing or directing employees of the Public Works Department . . . not to report to work in the usual and customary place and time." Loeb's lack of sympathy for the striking workers derived not only from his notions of the illegality of the strike, but also from his personal racial attitudes toward the overwhelmingly African American sanitation workers.[1]

The question of whether or not the city of Memphis would allow the American Federation of State, County, and Municipal Employees (AFSCME) to represent its sanitation workforce began as a dispute over working conditions, wages, and benefits. What initially appeared to be a question of union and labor rights quickly developed into a matter of racial equality. While national union officials of AFSCME maintained that the strike focused purely on a question of the legitimacy of its representing Memphis's sanitation workers, by the beginning of the second week of the strike, Memphis's local NAACP branch publicly stated its belief that the strike was inextricably linked to the fight for racial justice.[2] A 15 February 1968 statement from the Memphis branch of the NAACP introduced the issue of race into the situation in the following sentence: "[T]he type of work engaged in by these employees is only performed by Negro workers, [and] . . . the Memphis Branch NAACP calls upon the Mayor and City Council to act forthwith to eliminate these acts of racial discrimination and provide these workers with justice."[3]

As tensions mounted between labor officials and city government, and the strike negotiations seemed at a standstill, Memphis's black clergy reached out to its national network. After repeated pleas from religious leaders in Memphis to bring his name, influence, and inspiration to the city in an attempt to force city officials to end the sanitation strike, Dr. Martin Luther King, Jr., reluctantly entered the quagmire.[4] Memphis newspapers on 13 March reported that local Southern Christian Leadership Conference (SCLC) members had invited King to speak in support of striking sanitation workers later that week. The threat materialized into a reality when King made his first speech in Memphis on 18 March and called for a general strike. Within days, King led supporters of Memphis's sanitation workers on a march that became one of the more controversial and portentous of his career. The march on the twenty-eighth of that month became the first one he led that turned violent. It also became the only march in which King lost control of the crowd.

King viewed the Memphis sanitation strike as an appropriate location for the launching of his Poor People's Campaign (PPC). A project of the SCLC, the PPC had as its goal the amelioration of the problems of the country's poor, regardless of racial identity. Organizers planned to launch the project in late spring/early summer 1968. King believed that economic issues had bypassed racial ones in importance within the civil rights movement, primarily due to President Lyndon B. Johnson's shifting of federal funds away from his War on Poverty and into the space program and the Vietnam War. King argued that black Americans were disillusioned with Johnson's empty promises to help them and asserted that "bitter experience" had revealed that only "direct and dramatic" confrontation would sway the federal government to "correct a race problem."[5] For King, a strike of sanitation workers seeking recognition of their union offered the perfect opportunity to transcend his focus on rectifying the country's racial inequality and launch a campaign where race and class combined into one vast movement.[6]

Many Memphians believed that King's entrance into the city radicalized the leadership of the African American community. These leaders viewed King's appearance on behalf of a localized group of striking workers as legitimizing their cause, both locally and nationally.[7] Regardless of one's perspective, the 1968 sanitation strike brought Memphis, Tennessee, to the forefront of civil rights activities in the United States. Not only was the labor dispute one that resolved years of economic exploitation of Memphis's black municipal workers, but it also marked the end of a critical era in American history with the assassination of Dr. Martin Luther King, Jr. While the sanitation strike began as an attempt to address serious economic grievances among the city's sanitation workers, it quickly became an issue of civil rights.

Memphis's activist community joined the fray almost immediately, but the loudest voices of protest against the city's opposition to the strike emanated from the NAACP and Memphis's African American churches. While some African American women joined the activities of the white female activists that are the subject of this work, the majority of Memphis's African American female activists worked within the existing civil rights network dominated by African American members. Prior studies of Memphis during the 1960s have endeavored to examine civil rights activities in the city through the lens of these traditional organizations. And as the site of King's assassination, Memphis has a centrality to the struggle for racial equality that has resulted in a significant body of scholarship on the city. However, no previous study has focused solely on the role of Memphis's white female activists. As such, this work seeks to fill a hitherto unexplored gap in the voluminous historiography of Memphis during the tumultuous 1960s. These women operated in both leadership and auxiliary roles throughout the decade, serving as an important bridge between the African American and white communities. Their ties to Memphis's white political and social elite facilitated dialogues and programs denied to African American activists by the city's racial caste system. By focusing exclusively on the actions of this group of elite white women, I hope to build upon the existing work of such scholars as David Chappell and Mary Stanton on southern white sympathizers to the civil rights movement by examining their roles in the larger successes of the movement.[8]

I also do not want to minimize the work of African American female activists in both Memphis's and the larger civil rights struggle. Several works have initiated that process, namely Laurie Green's work on the Memphis movement and Sherry Hoppe and Bruce Speck's biography of Maxine Smith. I have maintained my focus here on white women specifically in order to tell this group's uniquely compelling story.[9]

During the first six weeks of the sanitation strike, few white women in Memphis voiced any consternation over it, save dismay at their own personal inconvenience. Yet one could see pockets of anger and embarrassment growing from Memphis's white community as the strike continued unresolved. It would take the growing spotlight of national media attention—and the entrance of King into the city—to force those in the middle of the road one way or the other.

Activists such as Jocelyn Wurzburg, Happy Jones, and Donna Sue Shannon point to the sanitation strike or, more dramatically, Dr. Martin Luther King, Jr.'s death as changing their worldviews forever. While some white women, such as Judith Sullivan, became involved in civil rights work after King arrived in Memphis, and the marches turned violent, many more did not begin questioning the city's racial problems until after his death and settlement of the strike. All the subjects of this study admit to experiencing an awakening of sorts after King's death. For those already involved in civil rights work, their time and personal commitment increased. For those women who had never volunteered for any civil rights organization, King's death was their impetus to join. Carol Lynn Yellin noted during an interview that she believed the strike and King's death rendered civil rights work a "respectable" endeavor for white Memphis women. Peggy Jemison went so far as to label these women part of the "silent majority," alluding to the moderate constituency President Richard Nixon claimed to represent in the 1968 election.[10] During the two years following King's death, Memphis's activist community, white and black, worked together to find answers to the questions raised about race relations in the city, namely the economic problems of Memphis's white and black poor, and the place of labor and union representation in a city, and region, traditionally resistant to organized labor. Perhaps due to the fact that private citizens and reformers alike feared Memphis's racial divide would widen after King's death, many reformers crossed racial and religious lines to build a new coalition of activists committed to constructing a better Memphis.[11]

Richard Pearce's 1990 film *The Long Walk Home* examines the 1955 Montgomery, Alabama, bus boycott through the eyes of two female characters, Odessa Cotter, a black domestic worker and boycott participant, and her white employer, Miriam Thompson. Soon after the start of the boycott, Miriam, faced with the prospect of having to perform domestic duties without the assistance of Odessa, begins driving Odessa to work each day. When Miriam's husband, Norman, discovers Miriam's activities, he condemns the boycott and Miriam's tacit acceptance of it, and forbids her to drive Odessa. Miriam justifies Norman's behavior to Odessa as typical of all the white residents of Montgomery, including herself, who are "scared" of what might result from the boycott. When Odessa counters that she too is scared, she also challenges Miriam to discover whether her fear stems more from who she is or who Norman wants her to be. The next scene features a defiant Miriam telling Norman that she will do whatever must be done to perform her job as housewife and mother to the best of her ability, including shuttling Odessa to and from work. Norman responds by moving out of the house, and Miriam increases her involvement in the boycott by driving in the carpool.[12]

This fictional scenario echoed the real-life experiences of white southern women who, like Miriam Thompson, began their journey into civil rights activism as a result of their commitment to traditional female roles. For example, apolitical endeavors, such as working on Memphis Junior League youth programs, propelled many of the subjects of the following study into civil rights activism. When faced with the realization that the number of black children taking advantage of these programs far exceeded the number of white children, these women began questioning this racial discrepancy, and their involvement in racial reform commenced. What originated as a way for them to engage in charitable work—society's prescribed public activity for white housewives and mothers—evolved into more substantive political action. These women, however, often paid a price for their newfound activism. Challenging the racial status quo was controversial for elite white women whose participation in political and social reform ultimately involved their stepping out of the traditional gender roles prescribed for women of the post–World War II era. Furthermore, daring to shake up the rigid racial lines that defined southern society was considered decidedly beyond the pale. Like the fictional Miriam Thompson, Claudia Davis and other women examined in this study began their adult lives conforming to the gender and racial standards of their time and region, but their conventional experiences ultimately led to a new gender and racial consciousness that ensured they would no longer be able to fulfill their prescribed roles so comfortably.

The following study will focus on a generation of female civil rights activists born between the two world wars and typically omitted from the historiography of the civil rights movement. Unlike the white women usually included in studies of the civil rights movement—college women who were born during World War II or in the early years of the postwar baby boom—the wives and mothers of Memphis did not jeopardize their lives by participating alongside black activists in sit-ins and freedom rides.[13] Older white women who were not in the front lines of the civil rights movement, however, deserve attention in a study of that movement. They may not have joined the dramatic wave of direct action protests that occurred in the early 1960s, but these women also aided in the movement's success. While involvement with groups devoted to feeding schoolchildren and integrating Bible study groups seemed apolitical on the surface, through these activities Myra Dreifus and like-minded activists experienced an awakening that led them to question the South's racial hierarchy and ultimately engage in actions that challenged the region's racial system more directly. Specifically, for white women in Memphis, Tennessee, their newly discovered commitment to civil rights contributed to the success of a key event in the movement's history—the city's sanitation workers' strike of 1968. This particular case study of white female contributions to the movement warrants attention if for no other reason than that Memphis marked the end of Dr. Martin

Luther King, Jr.'s life and career. Indeed, his death during the height of the sanitation workers' strike resonated so deeply with the subjects of this study that they could no longer ignore the racial caste system from which they benefited. King's death compelled them to some type of action, ranging from passive discussion to active protest.

In examining the civil rights awakenings and activities of Memphis's white wives and mothers, such as Jeanne Varnell and Selma Lewis, this study builds upon the work of historians including Amy Swerdlow and Nancy Cott, who have documented the manner in which white middle- and upper-class women born before World War II utilized maternalist rhetoric for political and social reform. While Cott's work on the history of the early twentieth-century feminist movement located much of the suffragists' initial political experience in volunteer organizations or religious groups, Swerdlow's examination of Women Strike for Peace detailed that group's ability to "politicize maternal values" in order to influence decision making at the federal level. Although the subjects of this study participated in a different movement altogether from Cott's and Swerdlow's subjects, their work followed a similar trajectory.[14]

The experience of the subjects of this study carved out a unique niche within the historiography of white women of the interwar generation in the civil rights movement. Whereas black and white activists from the North as well as black activists from the South were the shock troops of the movement, who engaged in high-profile sit-ins, freedom rides, and freedom school projects, white southern wives and mothers—some ten to twenty years older than the majority of white southern activists—offered a quiet, yet key alliance to the movement through activities deemed acceptable within the confines of the postwar domestic ideal. Their movement into working for racial equality came not from some catalytic event while witnessing police brutality on the street or reading of yet another lynching. Instead, these women came slowly and gradually into this movement, almost happening upon it accidentally while they collected food and clothing for the working poor and their children or shuttled children to and from local historical landmarks. Once arrived at their expanded consciousness through recognition of the systemic impact of racism on African Americans' economic, political, and social inequality, these women moved into action, using their greatest political tool, influence. The seemingly conventional behavior and activities of white women marked a campaign for change that white southerners resistant to racial equality could more easily accept when compared to the demands of their African American contemporaries. This reality further warrants the need for this particular study of white women singularly. The legacy of these women lies not only in their contributions to the struggle for racial equality, but also in their long-term, progressive influence upon the general social and political attitudes of the community most reluctant to grant either equal opportunity or a sympathetic ear to African Americans—the southern white elite.

Chapter 1

"You Must Be from the North." "Yes, North Mississippi"
Women and Direct Action Protests, 1955–1964

Often labeled the "most northern city in Mississippi," Memphis has historically attempted to distinguish itself from the rest of the Deep South. Pointing to its position as a business center, a city with a large black middle class, and a culturally thriving metropolis, Memphis prided itself on its progressivism throughout the racial struggles of the twentieth century. The first protests of the 1960s civil rights movement in Memphis mimicked those of Greensboro, Nashville, Atlanta, and Birmingham, in that participants were primarily young, black college students. While there were isolated instances where white individuals contributed to the demonstrations, white participation did not occur in the southern United States en masse early in the decade. Still fewer examples emerged of southern white women becoming involved in these protests.

An examination of the involvement of southern white women in direct action protests—such as sit-ins, freedom rides, and economic boycotts—across the South yields an amalgamation of ages and educational and socioeconomic backgrounds. Southern women such as Casey Hayden, Sara Evans, Joan Browning, and Mary King (activists known to scholars of white women's participation in the civil rights movement, yet who did not participate in Memphis's struggle) entered the movement while college students. Radicalized by realizations that their white southern experience contrasted with the harsh brutality of life for black southerners, these women joined specific religious, charitable, and student political organizations that focused on leveling the social, political, and economic playing fields for African Americans.[1] These initial steps into social reform began lifelong careers in civil rights work for all of these women. For the older generation of activists such as Sarah Patton Boyle, Virginia Durr, and Anne Braden, realizations of the hindrances that the nation's racial hierarchy engendered for black Americans came through similar channels, although these awakenings occurred later in life.[2] The face of the average sit-in participant in 1960 appeared youthful and African American; it did not appear white and middle-aged, let alone female. Although a minority, several key figures in Memphis's civil rights history, women such as Margaret Valiant, Marjorie Cherry, and the members of the Saturday Luncheon Group (SLG) began their journey into civil rights activism through participation in physically challenging segregation by moving into all-black housing projects and slowly yet steadily integrating Memphis's restaurants. Their stories add a different perspective on the contributions of white southern women to the civil rights movement, debunking the stereotype that only young white southerners participated in the movement's sit-ins.

High-profile challenges to segregation began with the 1954 *Brown v. Board of Education* decision that unleashed efforts to desegregate facilities, public and private, in Memphis, much as it did throughout the entire South. Attempts to desegregate facilities receiving public money were the first targets for Memphis activists in the 1950s. A challenge to Memphis's Jim Crow laws occurred nearly two years prior to the Montgomery, Alabama, bus boycott of 1955. On December 18, 1953, two "special officers" of the Memphis Railway System (MRS) boarded a trolley and "demanded" that two black passengers give up their seats to standing white men. A witness to the event—a "white photographer"—claimed that the officers used "abusive language" toward the black men.[3] When challenged by city officials and local black leaders, a spokesman from MRS said the officer in question had been "reprimanded" after an investigation into the incident—prompted by press coverage of the event—yielded positive evidence that the men had used "unnecessarily harsh language," and that said officer's handling of the event was "wrong."[4] Nonetheless, Memphis's Mayor Frank Tobey pressured MRS officials to investigate the incident as rumors began to develop that a leading African American community organization was planning a boycott of the trolley system.

Maxine Smith, executive secretary of the Memphis branch of the NAACP from 1962 through the 1968 sanitation workers' strike, asserted that Memphis was right in step with—if not a step or two in front of—the rest of the South during the civil rights movement. She put the NAACP squarely at the center of these protests in the 1950s—as well as those in the early 1960s—and credited Memphis with being even more progressive than the rest of the South in desegregation since all public accommodations had desegregated officially by 1964. She herself participated in several high-profile sit-ins at local department stores in the downtown area in 1962, lent her support to the integration efforts at the Memphis public library system in 1960, and attempted to integrate Memphis State College, now the University of Memphis, in 1957.[5]

Memphis's opening salvoes of the post-*Brown* civil rights period mirrored those of other southern cities: African American activists organized and dominated them with only a few rare exceptions. One such exception came from the work of Mary Frances Lacey, a white native of rural Mississippi and a recent transplant to the city. Lacey, executive secretary of the Memphis branch of the YWCA in 1958, suggested that local municipal leaders integrate the city zoo—although she maintained she acted independently of the YWCA and that her calls for integration stemmed from her own principles, not those of the YWCA. She recommended that the zoo extend the number of days per week that black Memphians visited from one to two; in addition, she requested that zoo officials designate one day per week when both races could visit the zoo together.

Lacey illustrated her belief that the only solution to the "race problem" was to "avoid . . . litigation and violence" through her attitude toward integration. She maintained that she would not pursue her idea any further if the city commission rejected it, which it did. Lacey vanished from the racial reform landscape after this isolated foray, yet white reformers in Memphis mimicked her nonconfrontational tactic throughout the 1960s. Although it would take another five years for public areas of Memphis to desegregate, Lacey's voice was a very early and prescient one. Methodical, gradual persistence in matters of racial inequality characterized white women's activist style until the 1968 sanitation workers' strike imbued them with urgency.[6]

Memphis finally witnessed the full desegregation of its recreational facilities in 1965, but not without enormous resistance from city commissioners and white Memphians. When the United States Supreme Court labeled Memphis's response to the Civil Rights Act of 1964 inadequate—officials proffered the implementation of a ten-year plan to desegregate recreational facilities—the city commission closed all municipal pools (and seventeen playgrounds) while the "immediate" desegregation took place. Response from Memphis's African American community was angry, due to the fact that the majority of visitors to the city's swimming pools were black residents. Yet Mayor Henry Loeb and his commissioners remained unmoved on this and many other issues related to racial equality. Many pools, playgrounds, and parks previously designated for black residents only remained closed throughout the year.[7]

The first term in office for Loeb (1960–1963) revealed the depth of his dedication to segregation and highlighted his intransigence on guaranteeing black Memphians equal rights economically or politically. Perhaps one explanation for how any civil rights statute made it into the law books during a period when such a problematic official occupied the mayor's office resulted from the composition of Memphis's electorate. According to NAACP Executive Secretary Maxine Smith, Loeb's first term in office coincided with a period in Memphis's history when black Memphians voted as a bloc for candidates who supported civil rights. She estimated the total black proportion of the voting public to be nearly 30 percent in 1961 and 1962, and posited that, although the NAACP had a significant amount of effectiveness in pressuring city officials to enact civil rights laws, the laws' success came more from the ballot than from any particular political or social reform organization and its activities.[8] However, Loeb continued to do all within his power to obstruct the implementation of desegregation laws, while he also dealt unsuccessfully and unreasonably with an early attempt by sanitation workers to unionize in 1962.[9]

Meanwhile, the sit-in movement that began in February 1960 in Greensboro, North Carolina, spread to Memphis by the middle of March that year. Much like the students from North Carolina Agricultural and Technical College, Memphis's first sit-in participants attended two local all-black institutions, LeMoyne College and Owen College. Yet, unlike the Greensboro sit-in demonstrations, civil rights protests in Memphis waged a two-pronged assault on the city's segregation policies.[10] Within four days in March, students attempted to desegregate Memphis's public libraries and art museum, as well as a popular lunch counter in the downtown business area.

On 18 March 1960 twelve students from LeMoyne and Owen began a sit-in at the lunch counter at McLellan's—a sundries store—on Main Street, the first demonstration of its kind in the city. As the students entered the store and took their seats at a lunch counter that catered to a white clientele exclusively, waitresses abandoned their posts and headed to the employee lounge, as per the plan previously arranged by store manager J. D. Fields. When one student asked for a cup of coffee to be served to him at the white counter, Fields refused to serve the student, insisting that the student move to the counter that serviced black patrons instead. Upon refusal of Fields's offer, the manager closed the lunch counter, then the entire store, when protesters refused to leave. Following the lead of student activists throughout the South, students sat "quietly reading" after the store's closing, awaiting the inevitable arrival of local law enforcement. Eventually, the arrival of local policemen prompted the students to vacate McLellan's and avoid arrest.[11]

Meanwhile, the second flank of these initial sit-ins occurred four days later, when police arrested ten additional students from LeMoyne and Owen at the Peabody branch of the Memphis public library after they took seats and began reading. Across town at the Brooks Memorial Art Gallery, police arrested another seven students who were looking at an exhibit and six additional students outside the building for "loitering."[12] Following these arrests, police commissioner Claude A. Armour made an official statement that Memphis had hoped to avoid "this type of unlawful demonstration," but that a plan existed in order to deal with it: protesters would—and did—face charges that included disorderly conduct, threatening to breach the peace, and loitering. Lawyers representing those students arrested believed that the key to a successful push for integration in Memphis rested in putting pressure on institutions that relied on financial assistance from municipal and state governments, thus justifying the dual attack on Jim Crow laws in Memphis. The push to integrate Memphis's retail stores, restaurants, and publicly funded institutions continued for eighteen months.[13]

While northern white student involvement in direct action protests in the South is well known and well documented, Memphis's experience ran counter to this trend. Although little documentation existed, anecdotal evidence reported a white student from Philadelphia becoming involved in a sit-in at a downtown restaurant in September 1960 as part of a larger sweep he made throughout the southeastern United States. However, this isolated incident fails to support the notion that white college students participated in large numbers in any of these early direct action protests in Memphis. Perhaps one reason for this lack of white student involvement in Memphis's sit-in movement lies in the fact that education at the college level remained segregated in the city until the fall of 1959, when Memphis State College allowed eight black students to enter that school as per a court decision handed down in 1958. Attempts began as early as 1954 to desegregate Memphis State, with Maxine Smith and Laurie Sugarmon—both black women—at the helm, but the school resisted until a federal judgment mandated desegregation in 1958. In response, the Tennessee Board of Education demanded a year's "cooling off" period between the court's ruling and the entrance of the first black students into the college.[14] Much like what happened in the integration of public accommodations city wide, institutions of higher learning reacted to invocations from the upper echelons of regional and federal governments instead of initiating change on their own.

Regardless of the rarity of white student assistance, at least one direct action protest figured white students prominently. In May 1967 a group of black and white Southwestern students attempted to integrate the Givens Steak House after proprietors of the restaurant had refused entrance to a black Southwestern senior, Lorenzo Childress. Marty Frich, a white student from Arkansas, recalled campus-wide resistance to the action, including the student government's official stand condemning it. This stand marked the second time the government had become active—or vocal—in matters related to any type of protest movement. The first incident revolved around the integration of the privately funded college itself two years prior, in 1965, when students came out in support of the move. In an interview with Southwestern students, debate swirled around the question of whether or not animosity to integration represented a majority opinion. One interviewee, Bill Casey, remarked that what animosity existed characterized a minority voice, although that voice sounded particularly "nasty."[15]

This 1967 sit-in occurred one year prior to the infamous sanitation workers' strike and three years after Memphis officially desegregated all public accommodations. Such an isolated, and somewhat tardy, protest begs the question of why students at this socially progressive college joined the bevy of 1960s protest at such a late hour. A later chapter will explore Southwestern student attempts at integrating several local religious groups prior to this 1967 event, so we know a history of activism existed on campus. Perhaps an apathetic press corps helps explain this omission, since white civil rights activism simply represented the exception, and not the norm, in the city of Memphis. Regardless of the reason behind this oversight, the middle years of the 1960s witnessed a ramping up of political activism from all quadrants of the population, including from a hitherto unseen and relatively quiet demographic, white female housewives and mothers. These women joined the fray in 1963, when twelve women, six black and six white, decided to meet together for lunch at a local restaurant that still abided by the South's Jim Crow laws.

This group of women, who named themselves the Saturday Luncheon Group (SLG), did not intend to turn the world upside down by marching on city hall or picketing local restaurants that refused to integrate. They merely aimed "to remove some communications barriers by having lunch together monthly."[16] This variation—or lack thereof—on the "ladies lunching" concept opened up a critical dialogue between two racially disparate groups of women and served as a quasi consciousness-raising experience for its white attendees. Organizers and participants, black and white, debated the significance of the group's impact on Memphis race relations, but its legacy lies in the imprints emblazoned on the lives of its white members. For some of the white participants, these casual integrated lunches blew the doors off years of racist indoctrination and led them to question the very core of their moral belief systems. These awakenings then progressed into full-fledged careers in antiracist activism and political reform.

Marjorie Cherry, who had moved to Memphis in 1958 with her husband and two daughters, and Ann Johnston, a native Mississippian, started the group in 1963 after Cherry mentioned to Johnston how much she missed her African American friends in Virginia.[17] Cherry hoped to expand her circle of friends to include more African American members. She considered herself to be a fairly progressive-minded thinker, due to both her upbringing—Cherry's mother forbade her children to use racial epithets—and to her past experiences in civil rights activities and organizations in Virginia, including the NAACP.[18]

Marjorie Cherry began her involvement in civil rights work in the mid-1940s in Charlottesville, Virginia, when she protested segregation laws in that state by sitting in the back of city buses and refusing to move to the front. Although Cherry acted alone and independent of any civil rights organizations in these protests, she acknowledged that she capitalized on a wave of protests occurring in Charlottesville in 1946 and 1947. Cherry combined these actions with letters to the Charlottesville newspaper criticizing Virginia's segregation laws, hoping that her letters would generate a modicum of local press coverage for all of the sit-in protests of the city. She noted that local police made no arrests in these early sit-ins, but they served as seeds of the larger direct action arm of the movement that began in 1960.[19] While a small ripple in the larger civil rights movement, Cherry's involvement symbolized an important moment in her own, personal evolution. She risked her reputation as a law-abiding, upper-class, "proper" southern woman in participating in these protests. The primary political weapon of women living between the first and second waves of feminism emanated from the influence their reputation and class status afforded them.

Criticisms often abounded when women in their middle years suddenly became immersed in civil rights work after years of devotion to husbands, children, and volunteer work with charitable organizations. Insinuations of both complicity and "white guilt" from either side of the political and racial spectrum hounded these women as they put their ideals into practice by challenging segregation laws. Cherry characterized her affiliation with the Charlottesville chapter of the NAACP as problematic. She recounted an incident in which she attempted to attend a meeting, but, upon arrival, found no one there. Upon inquiring, Cherry discovered that members had relocated the meeting, neglecting to inform her of the change. She pointed to this incident as an example of the resistance she met from black activists early on in her career. Although not critical of the organization, its practices, or its ideology, Cherry attributed this indifference from NAACP members to distrust of white involvement and its potentially corrupting influence.[20]

Cherry admitted to no remorse for taking so long in life to become involved in the struggle. She posited that she "had no choice" in refusing to move to the white section of the bus once she realized that the inequities between black and white southerners derived from the fact that for segregationists, white skin color carried a badge of merit and superiority to that of black skin. The 1896 Supreme Court decision *Plessy v. Ferguson* institutionalized this belief by relegating African Americans to a secondary status economically, legally, socially, and politically. Cherry embarked upon her personal journey through questioning the racial status quo in 1940 when a friend who had relocated to Michigan from Charlottesville introduced her to the word "Negro" as an alternative to racial epithets and talked to her about the struggle for equal rights. Cherry thought, at first, that these activities provided yet another example of black Americans acting "ungrateful" for all that white Americans had done in the wake of slavery. Yet she soon discovered, through reading and educating herself on African American history, that systemic white supremacy, not the inferiority of the black race, crippled African American advancements in the United States.[21]

After five years in Memphis, Cherry felt compelled to renew her commitment to biracial dialogue and activism. At Ann Johnston's suggestion, she and Cherry planned an informal gathering for lunch at Johnston's home. Both women concurred that they would each invite other women, black and white, to join them. The women included Rachel Powell, Mary Kay Tolleson, Ann Willis, Margaret Valiant, and Maxine Smith.[22] Due to the success of this initial meeting, the women decided to continue meeting once a month, alternating from one individual's home to another's.

Within a couple of months, the women dared to take their dialogue into the public sphere, and headed to the Wolf River Society, a members-only, all-white dining club catering to businessmen in the downtown area. Both Johnston and Cherry belonged to this elite dining club, and they felt entitled to bring along several black women on their quests. The Wolf River Society luncheon marked the opening salvo of this association of women, and it included a roster of some rather prestigious diners, including Maxine Smith. With little fanfare and hubbub, the women met, enjoyed a noneventful lunch, and decided to expand their operations to other restaurants throughout Memphis.[23]

After the initial meal at the Wolf River Society, luncheon group members targeted the Flame Room of the Downtowner Motel; the women received a warm and positive reception. Although members of the

Saturday Luncheon Group held their meetings at those restaurants that welcomed black Memphians only as employees, the initial response from proprietors appeared neutral, and, in some instances, quite positive. This fact does not obscure the reality that Memphis restaurants did not officially desegregate until 1964, nor did all restaurants open their doors to the women wholeheartedly. The group booked the Flame Room, for example, after three other, unsuccessful tries at making a dining reservation.[24]

Within a few months of its first meeting, word of the Saturday Luncheon Group spread throughout the city's black and white reform networks. The group received no publicity in the press, yet members continued to join, informed of meetings, their times, and locations from friends and/or colleagues. A member of the group from the mid-1960s, Judith Schulz Sullivan, called it a "very informal, loose group" where that week's "hostess" called members and gave them the time and place for the next meeting.[25]

The "hostess," or social chairwoman, did not decide times and/or locations of individual meetings.[26] One of the original members of the group, LeMoyne College graduate Lorene Osborne, recalled that although the white "hostesses" contacted the restaurants to reserve a space for the diners, each actual meeting had both a white and black hostess. The week's hostess called the agreed-upon restaurant, made the necessary reservations, and circulated the details to the rest of the group. Each member then called a few friends and associates, seeking out only those women who she believed would be sympathetic to the group's work. Each woman called whomever she pleased, including women who had never attended a meeting before or who were totally unfamiliar with other members or the activities of the group itself.

The idea behind creating an informal organization originated largely from individual members' family and personal commitments, and less out of concern/fear of community reprisals. In fact, the women "drew straws" to see who would be in charge of making the reservations and arrangements/initiations for the next meeting. Members recollected an arbitrary, certainly ad hoc manner in the choice of leadership positions, a hallmark of such national organizations as Women Strike for Peace (WSP). SLG's networking and informal organization mirrored that of WSP, and it illustrates the similarities between this local coalition of female activists and their contemporaries in other regions and reform movements. The uniqueness of the Memphis cadre of female activists, however, derived from the focus of their reform efforts; whereas WSP focused its efforts on pacifism, SLG members targeted civil rights.[27]

The informal nature of the group was the brainchild of Johnston, due to the fact that many of the white women involved articulated concern that they were growing increasingly more "outstretched" in their commitments, both to family and to social justice. Saturday Luncheon Group members ranged the gamut of the female identity. Some unmarried members devoted themselves full-time to work and community and social reform activism. Other members juggled the tasks of maintaining professional lives apart from their responsibilities as wives and mothers, while another faction engaged primarily in domestic endeavors, peppering their days with the occasional foray into meeting a biracial group of women for lunch. Although some members brought friends and neighbors who did not work outside the home, these women did not attend regularly; many women who did not take part in any other type of activism—either within their own communities or as members of volunteer organizations—often shied away from repeat appearances at meetings, fearing reprisals from families or friends.[28]

Judith Shultz Sullivan represented that component of the SLG whose professional and activist commitments complemented their responsibilities as wives and mothers. While Sullivan recognized an awareness of racism from an early age, she credited the SLG as a critical step in the development of her antiracist consciousness. Born in Waco, Texas, in 1939, Sullivan moved to Dallas at the age of seven, attending that city's public, segregated school system until her graduation in 1957. She pointed to her upbringing in the public school system as seminal to her racially progressive politics. Southern public schools rendered students impervious, in her view, to the elitism of her contemporaries educated in Texas's private school system. While segregation prevailed, Sullivan never heard her parents speak "disparagingly" about African American people as a group, but she overheard racial epithets in school and on the Dallas streets. The streets, Sullivan believed, taught her about racism through the derogatory comments directed at both African American and Mexican American residents of Texas. In fact, Sullivan realized from an early age that white Texans' animosity toward Mexican Americans emanated from the economic threat posed by their work to the white Texas hegemony.[29]

The 1954 *Brown* decision came and went without much attention from Sullivan. Her moment of clarity with regard to race relations occurred much earlier in her life, at the age of eight. At a department store in Dallas, Sullivan begged her mother to allow her to drink from the water fountain with the "colored" sign above it, thinking that the water would be colorful, and, therefore, somewhat special and unique. Sullivan considered this moment a pivotal one in her ideological evolution. Just as her mother failed to explain to her eight-year-old daughter how an urban department store needed two water fountains dispensing an identical product, Sullivan struggled to decipher why one person held another in disregard due to the color of her skin.[30]

The true turning point for Sullivan came in 1961, when she began teaching in the Dallas public school system after graduating from North Texas State. While working, Sullivan earned a master's degree in speech and drama, eventually becoming a debate coach. She credited her experience as a debate coach as the source of the ease with which she listened to both sides of an argument, a characteristic she found essential as the 1960s wore on and her commitment to social reform increased. Sullivan's involvement with the Saturday Luncheon Group flowed naturally from her vocation. Just as she saw her classroom as the perfect place for students from a variety of ethnic and socioeconomic backgrounds to come together, listen, engage, and confront current issues, the SLG mirrored that spirit of dialogue that Sullivan cherished.[31]

Judith Sullivan's recollection of the group's members sheds light on the overall socioeconomic characteristics they had. Sullivan accurately characterized the group as an inadequate and unrealistic representation of the female population, black and white, in Memphis, due to the fact that working-class black and white women did not attend lunches. Only those members of the black and white Memphis communities who had attained middle- and upper-class status participated; Sullivan observed that she did "not remember anyone's maid coming to a lunch . . . or the cleaning lady at school."[32] Sullivan's insights offer us a glimpse into the inner workings of a group consistently criticized for its elitism by many of its black participants, yet her comments emanate from the lips of a white woman from a working-class background. Sullivan's analysis adds depth to the complex legacy of a group praised for its prescience in exposing the hypocrisy of race relations to its contemporaries, the southern white elite, while vilified for falling back upon that elitism in its approach to integrating Memphis restaurants and the group itself.

Ideologically, the black and white luncheon group members believed integration was going to be "slow" in Memphis. Because the group let the targeted restaurant know, on the front end, that the luncheon would be integrated, many restaurants during the first two or three years of the group's existence claimed they had no reservations available. Margaret Valiant, one of the original members of the SLG, claimed that resistance to integration was there, albeit under the surface. She recounted a response she received from a "prominent local businessman" who was a member of the Wolf River Society when she told him of the group's plans to integrate that club. He responded, "Don't tell me you're going into any nigger-white lunch group!"[33] However, by the time Sullivan began attending the luncheons, after the legal desegregation of Memphis's restaurants, she did not perceive any open hostility to an integrated group eating, although cordial welcomes rarely greeted the women. Restaurants would accept the reservation, but "the service would be extra-slow. You know, the good ole passive-aggressive Southern way of doing things."[34] Although the group did not take any specific political positions, nor did they back any particular candidates in political races, many members interested in Memphis politics—as well as other subjects regarding political and social reform—engaged in debates about such issues over lunch. Sullivan reiterated the fact that the group did not have any sort of a political "agenda"; they simply coalesced around their shared interest in challenging the segregation laws regarding restaurants in Memphis. These disclaimers are identical in nature to those of WSP members, who, according to Amy Swerdlow, illustrated "politicized maternal values" in order to effect political change.[35]

Members agreed that these luncheons demonstrated that white and black women could sit together, enjoy a meal, and engage in lively conversation, without creating any sort of controversy or chaos in the outside world.[36] Although many members stressed the simplicity of the luncheons' conversations, all women examined in this study agreed that if discussions steered toward more controversial topics, no members shied away from such discussions. They intended not to confront directly, but to "demonstrate to other people that black and white women could sit and share a meal without anything terrible happening, and that [segregationists] should get more comfortable with that happening."³⁷ Members united in this simple characterization of the group's goal.

Regardless of the humble intentions of the Saturday Luncheon Group's founders and members, the official desegregation of the city's restaurants in May 1964 confirmed its success. Memphis Chamber of Commerce president Wallace Witmer released a statement that month announcing "more than one hundred Memphis restaurant owners have agreed to open their doors, regardless of race"; restaurant owners had done so at the behest of city officials, the Memphis Committee on Human Relations, and the chamber of commerce in an attempt to maintain the municipal peace.³⁸ While restaurant owners publicly made clear their unhappiness with desegregating—they felt the chamber pressured them into this move—city commissioners pointed to repeated picketing of segregated restaurants, as well as the efforts of the SLG, as justification for integration. The group itself endured for several years following the 1964 integration, and it experienced a groundswell in membership numbers during the sanitation workers' strike. By 1974, the mailing list had grown to four hundred names with fifty women declaring themselves official members, but community activism had replaced the initial goal of lunch hour integration as the focus of the group.³⁹

While the SLG's forays into integration garnered the lion's share of media attention focused on white female activism through utilization of the direct action approach, the flamboyant, controversial Margaret Valiant often took center stage in Memphis newspaper accounts of individual examples of local civil rights activism. Her personal act of direct action protest came in the form of moving into the LeMoyne Gardens housing project in 1963, and, by doing so, becoming the sole white individual to live there in the 1960s. Valiant asserted that she moved into LeMoyne Gardens because she grew tired of being prevented from visiting with African American friends in her own home. The 1963 March on Washington proved to be her breaking point, when she was not permitted to watch the march on the television in the lobby of the Allen Hotel where she lived. She moved out of the hotel the following day.⁴⁰

Born on 22 February 1901 in Como, Mississippi, Margaret Valiant Brahan credited her experiences in Europe and the northern United

States while studying music with broadening the limited horizons of someone like herself who had sprung from a rural, deep southern background. After the loss of her mother at the age of two, and because of her father's inability to care for her due to mental illness, Valiant relocated to Texas. She lived with an aunt there for the next six years, and returned to Mississippi to live in Plum Point to pitch in with the work on her cousin Annie Davis's cotton farm and attend the small, segregated, one-room school in Plum Point. At the age of thirteen, Valiant moved to Memphis, graduating from Central High School in 1917. Her move after graduation to Cincinnati, Ohio, to study voice and piano at the Cincinnati Conservatory of Music emblematized the birth of her awakening consciousness to the perilous circumstances created by racism.[41]

Through exposure to African American opera singers, intellectuals, and artists, both in Ohio and throughout her extensive travels in Europe, Valiant began challenging the racism the South had indoctrinated into her. Her interest in social reform accelerated after a brief marriage to Edward Mims, Jr., during the 1920s ended in divorce, and Valiant began work as a folklorist for the Agriculture Department's Resettlement Administration in the mid-1930s. While her involvement in racial reform did not begin officially until the 1950s and her return to Memphis, Valiant's activities in Washington, D.C., while working as an organizer for the National Youth Administration's youth symphonies, advocating for voluntary motherhood as a solution to the inequality of women to men, and developing a friendship with Eleanor Roosevelt, laid the foundation for her eventual foray into civil rights activism.[42]

Upon returning to Memphis in 1950, Valiant became involved in both community and political activism. She maintained memberships in several different organizations involved in civil rights work, and she also tried her hand at more traditional political reform by working to oust Mayor William Henry Crump in the city's mayoral election. The year 1950 marked a turning point for Valiant personally and politically as she grew increasingly invigorated in her dedication to political and community activism. By 1953, Valiant combined the physical act of integrating a segregated housing project with the cerebral satisfaction engendered by sharing ideas with other like-minded individuals. Her ideas about and analysis of the pernicious effects of racism developed and matured through her participation in a biracial discussion group at LeMoyne College.

LeMoyne College, located across the street from her home in LeMoyne Gardens, consisted of a student body of African Americans with a virtually all-white faculty pool. Faculty members created this discussion group in 1950 to encourage dialogue between the races, but Valiant believed that the group's effectiveness was minimal—due to the fact that the meetings received no publicity in the white press—and that her participation within it had little impact on race relations in the city. While her insights into the effect her attendance had on the relationship between the city's two races rang true, the group itself served the vital purpose of opening up conversation on various and sundry topics. A typical topic discussed in the LeMoyne group concerned an early 1960s boycott of the Memphis *Commercial Appeal* and the *Memphis Press-Scimitar* over issues related to courtesy titles for African American women. A female professor at LeMoyne, Juanita Williamson, contacted the publishing company of the papers, Scripps-Howard, and informed them that until print references to black individuals began with the titles "Mr." and "Mrs.," Memphis's black community was boycotting both newspapers. The boycott resulted in forcing both the *Commercial Appeal* and the *Press-Scimitar* to utilize courtesy titles when referring to married people of color. The papers did not, however, utilize courtesy titles for unmarried women of color. Nonetheless, the process of shattering the racial sexual double standard began with the revolutionary act of bestowing courtesy titles onto a group of women southern white journalists deemed unworthy of respect. Valiant did not discount this triumph, but she did maintain her skepticism—and rightly so—that white activists did much to implement this change. While the idea may have gathered steam from a biracial discussion group, black readers organized and carried out the boycott, and thus facilitated the victory.[43]

Valiant initially limited her public engagements with antiracist activism upon first moving to LeMoyne Gardens in part due to the unsurprising resistance she faced from both the white and black communities. Several of her neighbors believed her to be a "spy" from the welfare department, sent to check up on fellow residents to make sure they were abiding by all the stipulations mandated by the federal government to remain living in subsidized housing. The 1950s was an exceptionally volatile period in Memphis with regard to questions of housing and neighborhood segregation, so a white resident voluntarily living in a black neighborhood certainly warranted suspicion. Beginning in 1953, individual black families began buying homes in traditionally white-only neighborhoods on the heels of a recent Supreme Court ruling prohibiting racial discrimination in the buying and selling of real estate properties.[44] An interesting perspective on this situation came from the *Tri-State Defender*'s journalists who wrote that the reason why many of these families involved in the 1953 integration drive moved into formerly all-white neighborhoods was due to the fact that "unscrupulous" realtors had duped black buyers into purchasing homes in these areas. Indeed, a real estate company, the Weston Morgan group of Memphis, faced accusations of this very "crime" in the wake of a bombing in early July. Death threats, bombings, arson, and verbal and physical harassment during the first year of this push toward integration prompted city officials to become involved by increasing police patrols in those neighborhoods where integration occurred. This climate created the mixed responses Valiant encountered upon arriving at LeMoyne Gardens, yet she remained. As the years progressed, so did Valiant's involvement in the civil rights movement.

By the early 1960s, Valiant had gradually increased her activities in the civil rights movement, and her dedication throughout the decade culminated in her participation in several of the marches and mass meetings held during the sanitation strike in 1968. In 1963, however, Valiant virtually stumbled into a sit-in at a Walgreen's drugstore. She joined one of the students at the lunch counter for a cup of coffee, yet, not surprisingly, failed to receive service. Amid taunts of "nigger lover" hurled at her by white youths protesting the sit-ins, Valiant approached a white female clerk to purchase a package of cigarettes. The young woman remarked, "You must be from up north." Valiant responded, "Yes, north Mississippi."[45]

Although Valiant's response was not as radical, organized, and aggressive as those of her young contemporaries throughout the South, the ideas she embraced and put forward in her daily actions had much in common with her contemporaries in Memphis during the 1950s and early 1960s. The 1968 sanitation workers' strike radicalized countless Memphians of all races and ages, yet quiet, methodical protests, enacted both by individual members of the white and black communities and by Memphis chapters of the Fellowship of Reconciliation, Congress of Racial

Equality, National Association for the Advancement of Colored People, Southern Christian Leadership Conference, and Student Nonviolent Coordinating Committee typified Memphis's civil rights movement prior to 1968.[46] A city with its fair share of serious racial problems, due to the intransigence of the white community to give in to any demands from the federal government to implement its legislation posthaste, Memphis mirrored the rest of the South in the tenor of its movement for racial justice. White female participants in direct action protests surfaced sporadically, in isolated, quiet pockets, but they nonetheless exerted an influence on the movement by making small inroads within both the white and black communities. Memphis's white female civil rights activists entered the public arena of the movement through the back door, through volunteer and religious organizations. They faced resistance from all quarters, white and black, as they broke through these barriers to challenge a status quo many of them had accepted unquestioningly their entire lives.

Chapter 2

"All Are Worthy"
"Woman's Work" as a Catalyst for Civil Rights Reform

Married middle- and upper-class white women of the postwar period filled the role of volunteer worker regularly. American society praised housewives and mothers who transplanted their nurturing, maternal abilities from the home and hearth into the public sphere. For some women, this volunteer work took the form of wage earning in the fields of social work or education, and for others, it evolved into tangible political activism. Women activists since the beginning of the twentieth century often began their careers in reform work through involvement in volunteer organizations devoted to causes superficially deemed "nonpolitical." Nancy Cott's research on the growth of the feminist movement in the 1920s placed the League of Women Voters firmly within this tradition. Cott asserted that dismissing women's activities within volunteer organizations as nonpolitical discounted activities that consumed female activists prior to their acquisition of the vote in 1920. If such activity were nonpolitical, therefore, the work of women such as Florence Kelley, Eleanor Roosevelt, and Rose Schneiderman in the early decades of the 1900s—endeavors that yielded concrete, protective legislation for female workers in industry as well as federal programs guarding the health and welfare of women and children—had no political relevance.[1]

The problematic notion that acquisition of the vote marked the entry of American women into the political sphere belied the reality of female activists before and after 1920. Society condoned the activities of women who contributed their free time to volunteer work as long as husbands, homes, and children remained their first priority. As Cott and other scholars discovered, volunteering for causes easily construed as charitable and benevolent often safely disguised women's political work. Indeed, for many female volunteers their devotion to volunteer work simply served as a launching pad for more overtly political activities, including civil rights work.

The life and career of Virginia Foster Durr provide an excellent illustration of the historical trend observed among women active in volunteer work who eventually move into activities more squarely within the formal political arena. A woman situated in the center of the civil rights movement through her involvement with Dr. Martin Luther King, Jr., and the Southern Christian Leadership Conference, Rosa Parks, Ella Baker, and the students of the Student Nonviolent Coordinating Committee (SNCC), Durr and her exceptional life deserve a brief mention in an analysis of elite white women's work with volunteer organizations.

Born to an upper-class family of former slaveholders and planters from Alabama, Durr entered higher education at prestigious Wellesley College in 1921, becoming aware, for the first time, of the uniqueness of—and the problems with—her upbringing as a southern woman. Durr wrote in her autobiography of the "first time . . . my values had ever been challenged" when she faced the decision of either dining with black women in the cafeteria or facing expulsion from the college. Her roommate pointed out that Durr had no problem showing affection to the black men and women who had worked for her family, serving as her nursemaid and cooking her meals, but was quite irrational in her refusal simply to eat in the same room with black students.[2]

Durr's volunteer work began during the 1930s, when she worked with the Birmingham, Alabama, chapter of the Red Cross. She viewed this move as the next natural step from her membership in the Junior League, unaware of the role such volunteer work would play in her trajectory into civil rights activism. Within two years, Durr and her husband, Clifford, relocated to Washington, D. C., and Durr's career in volunteer and political organizations exploded. She worked with Eleanor Roosevelt in the Women's Division of the Democratic National Committee when that division was in the process of implementing gender parity within Democratic Party committees. It was through this group that Durr first became interested in amending the poll tax laws throughout the South. Her intentions, however noble, centered less on the unfairness of the poll tax to black southerners and more on the impediment the poll tax presented to white women interested in casting their votes in local southern elections.[3]

Durr's integration into civil rights work came slowly. She began working with labor organizations, limiting that involvement to groups aiming to ameliorate the poverty of southern whites. Her association with the Southern Conference for Human Welfare (SCHW) marked the beginning of her work with integrated groups. A disparate collection of fifteen hundred reformers, from southern "New Dealers" to civil rights activists, met in Birmingham in November 1938 to formulate a plan to address the South's economic situation and the federal government's apparent neglect of that problem. The infamous Eugene "Bull" Connor attended the meeting, hoping to enforce Birmingham's segregation laws. When Eleanor Roosevelt refused to sit in the center aisle of the auditorium—and respect the city's segregation laws—Connor failed to arrest her. Durr pointed to this episode as another impetus for her ideological shift from labor to race: "I c[a]me around to thinking that segregation was terrible. Just by osmosis really."[4]

The SCHW focused initially on the abolition of the poll tax as one of several issues, yet, within three years, the issue of the poll tax dominated the work of the conference, and led to an organizational split in August 1941. Durr became vice-chair of the National Committee to Abolish the Poll Tax (NCAPT) at that time. By 1948, both the SCHW and the NCAPT were defunct, primarily due to consistent red-baiting of members. Accusations of Communist tendencies squelched the activities of these groups and Durr's volunteer work as well. During the decade of the 1940s, Durr worked with several groups considered to be "Communist" by forces within the federal government, including the Women's International League for Peace and Freedom (WILPF) and the Highlander Folk School. Although she temporarily left the WILPF during World War II, Durr launched a failed attempt to organize a chapter in Montgomery after the war that would focus on civil rights work. Durr believed much of the animosity she faced within her own community came from her association with these groups, both frequent targets of anti-Communist forces of this era.

The next journey she embarked upon began with Rosa Parks's arrest in 1955, and from that point on, Durr devoted much of her energy to the civil rights movement.[5] Durr's life provided a model of the typical white southern female activist involved in the civil rights movement in that her initial steps into reform came from involvement in groups that did not have racial reform as the focus of their activities. Certainly not all of the women involved in volunteer work in Memphis during the 1960s moved into civil rights work; indeed, few did. However, several key figures in Memphis's civil rights movement got their start in activism by working as volunteers with local community groups. Three women in particular, Frances Coe, Myra Dreifus and Anne Shafer, became formidable and vocal opponents of the South's racial hierarchy in the 1960s, yet they began their careers as volunteers who assisted and fed needy schoolchildren and who beautified the city.

Frances Edgar Coe laid the foundational infrastructure Myra Dreifus needed to launch her campaign to help Memphis's hungry, primarily black, schoolchildren. Coe's attempts at assisting underprivileged children began in 1955 when she campaigned for a seat on the Memphis Board of Education. A native of Memphis, this Vassar College graduate announced a campaign platform that included attempts at decreasing the average size of schools, classrooms, and districts, allocating additional money and manpower earmarked for children with special physical and emotional needs, as well as the addition of cultural coursework, such as art and music, and physical education. The key to improving educational standards in Memphis's schools, according to Coe, lay in increasing teacher salaries, accomplished by adding only "a few pennies to our school tax." Although many of Coe's critics—and school board members—warned that this call for additional "pennies" portended bigger tax increases in years to come, Coe persisted, running for one of sixteen possible seats on the Memphis school board in 1955 in the first school board election after the demise of the local Crump machine and the termination of Crump's policy of appointing members to the school board.[6] Although many board members and local politicians considered Coe quite a controversial figure, her success in persuading reluctant board members to adopt her ideas, regardless of the political outcome, remained evident through the six terms she ultimately served on the board.

Frances Coe enjoyed a substantial public career prior to her election to the Memphis school board. As the granddaughter of a former president of the University of Arkansas, Coe recalled intellectual pursuits and conversations on politics and literature permeating her childhood memories. She attended Miss Hutchison's School for Girls, a private college preparatory school for the children of Memphis's wealthier classes, before entering Vassar College in the middle 1920s. While Vassar opened her eyes to social work through her experiences working at a settlement house in Poughkeepsie, Coe also had an interest in the law. She attended law school for one year before deciding law was not the career for her. She wrote for the society pages of the Memphis *Commercial Appeal* during the 1930s. When editors turned down her request to do more substantial pieces on "women's news," she resigned that position, disappointed in not receiving more substantive assignments. Coe claimed that her resignation stemmed from the nation suffering under the grip of the Depression, and, due to her financial situation, she "thought that other people needed the job more than [she] did." Soon thereafter, she married Lawrence Coe, yet, unlike many of her southern contemporaries, she did not abandon her career aspirations for marriage and family. She enrolled in the graduate program in education at Memphis State University, seeking to broaden her educational horizons with an additional degree, while also continuing the community activism she had begun while a student at Vassar.[7]

While Coe credited these early experiences in community activism as awakening her desire to become more involved in volunteer work, her experiences in Memphis during the 1930s and 1940s gave form and purpose to those desires, particularly in the area of helping Memphis's mothers and children. She cofounded the Memphis Maternal Health Association in 1936, becoming that group's vice president in 1940. This group consisted of female volunteers who staffed a free clinic at the John Gaston Hospital in order to provide new mothers with education on nutrition and child care.[8] Coe's work with birth control advocate Margaret Sanger in 1939 stemmed from many of these concerns for women and children. Indeed, Coe tied the misery of women struggling to find food and housing in the wake of the 1939 flood of the Mississippi River to their inability to adequately control their fertility. The inaccessibility of birth control not only created economic hardships for local flood victims, Coe believed, but for their children as well.[9]

Coe embarked upon graduate work in Memphis State's education department during the 1940s, persuaded the Memphis YWCA to integrate in 1940, served as president of the local Planned Parenthood organization, and was the vice president of the Memphis branch of the League of Women Voters at the end of the decade. She kept her foot firmly planted in traditional social work throughout this decade, serving as a citizen investigator of the removal of the Tennessee Department of Welfare's Shelby County office director, Mrs. Garnett McNeil Cooper in 1949.[10] From her public statements in support of women taking up arms if necessary to contribute to the war effort during World War II in 1941 to her championing women's participation in electoral politics in 1950, the decade of the 1940s marked Coe's bold steps away from advocating for improving the lives of mothers and their children and marching toward active political engagement.[11]

Coe's contribution to Estes Kefauver's 1948 campaign for the United States Senate proved monumental to this political evolution. As a member of the Women's Executive Committee of the Shelby County Citizens Committee for Estes Kefauver, Coe publicly spoke often in support of Kefauver's candidacy—the campaign was an attempt to break the domination of the Crump machine in west Tennessee—imploring both women and men to vote for someone uninfluenced by party politics, regardless of accusations circulating that he sympathized with Communists. Indeed, Coe believed that Kefauver's election, and his plans for reforming government once in office, protected the nation and the state of Tennessee from the alleged Communist threat.

Coe followed up her work with the Kefauver campaign with a trip to the 1952 Democratic National Convention, serving as a delegate from the state of Tennessee. While these early forays into decisive political organizing whetted her appetite for political work, she nonetheless maintained that her interest in running for the school board position came strictly from her desire to improve the school system once her own children had reached school age. Evidence of Coe's altruism revealed itself during the campaign for her second term on the school board. She argued that school board members perform their work without any financial compensation, volunteering their time out of a personal commitment to improving the lives of Memphis's schoolchildren.[12]

By the time she arrived on the Memphis school board in 1955, Coe's concerns focused primarily on resolving the inequities between Memphis's black and white schoolchildren. Within a few years, Coe expanded her rhetoric, linking inadequacies in educational opportunities to continued racial inequality and America's losing position in the cold war struggle for victory in the space race. In order to appeal to a white constituency that resisted equitable distribution of school resources to black and white children, Coe argued that increasing city allocations to the city school budget helped the school board better educate its students, by enhancing its math and science curricula in all its schools.[13]

She strove to insure that those black students attending segregated schools had access to the same materials as their white counterparts. Her investigations into these problems led her into work with the federal government's school lunch program, first proposed in 1946. The Fund for Needy Schoolchildren (Fund), Myra Driefus's central project throughout the 1960s, had its roots in this early program. A free breakfast program would also emerge from this early free lunch program. An early predecessor to Dreifus's Fund, this plan was patterned after a similar program in Kansas City that fed hungry schoolchildren before and during regular school hours. Initially, funding came from the Memphis school board, but the Better Breakfast Club, a group of private financial backers, began providing additional funds to offset some of the board's expenses.[14] These early efforts failed in the short term, but they established legal precedents and networks of donors that Myra Dreifus capitalized on in 1964.

Frances Coe's motivation behind her work with the Memphis school board stemmed from her desire to help Memphis's poor schoolchildren. Radicalized by her activism at Vassar, Coe believed she could effect positive change within Memphis's school system through her work on the school board. Coe dedicated herself to improving the environments of schoolchildren in the South, a safe and socially acceptable cause for a female reformer living in that region. In the process, Coe expanded educational opportunities for African American schoolchildren, since they constituted the majority of the recipients of these government-funded programs. Family contacts, personal financial resources, and influence allowed Frances Coe to occupy a valuable place in the history of Memphis's civil rights movement through her ability to provide the framework necessary for Dreifus's work with poor schoolchildren. Dreifus's actions on behalf of Memphis's poorest children, in turn, launched Dreifus's own civil rights activism as she continually confronted the connections between institutionalized racism and poverty and hunger.

Myra Finsterwald Dreifus's own plans for feeding Memphis's schoolchildren materialized in October 1963. Born in Flint, Michigan, in 1904, Dreifus graduated from the University of Michigan and completed some graduate work at the Merrill Palmer School—keeping her studies focused on "early growth" and child development—before moving to Memphis in 1936 after her husband had painstakingly researched which city would be the proper location for him to start his own jewelry business. Dreifus noted that she and her husband consciously chose Memphis over Terre Haute, Indiana, specifically because of what she described as the "positive" climate in the city for Jewish individuals. She admitted a degree of initial reluctance in moving to the South, due primarily to the region's racism, yet Dreifus viewed the relocation as an opportunity to continue the activism begun in Michigan—she served as chairperson of the Big Sister Project in Detroit (a combined effort of the Jewish Children's Bureau and the Council of Jewish Women) where she received much of the organizational training crucial to her later work—in Memphis. Dreifus immediately noticed upon her arrival in Memphis that while the population exhibited less racism than the one she had observed in Terre Haute, racism persisted.[15]

Dreifus described herself as a woman who liked the "creativity of something." She preferred dedicating her time and energy to a project in peril or disrepair, ironing out the imperfections, then passing the reins to another and moving on to some other project. Her work in the 1940s and 1950s included volunteering for the Memphis Junior Red Cross, the Board of Integration Service—a group that endeavored to "facilitate legally required school integration"—and the National Council of Jewish Women. She worked as a nurse's aide with the Red Cross during World War II and became president of the Junior Red Cross in Memphis in 1953. After that organization's chairman resigned due to Dreifus's persistent attempts to integrate the group, Dreifus served as president of the Junior Red Cross for three years, running an integrated organization and staff for the duration. Her lifelong crusade for children's nutrition and health began in the 1960s when she volunteered at the John Gaston Hospital's African American children's unit. She served as president of the Memphis Mental Health Association (MMHA), an organization that she cofounded. Dreifus's stint with the MMHA lasted five years and coincided with her work with the Fund as well as with her service as a board member of the Memphis Jewish Community Center.[16]

In October 1963, while working with the MMHA, Dreifus accepted an invitation from Frances Coe to attend a meeting of social workers from the Memphis area where Hollis Price, president of LeMoyne College, delivered a speech in which he discussed the plight of the American poor. Dreifus, shocked by what she learned at this meeting, embarked upon a search for the facts surrounding Memphis's free lunch program; she began at the Tennessee Department of Public Welfare.[17] Representatives from that agency shared data with her regarding the thousands of Tennessee children who had neither the money nor the means to eat lunch at school, regardless of the existence of a federal agency ostensibly created to deal with this problem. Dreifus's disgust with the allegation that the state's welfare department and school systems knew of this problem, yet neglected to rectify it, mobilized her to seek solutions independent of government agencies. She began questioning school officials as to the validity of these assertions, funding herself with financial support and logistical assistance from the Memphis Health and Welfare Planning Council. Problems quickly arose, however, due to the hesitation of several principals from schools receiving federal aid to talk frankly with her. Dreifus remarked that the only accurate answer she received in this early period came from a former principal unaffiliated with the school or program, who confirmed Dreifus's worst fears: the school system refused to utilize funds earmarked for feeding poor children, and no federal agency lifted a finger to help.[18]

The problem Dreifus discovered with feeding Memphis's schoolchildren stemmed from the age-old southern aversion to federalism. The Department of Agriculture gave Memphis just over 50 percent of what it needed per plate, per child for lunch, supplementing these contributions with a pittance for "milk money." The Memphis Board of Education made up the financial difference at the local level, yet it was reluctant to expend its own money for programs that primarily targeted the city's black schools. Dreifus uncovered another disturbing discrepancy as well.

The Department of Agriculture claimed that the state of Tennessee had returned some of the designated funds over the previous couple of years, arguing they were not needed, which, in turn, led to a lower allocation the following year, and so forth. This pattern persisted throughout the early years of the Fund's existence, continuing as late as 1967.[19] Of the forty thousand schoolchildren eligible for free lunches in 1964, only seven hundred actually took advantage of the program. Furthermore, school officials forced those children who did not qualify for free lunches, yet could not afford to eat during the lunch break, to remain in the cafeteria throughout the lunch period, surrounded by food unavailable to them. Dreifus noted that this "discovery . . . haunted" her.[20]

Armed with these alarming facts, Dreifus and her friend and fellow activist Selma Lewis, along with eleven female volunteers from the Tennessee Department of Public Welfare, formed the Food for Fitness program and began offering their assistance with staffing these lunch programs to local principals whose schools received federal lunch money.[21] Four such schools existed in 1964; by 1965, an additional ten schools met the school board's criteria for eligibility. Membership grew through a grassroots organizing process. New members attended meetings through invitations from veteran members; those new members invited someone new to the next meeting, and so forth. When the loosely organized group of black and white women began in 1964, it focused its efforts on ensuring that schools utilized the appropriate funds allocated to them by the federal government in order to provide nutritional, healthy lunches to qualified children.[22]

Funding came from private donors, religious organizations, and community sources locally, and the addition of Selma Lewis to this project certainly did not hurt. Elected the first female president of Memphis's Jewish Family Services in 1962, Lewis graduated with a bachelor's degree from Vanderbilt University in 1942 and earned her doctorate in history at the age of fifty. Lewis's influence within Memphis's Jewish community, and its attendant network of charity associations, helped in the solicitation of funds and membership necessary for the Fund's survival.[23] Dreifus also tapped into a national network that contributed to groups around the country trying to achieve goals similar to those of the Memphis group. The Lilly Fischer Memorial Fund based in Cleveland, Ohio, in particular, contributed a significant amount of money to the group in its early years. Nonetheless, donations for items from stationery to gas money came primarily from local, private donors.[24]

Bureaucratic constraints compounded monetary issues and impeded the plans of the women of Food for Fitness from the outset. The Department of Agriculture allocated money to individual students only after parents completed applications for their children. Principals either approved or denied the applications and sent those approved to the school board for final authorization. Dreifus and her initial volunteers began visiting parents of eligible schoolchildren and assisting in the process of completing the applications. Problems related to these applications were numerous. Application questions ranged from the benign—such as the father's name and place of employment and number of children living in the house—to the bizarre: "Does Father or Mother drink and/or smoke?" "Does family have a radio? Television? Automobile?" The school board often rejected applicants if one of the parents smoked cigarettes or drank alcohol, regardless of the principal's recommendation. The school board approved other applicants merely on the basis of the legibility of their handwriting; board members theorized that legible handwriting equaled literacy.

The applications attempted to sort out the supposedly "worthy" poor from the "unworthy" poor, and those families deemed "unworthy" became ineligible for assistance. The social and public welfare system in the United States differentiated recipients of assistance into the categories of "worthy" and "unworthy." The justification for this designation stemmed from the nation's earliest policies regarding federal assistance to veterans, widows, and mothers. Public and private agencies considered only those individuals who had truly fallen upon hard times due to circumstances beyond their control—disability caused by injuries incurred during military defense of one's country, death of a spouse—eligible for financial relief.[25]

Entry into these homes stirred the program's initial volunteers to action. Members recognized the outrageous and unscrupulous manner in which board members decided which students would and would not receive free school lunches. With Frances Coe at the helm of the Economic Opportunity Act's Memphis chapter of its antipoverty program in 1965, these reformers had an added edge in the fight against poverty. Recognizing the abject poverty so many of these children and families suffered, and equipped with statistical data to corroborate their claims, these women broadened the scope of Food for Fitness, changing the name of the group to the Fund for Needy Schoolchildren (Fund) as well as changing the group's goals. Volunteers funneled money into providing children with free lunches, but they also began distributing free and discounted shoes, coats, and clothing. Dreifus noted that the apparently arbitrary manner in which the school board selected children for the free lunch program contributed to her cynicism and suspicion surrounding the school board's allocation of these funds. She claimed these early realizations only fueled her desire to force the school board to distribute as much federal money as possible to Memphis's poor and hungry schoolchildren.[26]

In 1964, Selma Lewis implemented the Lend-A-Hand Club, where the mothers of children participating in the free lunch program received donated clothing items. Upon arrival, white volunteers from the Fund offered assistance in demonstrating how to sew on a button or mend a hem—"basic housekeeping skills"—to these mothers. Initially, meetings were held once a month, with the principal of the school, the school's PTA president, and a teacher always in attendance. Subjects covered at these meetings included basic nutritional information, workshops on sewing and knitting, suggestions on how to stretch a limited food budget by using alternative proteins to meats, and education regarding the food stamp program, complete with representatives from the Memphis welfare office.[27]

Regular attendance marked these early meetings in 1964, but by the end of the year, few women appeared. Lewis observed that the educational programs were relatively unsuccessful at this time as the result of "intimidation" and suspicion. Lewis acknowledged the problems inherent in teaching these particular "skills" to a group of impoverished women. She noted that the idea for teaching these skills came first from the principals of the schools/children involved, many of them African American. Lewis argued that these officials claimed donated clothing items would never last as long as needed because recipients were unaware of how to repair them. Although the validity of this claim has not been verified, it is important to point out that Lewis correctly recognized the criticisms such paternalistic behavior warranted, especially if one considers the racial makeup of the parties involved—white instructors who gave domestic advice to a predominantly African American group of women. It was just these types of activities that contributed to the chilly climate between black and white female baby boomers who organized for civil rights, as discussed by such authors as Lynne Olson.[28]

Both Lewis and Dreifus understood those black critics who labeled them paternalistic. Dreifus credited the problems in 1964 as coming partially from local principals, suspicious of these "white do-gooders" from the suburbs, as well as members of the school board whose sheer racism impeded the Fund's progress and the flow of money into its programs. Undeterred, the women of the Fund and their programs continued. However, by 1965, control of these groups transferred over to neighborhood women of these communities and schools, where they continued a modified version of the Lend-A-Hand programs for the duration of the Fund.[29]

By 1968, Dreifus continued to steer the Fund into numerous activities throughout Memphis and surrounding Shelby County aimed at ameliorating the hunger of Memphis's schoolchildren, and the group also moved into addressing other problems associated with poor diet. The Fund expanded that year to offer free breakfasts for children who qualified (the first year of the free breakfast program saw one school enrolled, and the following year an additional ten schools joined the program). That same year, private donors financed an elaborate transportation system for program participants. Fund volunteers provided transportation to and from free medical, dental, and psychiatric care, as well as offering transportation to locations where participants selected free shoes and clothing. A group called Faculty Wives and Women, which was a collection of area professors and spouses, together with the wives of local physicians donated their services to a tutoring program for Fund participants. Finally, private donations to the Fund supported those students who qualified for the "partial-pay" option of the free lunch program (implemented in 1967), but who were unable to pay any portion of the cost.[30] A 1967 move to working under the auspices of the Shelby County United Neighbors, a precursor to Memphis's United Way chapter, had already increased the Fund's coffers, while simultaneously allowing volunteers to move into even broader arenas of community work. Dreifus expanded the Fund's focus to include supplying eyeglasses to school-age children, as well as providing layettes and milk formula to new mothers.[31]

Opposition to the Fund persisted in the midst of its tangible accomplishments, and it occasionally emanated from unlikely sources. In 1968, the Social Action Committee of the Memphis Ministers Association concluded that, due to a "lack of interest on the part of some principals and teachers," the program reached "less than 25 percent of the number of poor children in the city schools."[32] This criticism stemmed from the expansion of the lunch program by 1968 into schools attended by white children, and the board of education's implementation of "reduced-price" meals. The Memphis school board adopted Amendment 25 of the 1946 National School Lunch Act in 1968, allocating money for additional commodities such as milk to the preexisting money for lunches and breakfasts. Parents began lodging formal complaints to the Memphis school board that, due to the federally funded program, the quality of food for all students suffered and the cafeterias earned less revenue than before the implementation of the programs, since fewer students actually purchased their meals and more qualified for the free lunches. Predominantly white critics of the lunch program charged that local schools served less expensive and less nutritional meals to students in an effort to save money. In her testimony before the school board later that year, and before the Shelby County Quarterly Court in 1970, Dreifus argued that the policy of "reduced-price" meals was quite effective.[33]

The "reduced-price" meal plan allowed the Memphis school board to limit its financial expenditures on the free lunch program. The board utilized other approaches to decrease its financial commitments to the program as well. For example, the school board "matched" schools and churches throughout Memphis. Local churches provided the proceeds from their bazaars for these meals, an attempt to offset the school board's estimated four million dollar cost of the 1970 free lunch program. Churches also provided fund-raising activities for the Fund's clothing, shoe, and toy drives.[34]

Discussions about the different types of activities financed by the Fund and its private donors prompted a group called the Citizens' Committee to Study Poverty to press all municipal, county, and state agencies in Memphis, as well as the federal government, to increase the amount of money allocated to Memphis for the free lunch program.[35] Heightened scrutiny of the Fund's activities corresponded to rising numbers of white households in poverty. Once white children competed with African American children for the slice of an ever-dwindling financial pie, white outrage rose and the tug of war over the allocation of money to Memphis's children in need escalated.

Nonetheless, the Fund garnered unquestionable accolades at both the municipal and national levels, and one cannot question its success at moving money allocated to children from government bank accounts into the lives of those hungry children. What began as a small group of volunteers from the Memphis community emerged as the model for the National School Lunch Program once the Memphis school board agreed to finance and sponsor the organization.[36] Perhaps another testament to the Fund's success in Memphis was the fact that by 1969, fewer than five schools in the Memphis city school system refused federal funds for free lunches. By 1972, what had been twelve volunteers in four schools in 1964 had grown to over four hundred volunteers working in fifty-seven schools around Memphis and Shelby County, and enrollment in the National School Lunch Program jumped from seven hundred students in 1968 to twenty-five thousand five hundred students by 1974.[37]

The Fund followed the model of its contemporary, the Saturday Luncheon Group, as well as the national group Women Strike for Peace, in its efforts to avoid any sort of formal designation as an activist association with organized leadership. Dreifus served as the chairperson throughout the 1960s, guiding other members from a central committee, with the assistance of a Memphis social worker, Elizabeth Jones. Dreifus enjoyed the intimacy such a small group afforded—in that members respected the domain of the other volunteers—and she credited the group's success by 1968 to this fact.[38] Membership in the Fund did not raise eyebrows in an elite southern white woman's social circle. Helping to feed children too poor to have nutritional food available to them at home had nothing but noble connotations, even to people averse to private citizens engaging in any type of political activism. However, the Fund offered many of Memphis's white female activists both an ideological and logistical training ground for antiracist work. As the coffers and volunteers grew, so did the awareness among its members that poverty and racism were interrelated, with one begetting the other in an endless cycle that privileged the white elite over its African American counterpart.

Dreifus went on to enjoy national recognition for her work with the Fund. In February 1968 she appeared before the Women's Committee of the United Community Metropolitan District of Detroit, delivering a speech calling for additional federal money for the subsidizing of low-income housing, education, and food for underprivileged children. She was critical of President Nixon's failure to expand upon Lyndon Johnson's community-level antipoverty programs, pointing to her work in Memphis with the Fund as evidence of the inability of federal agencies to address the problem in the United States.[39]

In November 1969 Dreifus received an invitation to the White House Conference on Food, Nutrition, and Health scheduled for December 2 and 3, 1969. President Nixon wanted participants to attempt to monitor the problem of "malnutrition" in the United States, or at least to provide him with a theory on how to implement and organize such a program. Delegates from numerous women's, volunteer, labor, and religious organizations submitted a Task Force Action Statement to the conference that called the levels of hunger and poverty a "national crisis." Among the requests were demands for Nixon to release food stamps to all who needed them and expand the nation's free lunch program to schoolchildren immediately.[40]

Dreifus's career illustrated the ease with which some women engaged in volunteer work extended that activity into the political arena. What began initially as one woman's crusade to level the educational playing ground for Memphis's poor, primarily black children quickly evolved into a demand to extend those benefits to all of the nation's schoolchildren with the help of the federal government. Dreifus transformed a seemingly benign cause, feeding hungry schoolchildren, into a call for President Nixon to renovate one aspect of his domestic policy. While she recognized her inability to eliminate the problem of poverty among America's children, Dreifus believed that she had a duty to try to help whomever she could with whatever resources available to her. Her goal for the Fund was to make such an organization obsolete.

Much like Myra Dreifus with her involvement in affecting public policy at the state and national levels, Anne Whalen Shafer helped change the Memphis city government. Shafer's work on the Memphis City Beautiful campaign facilitated the upgrade of the infrastructure of decaying black neighborhoods, as well as that of the poor, predominantly white areas. Shafer's tenure within the city government culminated a lifelong desire to assist Memphis's urban poor.

Shafer's career in civil rights activism began when she was a child riding the segregated streetcars to the Catholic Sacred Heart School. Born in 1923 to working-class parents in Memphis, Shafer rode the streetcar to school each morning. Every day she witnessed black riders forced to sit in the back of the car, and she believed from this young age that such a policy was "abusive" to the black riders themselves, as well as to her as a human being. Shafer understood that any white patron had primacy over a black patron in obtaining a seat on a streetcar, and she thought her actions might avoid a confrontation between a white driver and a black rider unwilling to abandon her/his seat. In an interview, Shafer elaborated on other unfair practices she observed while riding the streetcar, including the fact that drivers did not honor transfers from black passengers if they presented papers in anything but pristine condition. Although her ideas did not translate into major acts of protest while she was an elementary school student, Shafer recalled consciously relinquishing her seat and moving forward as seats became available, in an attempt to assist in any way possible by providing seating in the rear of the car. She pointed to these experiences, coupled with her ardent commitment to the Catholic Church, as the primary catalysts for her activism.[41]

Shafer's family background laid the groundwork for her later activism as well. Her father immigrated to Mississippi from Ireland and worked as a building trade union official throughout her childhood. Although her family resisted her civil rights/integration work from the start, she believed their support of the unpopular notion of labor organizing softened the blow delivered by her later community activism. While Shafer's parents and grandparents believed she was too "outspoken" in her activism as an adult, her siblings had harsher commentary on her earlier responses to segregation on streetcars. They labeled Shafer and her activities "ridiculous."[42]

Regardless of the tangible examples of Jim Crow that Shafer observed as a child and young adult, the strongest influence in her life's work with civil rights came through religion and prayer. A devout Catholic all her life, Shafer dedicated her hours outside of school to studying the Bible and the tenets of the Catholic Church. Shafer noted that her reading of a book entitled *Imitation of Christ,* which called on individuals to imitate Christ in their daily lives, motivated her from an early age to question the validity of segregation. She brought her concerns to the attention of her priest, who responded by informing Shafer that the Bible sanctioned slavery; he argued, therefore, that God ordained segregation and the relegation of African Americans to the status of second-class citizens. Puzzled and dismayed, Shafer repeatedly meditated and prayed, asking God to show her how to live in his path and "imitate" Jesus Christ in her daily life.[43]

The 1950s marked a decade of intense involvement in community activist and religious groups for Shafer. She belonged to the Catholic Human Relations Council, United Church Women, and numerous Catholic charity groups, following along in a tradition of interracial coalitions of women in Memphis from the early twentieth century. By 1958, Shafer had become active in the Memphis chapter of the League of Women Voters (LWV), and the group elected her president in 1959. Although the Memphis LWV integrated prior to her joining, municipal segregation laws limited meetings to only three public venues: the YWCA, the Unitarian Church, and LeMoyne College.[44] LWV projects stayed true to the organization's founding roots; its programs targeted women and women's issues. It came as no surprise, then, based upon Shafer's desire to elicit some sort of change in Memphis's racial hierarchy, that she soon broadened her horizons. By the dawn of the 1960s, Shafer moved into activism more directly related to issues of civil rights and community improvement.

Although Shafer's involvement in direct action desegregation attempts began with her participation in the Saturday Luncheon Group, it was her tenure as chairperson of the Memphis City Beautiful Commission (MCBC) from 1964 to 1966 that garnered her public notoriety as a woman devoted to integration of the city of Memphis, publicly and privately, at any and all costs. As an outgrowth of the Progressive Era's drive toward municipal housekeeping, the MCBC had begun operation on 30 July 1930—under the auspices of the city's Public Works Division—operated and staffed exclusively by women volunteers, with a chairwoman appointed by the mayor and his commissioners. The domination of the MCBC leadership by women prevailed until 1980, when Mayor Wyeth Chandler appointed the first male chairperson, Peter Pettit, to that office.[45]

The first mayor to implement the MCBC was E. H. Crump. Shafer appeared to be quite a fan of Mayor Crump's. Throughout interviews with Shafer, she repeatedly stressed her belief that Crump's policy of getting out the black vote, at a time when other southern cities comparable to the size of Memphis refused to do so, played an integral part in both the success of the civil rights movement in Memphis and in the city's relatively peaceful integration of public accommodations. Although Shafer recognized Crump's duplicitous tactics in mobilizing the African American vote—he believed in the power of any vote, regardless of the voter's skin color—she believed that the ends justified the means in Crump's inclusion of black Memphians into the electorate.[46]

Each ward in Memphis had its own watchdog group that reported to the central MCBC the problems a particular area encountered. From school grounds that needed maintenance or landscaping, to potholes and clogged drains in the city's sewers, MCBC volunteers addressed varied problems by requisitioning supplies and delegating tasks to employees of the city's Public Works Division. From 1930 until 1964 there were an equal number of groups monitoring black and white neighborhoods, but the MCBC itself remained a segregated organization. The black group and its white counterpart worked together effectively, and their efforts did not go unnoticed. The MCBC at this time consisted of approximately 150 civic clubs in black and white neighborhoods, all dedicated to "keeping the city safe and clean." Memphis received the Ernest T. Trigg "Nation's Cleanest City" award an unprecedented four times throughout this period, a testament to the commitment of the MCBC to improve the aesthetic qualities of the city.[47]

Mayor William B. Ingram, Jr., appointed Shafer chairperson of the MCBC in 1964. On her first day at the Commission, Shafer entered her office in city hall and discovered, much to her shock and horror, that the two staff members of the black division of the MCBC shared one office that had formerly been a closet—complete with coat rack—and was wide enough for two desks and a file cabinet. Shafer's own full-time secretary and the other four white staff members had a much larger work area than her African American counterparts. The following day, Shafer moved the black secretary and white secretary into the same office without asking anyone's permission, effectively desegregating the MCBC and city hall. Not only did Shafer integrate the actual offices of city hall, but she also integrated the activities of the MCBC itself. Instead of holding two, segregated Clean-Up, Fix-Up, Paint-Up parades, as well as two contests for poster art, Shafer insisted and saw to it that these activities be integrated. Invigorated by these victories, Shafer launched an unsuccessful campaign to have one Miss City Beautiful contest as well.[48] Such enterprises may not have yielded dramatic steps forward in the fight for racial equality, but they did illustrate Shafer's contributions to shifting social attitudes toward biracial cooperation, if only in the world of city beautification, culture, and beauty pageants.

Although Shafer's involvement in community and civil rights work accelerated after her stint with MCBC, one can squarely place her civil rights work as beginning with the MCBC. Not only did her integration of the organization gain her powerful allies in the civil rights community—as well as equally formidable enemies within the city government—but she also spoke publicly in her capacity as chair of the MCBC in Memphis's black churches. Those speaking engagements were critical to the network she relied on during the 1968 sanitation strike and afterward.[49]

Shafer remained chairperson of MCBC until 1966, garnering her share of recognition for the commission's beautification projects, including the 1965 designation of Memphis as America's "Cleanest City" by the First Lady, Lady Bird Johnson. However, Shafer soon left the MCBC to try politics. In 1965, the state of Tennessee called a limited constitutional convention with the intention of reapportioning the legislature. Eight delegates attended from Shelby County, including one African American representative, Jesse Turner. Out of a total of ninety-nine representatives, only three women, one each from west, middle, and east Tennessee attended. Shafer served as the lone female representative from the western third of the state. With this experience under her belt, she campaigned, unsuccessfully, for a seat on Memphis's city council in 1967.[50] Her defeat did not deter Shafer from her activism; her commitment to antiracist work merely escalated from 1967 onward.

Traditional "woman's careers," such as social work, education, and beautification, led upper-class and upper-middle-class women such as Myra Dreifus and Anne Shafer to public careers as reformers. For Dreifus and Shafer, involvement in reform activities did not stem from an impulse to contribute to any pathbreaking social movement, nor did these women possess the kind of radical political consciousness that one typically associates with civil rights activists. Rather, their civil rights work organically developed from prior activities in less politically charged social welfare programs and organizations, and reflected their increasing awareness of the systemic racism of the South and its role in the perpetuation of poverty. While Dreifus's activist career initially began with her association with Jewish women's groups in Michigan, her involvement with organizations targeting the South's poor naturally led to an awareness of the racial hierarchy of Memphis. Alternatively, Shafer acknowledged a call to action through her interpretation of the nature of Christian charity.

The women involved in volunteer activities in the years leading up to the modern civil rights movement rarely labeled their work anything other than community activism and/or charitable work. Those women who opted for charity work organized through their churches and synagogues experienced a similar awakening. For both groups of women, their work served as a direct route from aiding the poor, regardless of race and ethnicity, to the struggle for civil rights.

Chapter 3

"The Message Came on a Beam of Light"
Women in Religious Groups

A strong belief in God proved to be yet another motivating factor in drawing female reformers into civil rights activism. Women coming from both Jewish and Christian backgrounds echoed the claim that since all human beings belonged to a universal brotherhood, the unjust treatment of one of God's children constituted a sin against God. Memphis's activist community took no exception to this rule. Following in the footsteps of female activists from the nineteenth century, a number of women central to Memphis's civil rights movement began their journey into social reform from a deep-seated religious faith.

Although many historians have explored the connection between religious conviction and reform work, Anne Firor Scott initially isolated the direct connection between white southern churchwomen and civil rights activism, situating that connection as far back as the antebellum period. Scott's significant contribution stemmed from her work in the postbellum South, when "race work" occupied the careers of reformers concerned about the restrictive race laws that appeared on southern law books during Reconstruction.[1]

An understanding of the nexus of civil rights work and religion occupied a central place in the work of two influential civil rights activists, Anne Braden and Lillian Smith, and the catalyzing role of religion in their activist lives serves as a useful framework in examining the impact of religion on Memphis's female activists. While the two women had somewhat different careers—Braden's devoted to political organizing and Smith's devoted to writing—both women located the first awakenings of a progressive consciousness within their early religious development in childhood. Anne Braden, a native of Anniston, Alabama, spent the bulk of her activist career working for the Southern Conference Educational Fund (SCEF), a group involved in a multitude of projects committed to racial justice and labor organizing. Although employed as a staff member of SCEF throughout the 1950s and 1960s, Braden began to focus her energies and writings primarily on race while she worked as a journalist in Louisville, Kentucky, in the late 1940s.[2]

Braden began contributing to the *Louisville Times* in 1947. Shortly after her move to Kentucky, she facilitated discussions on segregation in the local Department of Christian Social Relations of the Episcopal Church. Braden noted in her autobiography that she recognized, albeit subconsciously, that the God she learned about in her Episcopal church did not resemble the God of her upper-class parents and their white southern neighbors. This early realization, Braden maintained throughout her life, propelled her into the illustrious career she enjoyed within the civil rights movement.[3]

Lillian Smith's motivation behind civil rights work bore similarities to Braden's. An eloquent writer, Smith recounted in her autobiography the confusion she experienced as a young, white, southern woman, born in 1897, and thus growing up in a region and country that defined very limited roles for women in society. Among the confusing elements she struggled with during the indoctrination process she called childhood were the lessons she learned in her church about God and love. Smith grew up in an extremely devout, Southern Baptist household, where she participated in Bible readings and church affairs regularly, and where, according to her parents' assertions, God lived along with Smith and her family. According to Smith, the first lesson southern children learned was that all God's children were one in God's love, but each one had her/his (segregated/separate) place.[4] Smith believed the powerful force of religion gave both sides of the segregation debate considerable strength.[5] Both Smith and Braden found the empowering message of Christianity liberating for both the black and white faithful, yet many southern Protestant churches resisted integration.

Numerous surveys exist on the official policies of southern churches, black and white, toward integration as the civil rights movement began.

An extensive historiography chronicles the strong tradition of the African American church and the pivotal role that institution played in both the modern civil rights movement and the larger struggle for African American freedom from Emancipation onward.[6] The southern white religious community, on the other hand, relied on individual church groups for any social reform work.

Perhaps the most progressive of the Memphis Protestant denominations, the Unitarian Church—of which there was only one congregation in the city in the 1960s—participated consistently in numerous activities throughout the civil rights movement in Memphis, by holding discussion forums and engaging in public projects and actions. The biracial Unitarian Fellowship met weekly to discuss religious and secular matters, ranging from the tenets of Islam to the emergence of black power, and Margaret Valiant regularly attended these meetings.[7] The youth groups of Memphis's Unitarian Church worked in conjunction with several African American student groups around the city during the first foray into bus desegregation in Memphis in the early 1960s. According to Marjorie Cherry, one of the founders of the Saturday Luncheon Group, the Social Action Committee of the Unitarian Church, of which she was a member, worked alongside these youth groups as well in the early stages of Memphis's desegregation by writing letters to the primary department stores in Memphis asking them to desegregate.[8]

Cathy Cade, an active member of the Student Nonviolent Coordinating Committee (SNCC) in its early years, belonged to the Memphis Unitarian youth group while in high school, and her experiences within the civil rights movement typify her generation's contributions. Cade believed her awakening to the similarities between black and white Americans occurred during the integrated meetings of this church group and other black student groups. Growing up in a family that condemned racism, Cade nonetheless noted that she had never spent any time with a black individual, and, to her shock and delight, she found that she had more in common with some of her African American colleagues than with some of her white ones. Cade also credited her experiences with the Unitarian group as seminal to her decision to enroll in a student exchange program with the historically black Spelman College in 1962. Within two days of her arrival in Atlanta, Cade became active in the sit-in movement there when she participated in a sit-in at the Georgia state legislature.[9]

The Unitarian Church's outreach program to church groups within Memphis's African American community functioned well in its limited space, but overall, Memphis's churches transitioned roughly into integration. A rift developed within the city's largest Presbyterian church over the issue of whether or not to allow black congregants into Sunday services. Like several other churches in Memphis during this period, Second Presbyterian had allowed black worshippers into its services, provided they sit in a segregated area. Yet even this action proved to be too much to bear for some. In 1965, several Second Presbyterian Church members opposed to integration formed a separate church devoted to Bible instruction free from political discussion, and funded with "no outside interference." Although this breakaway group, which eventually became the Independent Presbyterian Church, never commented on whether or not they were taking a stand against integration, the timing of the split confirmed many congregants' suspicions that the break did in fact center on the question of integration. The fracture occurred shortly after Second Presbyterian had increased its contributions to various civil rights groups.[10]

Second Presbyterian's experience mirrored that of other Protestant churches in Memphis that had splintered in the early 1960s over the question of integration.[11] Several large national women's groups associated with these Protestant churches increased their civil rights activism at the same time these rifts developed, both at the national level and throughout the city of Memphis. One of these groups, the United Church Women—also referred to as Church Women United (CWU)—included women from both Protestant and Catholic backgrounds, black and white, and it influenced the civil rights movement both in Memphis and throughout the South as a whole.

The CWU represented the final stage in an evolution of numerous women's organizations affiliated with the National Council of the Churches of Christ in the United States. Its earliest predecessor, the United Council of Church Women, began in December 1941 as an organization devoted to "world peace, human rights, and Christian unity."[12] An obvious reference to the problems emerging in the early years of World War II, "human rights" became a euphemism for civil rights by 1944 when members of the biracial United Council of Church Women took public stands against segregated facilities across the South. The organization, an amalgamation of women's church groups that had existed since 1901, historically had embraced a variety of reform causes, including civil rights and pacifism. Although the group acted independently of other church and secular bodies, CWU maintained an enduring and prosperous alliance with the National Council of Negro Women, the National Council of Jewish Women, and the National Council of Catholic Women.[13]

Civil rights dominated the national group's activities throughout the 1950s and 1960s. In 1954, the United Council of Church Women held a conference to discuss this dilemma, at which the council decried those Protestant churches that remained segregated. Furthermore, the United Council of Church Women condemned a new development across the South in the wake of the Supreme Court's 1954 *Brown v. Board of Education* decision—the phenomenon of Protestant churches opening private religious schools in an attempt to circumvent the entire integration issue. Some individual chapters, however, acted independently of the national organization and declined to involve themselves in the segregation debate entirely.[14]

Memphis's chapter of CWU, integrated from its inception, not only devoted a portion of its projects strictly to civil rights work, but it also attempted to integrate worship services, youth groups, and women's groups throughout the city in the late 1960s. CWU members repeatedly sought desegregation of both youth and women's church groups around the city in the 1960s.[15] The careers of CWU members Claudia Davis and Anne Shafer bear out a commitment to these goals and highlight the enormous impact religion had in the lives of these women.

Claudia Davis, a native of Little Rock, Arkansas, moved to Memphis shortly before Little Rock's Central High integration in 1957. She joined Memphis's CWU chapter upon her arrival, and became an influential member of the group. Although Davis acknowledged an awareness of the problems with the southern racial hierarchy from an early age, she situated the beginning of her public career of activism as coinciding with incidents at Central High. Like many of her peers, Davis recalled the instillation in her young mind of an "inferred" racism that differentiated between the proper places for black and white southerners, publicly and privately, yet she admitted to an equally powerful awareness of the problems such racism engendered. Although Davis failed to isolate any one conversation or incident that marked her conscious realization that a racial hierarchy existed in the South, she viewed her political "awakening" as akin to the inculcation of racist ideology southern children receive inadvertently from living in a segregated society. If the "teaching" of racism happened almost organically among white southerners, then the abandonment of subscribing to racism could occur just as naturally, Davis posited. Never one to label her actions politically significant, a typical response among her contemporaries, Davis believed her decision in the 1940s to deliver her first child in an integrated, yet inferior, medical facility in rural Conway, Arkansas, reflected an early manifestation of her dedication to racial equality.[16]

Davis articulated her decision to deliver her children in an integrated environment as a conscious attempt to avoid "handicapping" them with racist ideas, and dedication to children's issues became a hallmark of her career with CWU and, later, the Panel of American Women (Panel). She continually noted that her sole motivation throughout her career stemmed from her desire to avoid passing along any racial hatred and bias to her children. Indeed, Davis carefully weighed each decision she made as she scripted her activism, taking great pains to avoid doing any irreparable harm to her children. She professed her belief that by limiting the experiences of one's children, especially by exposing them to only one group of individuals—in her instance, middle-class white southerners—a parent did a great "disservice" to her/his children. These statements revealed the centrality of her own children to her work, while her work exposed the importance of other people's children to her as well.[17]

One of Davis's early projects illustrated the place religion occupied in her life. The St. Luke's United Methodist Church–sponsored Outpost Sunday School lasted from 1965 until 1970, and functioned as a quasi vacation Bible school. Staffed by various members of St. Luke's and CWU, Outpost Sunday School consisted of integrated groups who met weekly in neighborhoods around Memphis where residents did not have access to a Sunday school for their children. Although this project seemed politically benign on the surface, it nonetheless began the critical bridge-building process so necessary to keep the peace in a city where racial tensions maintained de facto segregation after the federal legislation of the 1960s. It also enabled Davis to establish vital contacts within Memphis's African American religious community that she would find invaluable during her work with the striking sanitation workers in 1968.

Another CWU-sponsored activity that Davis took part in was the Mothers of Young Children program. This project matched individual churches to individual schools, with volunteers staffing nurseries, serving as teachers' aides, tutors, kitchen workers, and so forth. Regardless of the inexperience of the workers, the Mothers of Young Children flourished and served as a model for later programs instituted by both the Fund for Needy Schoolchildren (Fund) and the Panel. Many of the activities CWU women engaged in through the Mothers of Young Children organization mirrored those of the Fund, such as transporting mothers and their children to dental and medical appointments. However, the CWU group's activities predated the Fund's by four years.[18]

CWU activists expended a considerable amount of time and effort building bridges between the black and white communities.[19] Anne Shafer, whose work with the Memphis City Beautiful Commission set new standards for race relations in Memphis's city hall, became involved with the civil rights movement purely because of her religious beliefs. Her commitment to the Catholic Church did not waver throughout the majority of Shafer's life. Both a cousin and an aunt belonged to religious orders, and, as a child, Shafer herself had planned on becoming a nun. She placed the beginning of her awareness of racial inequalities in the South as early as elementary school, due to events she observed in Jim Crow trolleys, as well as to her childhood understanding of Jesus Christ. A witness to racism while her husband worked in the military, Shafer pointed to a hunger strike among black veterans stationed at a Missouri military base with her husband as a radicalizing experience in her adult life. The men protested the inferior living conditions afforded them due simply to their race, and, when they refused to eat, their commanding officer forced them to dig trenches until they "got hungry."[20]

Perhaps the single event that most displayed the manner in which religious belief motivated Shafer occurred in a California church in 1952. That morning, Shafer had what she described as a vision in which a loud, clear voice told her, "All people are my people. What you do to the least, you do to me." Shafer returned to Memphis several months after this mystical experience, convinced that God had spoken to her and given her a mission to rid the world of racial prejudice. She immediately increased her involvement with the Catholic Church, local Catholic women's groups, and the Memphis diocese. At this point, however, Shafer began encountering hostility from local Catholic leaders and clergy who believed her outspokenness inappropriate for the venues in which she spoke; they attempted to silence and excommunicate her for what they characterized as her Communist beliefs.[21]

Shafer faced a familiar accusation leveled at civil rights activists of her era. The postwar period marked yet another "red scare" in twentieth-century American history, and accusations of Communist infiltration into civil rights organizations persisted as a popular tactic of pro-segregationists. The FBI launched sweeping investigations into numerous organizations from the late 1940s through the late 1960s, including the Highlander Folk School, the Fellowship of Reconciliation, the Congress of Racial Equality, and the Southern Christian Leadership Conference. Many individual activists faced allegations of Communist connections within their own communities as well; Shafer endured the greatest harassment of all the Memphis activists in this study.[22]

Shafer responded to these claims with a series of letters addressed to a variety of leaders within the Catholic Church, starting with state leaders and moving straight to the top of the Catholic hierarchy, Pope Paul VI. Shafer cited this experience as central to her eventual exodus from the Catholic Church, but she felt vindicated by the public stance of Bishop William L. Adrian of Nashville.[23] Bishop Adrian released the official statement of the Tennessee diocese regarding the civil rights movement in August 1963. He echoed the sentiments of many other religious leaders of the decade, black and white, who placed the race issue within a "moral and religious" context; he called any inhumanity toward another human being a violation against Christ. The statement went further in calling upon all Christians to reach across racial lines at their work, within their churches, and in the political arena as well, in order to fulfill Christ's vision of harmony on earth among all God's children.[24]

By 1962, Shafer lost her position on the board of the Council of Catholic Women; she occupied the chair of the vice president of the organization at the time. She had worked with the council since 1952, yet she blamed the removal on her persistence in addressing issues regarding civil rights throughout her tenure on the board. Although Shafer claimed that the council unanimously accepted her 1961 suggestion that it form a committee to study race relations in Memphis, the committee never materialized since the proposal never appeared on the agenda for the meeting. Shafer blamed this omission on the continuing allegations of her supposed Communist sympathies, maintaining that the red-baiting she had discussed with the bishop of Nashville contributed to her removal from the board.[25] Undaunted, Shafer continued her work within the Catholic Church, becoming a cofounder of the integrated Catholic Human Relations Council in 1963.

Shafer's religious beliefs catapulted her into work for racial justice, and her ideological evolution mimicked that of southern women of all ages who participated in the civil rights movement. Sara Evans's work on southern white women within the civil rights movement, *Personal Politics*, combined oral histories with critical analysis—based on the author's own experiences as a southerner within the movement—to illuminate the unique position of these women of the baby boom. Religion, Evans maintained, centered her subjects' activism. Placing this tradition as far back as the late nineteenth century, when white women joined missionary societies and the YWCA and began their critical training in political activism, Evans linked the Protestant church in the South directly with white southern women's involvement in the movement.[26]

The majority of Evans's subjects began their activist careers while enrolled in colleges and universities, and Evans discovered that a common thread of membership in Christian student groups defined her protagonists. Perhaps one of the largest religious groups active on southern campuses during the civil rights movement was the Methodist Student Movement (MSM). According to Evans, the MSM, based in the Bible Belt enclave of Nashville, Tennessee, "harbored the most radical groups on [southern college] campuses" in the late 1950s.[27]

The MSM advocated the radical nature of Christianity—the assumption that the teachings of Jesus Christ characterized a liberation theology—in its own organization. The group felt mainstream "institutional" Christianity lacked this religious interpretation. Evans's work included documents from the Study Committee of the United Student Christian Council, a group affiliated with MSM and to which many female activists in Evans's study belonged. The committee's *Theses for Study and*

Debate stated, as early as 1958, that the "Christian group on campus which does not promote involvement in political affairs denies [God's] authority in that area of life."[28]

MSM, with branches across the country, dedicated itself to addressing numerous social ills through its ministry, and during the 1960s, the majority of its personnel and finances focused on the civil rights movement. Both black and white students felt drawn to MSM, particularly in the South, and these activists utilized the resources and contacts MSM made available to them to further civil rights work on their respective campuses. Memphis's Southwestern College housed a large branch of MSM during the 1960s, and that group achieved a significant amount of visibility through its work with the school's branch of the Southern Student Organizing Committee (SSOC) during the 1968 sanitation strike.[29] These students followed in the footsteps of nationally known figures of the era who embarked upon civil rights work while affiliated with MSM.

Perhaps the strongest argument for the interconnectedness of the civil rights movement and Christianity came from the architect of SNCC's nonviolent ethos, James Lawson, writing in the pages of MSM's *Motive*. Not only did Lawson place the civil rights movement firmly within the tenets of Christianity, he also considered the sit-ins to be a form of protest that illustrated God's commitment and devotion to believers. Lawson believed that direct action protests such as the sit-ins were "God's promise that if radically Christian methods are adopted the rate of change can be vastly increased."[30] He asserted that the more entrenched the segregationist was in his or her ideas, the easier it was for an argument echoing the tenets of Christianity to break through those barriers. Indeed, Lawson argued that Christianity allowed for easier conversion of segregationists to the civil rights cause specifically due to the South's professed devotion to religion.

An influential figure in the feminist movement of the 1970s, Gayle Graham Yates, found her impetus to activism within MSM. Writing in *Motive*, the official magazine of MSM, Yates recounted her conversion to activism at an integrated church service in her native Greenwood, Mississippi, in the 1950s. A fellow member of the Methodist Youth Fellowship invited Yates to accompany him to an African American church for a meeting intended to open up lines of communication between black and white residents of Greenwood. Yates, like many others compelled to activism through their involvement in religious organizations, credited this meeting as the first time she realized that her southern friends and family members had taught her an unfounded and false belief in the inherent inferiority of African Americans. The African American residents of Mississippi attested to Yates's conviction, as they demonstrated more cordiality and education than the white citizens she knew.[31]

Texas native Casey Hayden, perhaps one of the best-known civil rights and feminist activists of the era, began her prestigious career through the MSM, the YWCA, and the Christian Faith and Life Community (Community) while a student at the University of Texas in Austin in 1959. Hayden considered the head of the Austin, Texas, YWCA, Rosalie Oakes, to be an inspirational woman who stressed the importance of southern white men and women rooting their convictions about racial harmony firmly within their "southern-ness" as a way to legitimize and empower their arguments.[32]

Hayden, born Sandra Cason in 1942, moved into the housing facility of the Community shortly upon her arrival at Texas, specifically because that dormitory allowed black and white students to live together on campus, the sole domicile to do so at this time. The Community's leader, a Methodist minister named Joseph Matthews, believed that Christians were to be active and involved; followers were to "witness" on earth to facilitate God's message throughout the world. Publicly exposing examples of racial prejudice figured prominently in Matthews's definition of Christian witnessing.[33]

While these individuals embodied the standard use of Christianity in dedicating one's self to civil rights work, Christian women did not monopolize the reform work arena. Jewish women made up a sizable proportion of Memphis's civil rights community. Their entry into civil rights work arose through a variety of channels, yet a significant number of activists credited the Holocaust with radicalizing them both personally and within their professional activism. One of the pioneers in stimulating discussion and cooperation between Memphis's African American and Jewish communities, Nina Katz, occupied the position of the first female board chairperson of the Memphis chapter of the National Conference of Christians and Jews (NCCJ), and she herself survived the Holocaust. Her devotion to the cause of adult literacy expanded, as it did for many other southern activists who began working exclusively with the poor, into civil rights work.³⁴ Organizations such as the NCCJ and the National Council of Jewish Women (NCJW) dedicated themselves, their projects, and their finances to a variety of civil rights causes during the movement. The NCCJ Memphis chapter sparked integration efforts as early as 1946 with their "Negro History Week," cosponsored with the *Memphis World* and the *Mid-South Courier*, two of the city's larger black-owned and -operated newspapers.³⁵

Historians continue to debate the shared history of oppression of African Americans and Jewish Americans. While some posit that the alliance one witnessed during the civil rights movement grew naturally from Jewish survivors of the Holocaust committing themselves to fighting any injustice based on ethnicity, others posit that the alliance was tenuous at best, hostile at worst.³⁶ Myra Dreifus attributed some of the impetus for her activism to the teachings of her faith. The recipient of numerous awards and honors from Memphis's Jewish community and organizations, Dreifus did not consider herself a deeply religious person, but she placed the root of her reform work squarely within the teachings of Jewish laws that encouraged human beings to be compassionate with one another.³⁷

Myra Dreifus cofounded the Fund for Needy Schoolchildren and was an active member of the NCJW. Dreifus's work with both groups repeatedly overlapped and proved quite successful due to her effective utilization of the financial and human resources of the groups. One such program educated parents in basic parenting skills and utilized many of the same tactics of some of the Fund's projects. The project at the Wisconsin Elementary School became the standard for later community action endeavors undertaken by women activists in Memphis. The Wisconsin project attempted to assist the entire family unit by educating parents as well as children; many activists considered the project innovative due to this unique aspect.³⁸

Memphis's largest Jewish synagogue, Temple Israel, joined such local groups as the NCJW, the black-owned and -operated radio station WDIA (whose contributions made up the largest single donation), the Food for Fitness Committee, the Memphis and Shelby County Health Department, and the Memphis Council of Parents and Teachers in loaning its resources to the Fund's cause. By 1968, Temple Israel Sisterhood members provided money for buses that brought tutors to the Kansas Street School, a school with a majority African American student body that Fund members worked closely with throughout their duration. This program marked the first occasion where Temple Israel opened its doors to community-based programs; its prior charitable work focused on Jewish community outreach. Dreifus's membership undoubtedly played a significant role in Temple Israel's involvement with the Fund.[39]

Jeanne Dreifus, Myra Dreifus's daughter-in-law, contributed significantly to the civil rights movement through her work with the NCJW as well as the YWCA. A 1951 graduate of Radcliffe College, Dreifus converted to Judaism shortly before her marriage and relocation from her home in New York City to Memphis in 1952. Myra Dreifus encouraged Jeanne to join the NCJW immediately upon her arrival in Memphis, not only to establish a network of friends in both intellectual and activist pursuits, but also to create a social network within Memphis's Jewish community. Dreifus felt as though the NCJW succeeded in both endeavors; it instilled an identity in her, both within the Jewish community in Memphis and globally. The NCJW educated Dreifus in "social issues," facilitating discussions on the root causes of poverty, problems with access to day care, and racial inequality, all the while couching the instruction within a Judaic framework. Dreifus pointed to this early experience in the NCJW as a formative one and a seminal component to her richly filled activist career.[40]

One of Jeanne Dreifus's earliest forays into racial reform occurred at the behest of Frances Coe. In 1953, Coe, a mentor to numerous Memphis activists and a central figure within the city's civil rights community, encouraged Dreifus to co-teach a class with her on American government at the YWCA. Coe offered the class to black and white students of all ages and backgrounds. This experience helped Dreifus tap into a rich network of well-established African American community leaders. Such contacts proved invaluable as Dreifus's career in reform work gained momentum in the coming years.[41]

In the 1960s, Dreifus plunged headlong into civil rights work. In the wake of President Kennedy's 1963 assassination a multitude of reform organizations throughout the nation, including the NCJW, converged on Washington, D.C., to lobby Congress for passage of what would become the Civil Rights Act of 1964. The Memphis chapter of the NCJW chose

Jeanne Dreifus and Judy Korones, both native New Yorkers, to represent it in Washington. Dreifus and Korones faced ridicule and disdain from the northern delegates who considered them complicit in the race problems in the South. Dreifus pointed to this experience as both an eye-opening and a radicalizing moment for her. She believed her role as a northern transplant compelled her to work harder for racial equality. Living in the North, according to those critics, meant she knew better. Dreifus felt vindicated by the fact that the act passed months after this trip to Washington, and Dreifus felt as though she had made a tangible difference in public policy.[42]

These discussions only accelerated the pace of Jeanne Dreifus's activities over the next decade. The NCJW launched a national campaign to investigate, fund, and improve inferior day care facilities during the 1960s and 1970s. Dreifus spearheaded the NCJW's attempts to expand adequate daycare services for all children throughout the 1970s, leading that struggle from the synagogues and Jewish groups in Memphis and Shelby County.[43] Dreifus's initial steps into exploring the tenets of her new religion facilitated an enduring dedication to civil rights work and community activism.

Many of the female activists drawn into civil rights work, both in Memphis and beyond, felt compelled to do so through deeply held spiritual beliefs. Sara Evans categorized religion as both a liberating force and a reflection of the "paradoxical reality" in which southern white women lived.[44] For these women, many of whom came from an earlier generation than Evans's subjects, religion served as a liberating mechanism that allowed them to transcend their circumscribed roles in southern white society and question the racial, and eventually for many, the gendered status quo. A backbone of faith and religiosity gave all of these female activists the fortitude and dedication needed to struggle with Memphis's omnipresent racial tensions exacerbated by the city's sanitation workers' strike in 1968. For those women involved peripherally in civil rights work, the strike only accelerated that pace and commitment. For women who dabbled in charitable work yet remained firmly seated on the fence when considering race relations, the strike forced them to take one side or the other.

Chapter 4

RAISING A GENERATION THAT DOES NOT HATE
The 1968 Sanitation Strike and the
Radicalizing of Memphis Activists

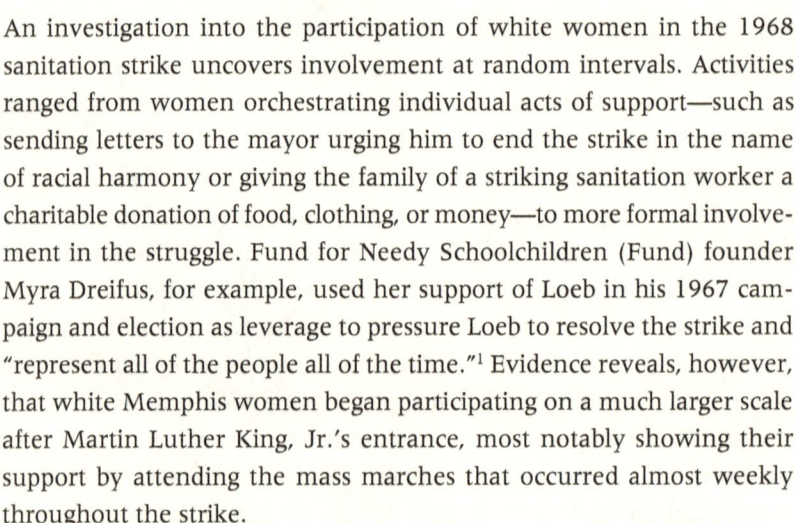

An investigation into the participation of white women in the 1968 sanitation strike uncovers involvement at random intervals. Activities ranged from women orchestrating individual acts of support—such as sending letters to the mayor urging him to end the strike in the name of racial harmony or giving the family of a striking sanitation worker a charitable donation of food, clothing, or money—to more formal involvement in the struggle. Fund for Needy Schoolchildren (Fund) founder Myra Dreifus, for example, used her support of Loeb in his 1967 campaign and election as leverage to pressure Loeb to resolve the strike and "represent all of the people all of the time."[1] Evidence reveals, however, that white Memphis women began participating on a much larger scale after Martin Luther King, Jr.'s entrance, most notably showing their support by attending the mass marches that occurred almost weekly throughout the strike.

Women gave a variety of reasons for why they became involved in demonstrations in support of striking sanitation workers; justifications ranged from Christian charity to feelings of guilt at not doing enough to resolve the problematic race relations in Memphis prior to the strike. Regardless of their motivations, Memphis's activist community experienced a groundswell of additional shock troops to fight racial injustice in that city at several key intervals during the 1968 strike.[2] For all of the subjects of this study, the strike represented a dramatic turning point in their lives, one that forced them to confront southern racism and take a stand one way or another.

One woman present throughout the strike's duration was the solitary female member of the Memphis City Council, Gwen Robinson Awsumb. Calling itself the "Businessman's Council," Mayor Henry Loeb's city council consisted wholly of individuals with "business connections," including Awsumb, whose business ties apparently came from her identity as the wife of a locally prominent architect.[3] The first woman elected to office in Memphis city government, Awsumb, a native of Marshall, Michigan, born in 1915, relocated with her family to Memphis in 1930. She attended both public and private high schools there, and she graduated in 1937 from the Presbyterian Church–affiliated Southwestern College. Before her election to the council in 1967, Awsumb worked as financial secretary of the Episcopal Diocese of Tennessee from 1956 until 1966. She also ventured into public office at the state level, running for a position in the Tennessee state legislature in 1956.[4]

Awsumb's first taste of politics materialized in 1951, while she canvassed her neighborhood for registered voters for the Civic Research Committee. The committee embarked upon this endeavor in an attempt to "shak[e] citizens out of the political apathy" engendered by years of the Crump political machine. Much to Awsumb's chagrin, she discovered that the majority of her neighbors in an affluent Memphis suburb had never registered, and many women she interviewed saw voting as an improper activity for women.[5]

A self-described "moderate Republican," whose entrance into political life began with her work on Eisenhower's 1952 presidential campaign, Awsumb articulated positive feelings toward labor representation, although not for city employees. While this enthusiasm for labor representation on a minimum scale ran counter to Republican Party ideology, Awsumb experienced little criticism during both terms on the council. Her conservative political views undoubtedly protected her from much of the criticism and ridicule one would expect for a woman in her public position. An interview with Mayor Loeb's wife early in her husband's tenure as mayor in 1967 illustrated the views of the majority of Memphians who found a woman with conservative views far more attractive a political animal than one who was outspoken and expressed ideas contrary to the mainstream. Mary Loeb herself saw women as a positive addition to the political structure, and she pointed to their involvement in civic activities, such as the Memphis City Beautiful Commission, as evidence of their capabilities.[6] Awsumb understood that her voice represented—if in name only—all women in Memphis and all issues related to "God, country, [and] motherhood." Her public record, however, contradicted those stereotypes. While on the council, Awsumb voted to support a relaxation of Memphis's liquor laws, a move many deemed "unwomanly."[7]

Awsumb's opposition to union representation for city workers stemmed from her belief that unions in city services had "destroyed" the United States. She used her disdain for unions in city services as justification for her support of Mayor Loeb early in the strike. Her divergence from Loeb later in the strike came from his intransigence in negotiating with the strikers and representatives, not from Awsumb's opinions of organized labor.

Marjorie Cherry shared Awsumb's views on union representation, and, in particular, Cherry believed the local and national American Federation of State, County, and Municipal Employees (AFSCME) leaders greatly exacerbated the tension in the city. Cherry's perspective on the intrusiveness of these "outside agitators" demonstrated the traditional southern resistance to organized labor. Another unseemly characteristic of Cherry's emerged at this time also: her paternalistic ideas regarding African American sanitation workers. Cherry initially did not support the strike, because she considered striking workers' grievances frivolous. Although sanitation workers remained among the highest paid African American workers in Memphis at that time, their salaries still fell below those of their white contemporaries in similar job categories at the municipal level. These two women shared an opposition to the 1968 strike early in its life, yet their reasons bore little resemblance to each other. Cherry believed racism created social, political, and economic inequality; Awsumb believed in the notion that the American meritocracy did not discriminate. Both women eventually met on common ground in their opposition to the strike as they realized that the unfair labor practices had little to do with the legality of municipal workers joining unions, and everything to do with the color of their skin.[8]

While some observers within Memphis and at the national level thought that King's entrance onto the scene caused the city government to begin viewing the strike as primarily a struggle for racial justice rather than one focused on labor organization, Awsumb maintained that the shift occurred far earlier. Awsumb claimed that the city's three black councilmen, Fred Davis, James Netters, and J. O. Patterson, warned fellow council members early on of the strike's potential to escalate into a racial issue. Although council members initially discounted the councilmen's claims as simply nervous reactions, once the black community began to rally around the strikers, the council realized the shift had already occurred.[9]

As the national spotlight began squaring its attention on Memphis and the strike, Awsumb assumed the unenviable position of official liaison between the council and Mayor Loeb. As such, Awsumb met with Loeb before council meetings on a weekly basis to discuss that week's agenda prior to the public meeting. On the fateful day of what came to be called the "miniriot"—23 February—Awsumb chastised Loeb for impeding the council's progress in resolving the strike. Awsumb understood what Loeb and many of her white colleagues did not. The strike did not ameliorate the economic problems within Memphis's African American community; on the contrary, it merely exacerbated them. Furthermore, racism on the part of the Memphis police department and within the white civilian population added fuel to the fire.[10]

Gwen Awsumb filled a unique spot in the history of the sanitation strike. She sat at the nexus of two key groups in the strike's history, the city council and civil rights reformers. As a council member, she provided an additional rational voice amid the shrill ones supporting Loeb's stand in the strike. As a community member, her reach extended into the community of women who effected a degree of change within Memphis's white community as the strike intensified. Several white activists who later participated in a number of the mass marches in support of striking sanitation workers credited Awsumb's detailed descriptions of council meetings in St. Mary's Episcopal Church Woman's Bible study group as serving as a consciousness-raising moment for their decision to demonstrate in support of the strikers.[11] Linda Allen, an early participant in the Saturday Luncheon Group (SLG) and a woman motivated to antiracist activity through her work with the Episcopal Church and the Junior League, prided herself on her access to the latest updates during the strike, since Awsumb, a member of Allen's Bible study group, kept the group abreast of developments from the council's perspective. For Awsumb and the majority of Memphis's white female reformers, the police brutality displayed in the 23 February protest marked a turning point in their ideological development on the relationship between racism and the demands of striking sanitation workers.

Memphis police utilized Mace in order to disperse some twenty-five hundred marchers in support of striking sanitation workers on February 23. The first large-scale protest of Loeb's policies in the strike turned violent, hence the moniker "miniriot." Apathy turned to rage, and indifference evolved into action when those involved in this nonviolent display of solidarity encountered a resistant and annoyed police force. Margaret Valiant participated in this march, having declared her unity with striking sanitation workers early on in the strike. At a meeting at the Mason Temple—the central location for weekly meetings to inform the community about the strike's progress—following the march, Valiant spoke to a largely African American audience about her firm commitment to assist the sanitation workers in receiving the "consideration" they deserved. Valiant considered herself to be quite the instigator in African American community organizing, boasting that her neighbors who attended meetings throughout the strike did so at her behest. She maintained that within the black community in which she lived, the older individuals appeared motivated to fight for social justice, while the younger residents concerned themselves more with "militancy" and protest as fashion.[12] Valiant always felt more connected to the older generation than to the younger one, and this philosophy affected her allegiances at various junctures in the civil rights movement. If black self-determination dominated, Valiant turned away from that project, and if biracial cooperation prevailed, Valiant supported the endeavor wholeheartedly. Mainstream Americans and Memphians alike shared this philosophy.

For another SLG member, Peggy Jemison, the 23 February macing shifted her perceptions about the strike. This Memphis native wore a number of hats during the sanitation workers' strike that undoubtedly colored her perceptions of Loeb's handling of the dispute. In 1968, Jemison was the wife of a prominent Memphis realtor, Frank Jemison, the mother of three children, the president of Memphis's Junior League chapter, and a friend to Loeb's wife, Mary Gregg Loeb. As with many of her Memphis contemporaries, Jemison's volunteer work—hers with the Junior League, specifically—laid the foundation for a move into antiracist activism, but an adult education course named Oriental Heritage lit the spark. This interdisciplinary course, taught at Southwestern, included discussion about events other than "Oriental" philosophy, religion, and history. Course instructor Ray Hill often expended a considerable amount of class time talking about current events, including the strike, and participants like Jemison and her new acquaintance, Mattie Sengstacke, utilized the space to engage in frank dialogue about the health of race relations and the nuances of Loeb's position.[13]

Jemison readily admitted her unquestioning support of Mayor Loeb at the outset of the strike, primarily due to her long-standing friendship with his wife, yet she experienced a dramatic shift in thinking around the time of the macing on 23 February. Although Jemison hesitated to pinpoint an actual date at which she became convinced that the strike comprised more than just a labor issue, she did proclaim that "perhaps we [were] closing our eyes to something. . . ."[14] The popular isolation of this pivotal moment occurring with the macing came from Maxine Smith, executive secretary of the NAACP. Smith viewed the macing as the point at which union officials realized they could no longer handle the strike purely from a labor perspective, and that they had to consider the racial element within it in order to succeed in receiving the city's recognition.[15] Mattie Sengstacke, an African American member of the Saturday Luncheon Group and wife of *Tri-State Defender* editor Whittier Sengstacke, similarly pointed to the macing as a turning point in the strike. The event prompted a boycott of the Memphis *Commercial Appeal* within the city's black community that eventually exerted pressure on that publication to temper its openly hostile stance toward the strike.[16] The boycott was one of several moves within Memphis's black community that agitated and worried its white counterparts.

Within a week of the macing, the protest at city hall on 2 March by strikers' supporters represented one of the earliest large marches against the mayor's resistance to union demands. The thousand-person march included a contingent of fifty white students from Memphis State University and Southwestern. Although it did not draw the numbers that the city witnessed later in the strike, the march became the first one in which large numbers of white strike supporters participated. Not surprisingly, the white Memphis press gave it scant coverage.[17]

One march to city hall that did draw considerable attention in the local press transpired during Loeb's open house on 7 March. A group of eighteen white women arrived together and as one group; they claimed to represent Memphis's white, middle-class community. Of the eighteen women who attended, decked out in hats and white gloves, sixteen openly disagreed with Loeb. The two lone dissenters justified their support of Loeb because of his argument that the illegal strike endangered the health of the city and its inhabitants.

The controversial issue for these women—as well as other Memphians and certain members of the city council—centered on the matter of the dues checkoff. Loeb claimed that his opposition to the dues checkoff reflected that of the larger Memphis community, and he vowed never to acquiesce to the union's demand to provide for an automatic extraction of monthly dues from union members' paychecks. Even those women who agreed with Loeb's stand on the dues checkoff articulated, nonetheless, their primary concern that the city's racial harmony was suffering during the sanitation strike, and Loeb's continued resistance to resolution of the strike was fomenting far more animosity and ill will between Memphis's black and white communities than the actual strike itself. All eighteen women, regardless of their opinions of Loeb and his handling of the strike, repeated their skepticism of the danger of the strike to the city's financial and physical health, maintaining that the damage occurring to Memphis's racial health was far greater and posed a far more immediate threat to Memphis's citizens than the health risks associated with piles of uncollected garbage.[18]

These women included members of the Memphis chapter of a burgeoning national program, Rearing Children of Goodwill (RCG). Although this group did not involve itself in many activities during the strike itself, and moved into the center of Memphis's reform community in the strike's wake, the RCG workshops began on 19 February 1968. Cosponsored by the National Conference of Christians and Jews, the Catholic Council on Human Relations, and the Anti-Defamation League of B'nai B'rith, RCG workshops emphasized increased communication among mothers of different racial, religious, and socioeconomic backgrounds in order to transfer that open-mindedness to their children.[19]

Founders of the RCG workshops fashioned their group on the model of the Saturday Luncheon Group (SLG), in that the key to its success lay in establishing open communication between Memphis's white and black communities. This first meeting in February featured black and white supporters of strikers discussing their perspective on the strike. While the initial meeting suffered from sparse attendance, the publicity following their appearance at Loeb's open house contributed to an increase in participants in the months following the strike's resolution. However, the group's impact remained unfelt throughout the strike itself. In fact, RCG workshop members sent another two contingents of both black and white delegates to Loeb's office during his weekly open houses, yet he remained unmoved by their entreaties for him to end the strike.[20]

Joan Beifuss, one of the founders of the RCG workshops, orchestrated the "march" on Loeb's office that fateful day in March. It was during the initial February meeting that Beifuss spoke of the pressing need for Memphis's white community to make clear to the mayor that white Memphians did not constitute a bloc of solidarity behind him. Although black and white women participated in the 19 February workshop, Beifuss recalled that the group agreed to send only white women from the affluent and predominantly white suburb of East Memphis to Loeb's office, in order to reinforce the notion that the white community was not a monolith. She believed that a group of "East Memphis housewives" fit the bill perfectly.[21]

Several members of the SLG also attended Loeb's open house. While the women still held their monthly meeting that February, their wider involvement in the strike happened after King's arrival in Memphis. Even then, although some members praised the SLG for not folding or splintering during the strike, critics accused the group of remaining too uninvolved to have any impact on the labor protest. Dorothy Lawson, the wife of strike supporter James Lawson, expressed enormous dismay that at the February meeting, only six white women attended—compared to thirty-six African-American women, including herself—thus signifying a dramatic decrease in the number of regular participants at these planning sessions.[22] SLG members such as Linda Allen took umbrage with their critics. Allen excused her lack of involvement early in the strike because of her ignorance of the situation. She claimed ignorance of the deaths of Cole and Walker, yet she also believed that the health and safety of the Memphis community trumped any grievances workers might have. Many white SLG members echoed Allen's excuses when pressed to explain why their involvement was so minimal during the early weeks of the strike.[23]

Without a doubt, the inability of strike supporters to articulate the centrality of race to the conflict contributed to the failure of Memphis's reform community to embrace the strikers' position from the beginning. What support did manifest prior to the 23 February macing came from individual women who attempted to convince Mayor Loeb to acquiesce to union demands and end the strike in the name of public safety.[24] The entrance of Dr. Martin Luther King, Jr., into the dispute on 28 March when he led a public march in support of striking sanitation workers pushed the envelope even further, and at this point, the floodgates of participation from Memphis's white female reformers opened.

The experience of Joyce Palmer, an active member of the Shelby County Democratic Party and a recent transplant from Minneapolis in 1967, typified that of many white activists who tentatively took their first steps into the civil rights movement during the sanitation strike. Inspired by Sister Adrian Marie Hofstetter, a white Catholic nun featured prominently in the Memphis media's coverage of the mass marches throughout the strike, Palmer impulsively joined the protest march of 28 March at the last minute. The infamous march, initially scheduled for the twenty-first, became violent. King's abandonment of the march, due to prodding from his SCLC colleagues, numerous arrests, and the murder of a black youth by Memphis police marred the event.

Palmer stated that her desire to participate in the demonstration stemmed not from her faith—she, too, was Catholic—but from the fact that she believed there needed to be more public displays of white solidarity among the marchers. She became involved in the 28 March demonstration following a discussion group she hosted the week before (21 March) on behalf of the Shelby County Democratic Party. Anne Shafer, then president of the Shelby County Women's Club of the Democratic Party, attended the discussion group that month. Palmer also noted the fact that union representatives had vacated negotiations between the striking workers and the city in the week prior to King's arrival as additional motivation to join the march. She recognized that the time was ripe for a more forceful intervention by the citizens of Memphis between union representatives and the city government.[25]

Palmer actively sought out white faces in the crowd upon her arrival. She remained with a group of white marchers until the vandalism and violence began, and her white compatriots disappeared. Palmer continued the march until the entire group dispersed, and attended the nightly mass meeting at Clayborne Temple afterwards. It was at this event that Memphis police attacked attendees, including Palmer, with Mace.[26]

Joan Turner Beifuss's first march in support of striking workers was also that fateful 28 March gathering. Born in Fall River, Massachusetts, on 13 October 1930, Beifuss moved with her family several times before settling in Tulsa, Oklahoma. Beifuss had an extensive career as a freelance journalist after she graduated from MacMurray College in Jacksonville, Illinois, in 1952. She worked for the *Chicago Sun-Times* for several years after graduating before entering Loyola University for graduate work in English. Beifuss finished her degree in 1963 and spent the next few years engaging in social activism. She became involved in civil rights work through her local church in Illinois. In 1965, she participated in a march for open housing in Oak Park, Illinois; the Episcopal church she attended led the march protesting segregation in Oak Park's neighborhoods. Yet Beifuss did not gravitate toward religious groups upon her relocation to Memphis in 1966. For Beifuss, reform work through religious groups had failed by 1968, and she believed that marching was her only option.[27]

The violence that marked the march and the evening meeting at Clayborne Temple fulfilled many Memphians' worst fears. Nonetheless, it was not only city officials and their supporters who feared King would exacerbate racial tension; many of Memphis's activist community also dreaded King's entrance into the city.[28] Beifuss articulated a concern shared by many Memphians, as well as by King and the moderate civil rights leadership at the time: fear of the black militant contingent working in Memphis in general, and at the 28 March protest, specifically.

King called for a walkout of all concerned citizens from their jobs, homes, and schools that day, in order to demonstrate their solidarity with striking workers. Students from the predominantly black Hamilton High School walked out en masse that morning from their classes, against the protestations of their teachers, and later faced blame for much of the vandalism that occurred during the march. Young black marchers taunted the mayor by carrying profanity-laden signs. Glenda Moon, wife of Richard Moon, one of the religious leaders of the white community, attended the march with Beifuss, and she shared Beifuss's trepidation regarding the march and its youthful participants. Both women recognized that inflammatory rhetoric plastered on signs could only do more harm than good. They agreed that had King maintained complete control over the march and its logistical organization, the violent tenor of the march would never have occurred. This reality, coupled with King's call the night before for a mass commitment from all elements of Memphis's black and white communities, only fueled tensions within the white Memphis community, and among white reformers themselves.[29]

Maxine Smith, executive secretary of Memphis's NAACP in 1968, echoed Beifuss's sentiments regarding the strike and the inability of anyone, including King, to handle the turbulent situation once it began. The NAACP was in charge of distributing signs for the march, and the sticks that she saw attached to those signs did not adhere to regulations regarding width and weight. She called it an oversight that the city failed to utilize more police protection in the march, considering the sheer numbers expected to attend. According to Smith, who marched at the head of the crowd with King that day, the police did nothing to quell the vandalism once it initially broke out. This oversight undoubtedly contributed to the problems King faced that day in controlling the thousands of people marching in support of striking sanitation workers.[30]

Not only did the resulting violence of the 28 March assembly alarm city officials and the white residents who supported Loeb's stand on the strike, but several of the participants also expressed concern and anxiety in the wake of the chaos. Beifuss noted that she found herself afraid to drive through predominantly black neighborhoods after the march, fearing violent recriminations due simply to her skin color. She managed to control her fear by forcing herself to drive through these areas, especially if she was heading to a mass meeting.[31]

This reluctance to mingle in integrated environments that many activists displayed, both before they became involved in racial reform work and after they had joined the fray, stemmed from the socialization these women experienced growing up in a segregated society. Reformers such as Anne Braden, Virginia Durr, and Sara Patton Boyle have detailed their personal struggles confronting an upbringing that emphasized racial hierarchy as a way to maintain their own social status within southern society.[32] White Memphians involved in the civil rights struggle faced similar concerns.

Another contingent of white female marchers in attendance at the 28 March event clustered together at the rear of the crowd.[33] One of these marchers, Marty Frich, a native of Little Rock, Arkansas, had a history of activism during her stay at Southwestern College. As a freshman in 1967, she had participated in an integration campaign at a local restaurant. Now, flanked by two members of Southwestern's chapter of the Southern Student Organizing Committee (SSOC), Linda Alders and Rutledge Tufts, Frich positioned herself at the rear of the march because the majority of the young marchers had congregated there. These women detected a degree of hostility from the black marchers around them. Not only did signs contain inflammatory slogans, but many of the younger demonstrators grew increasingly rowdy, running on city sidewalks—expressly prohibited by the city in its parade permit—screaming obscenities at Mayor Loeb and tearing down road signs along the parade route. Frich claimed that while she perceived some animosity coming from a contingent of black marchers toward herself and other white participants, it was the white "derelicts"—homeless men who lined Beale Street to watch the march—who invoked more panic in Frich than any of the actual march participants.

The violent march of 28 March was not the first taste of strike activism for Frich. Frich's earliest public display of solidarity with striking sanitation workers occurred at a "youth march," held on 2 March and targeting black and white junior high, high school, and college-age students. Frich repeated the sentiments of other female activists in expressing her distaste for the disruption and negativity she believed young black students brought to the movement. In particular, Frich blamed the Invaders, a militant black youth group that styled itself on the Black Panther Party, as the primary culprit in the problems with vandalism and violence that characterized this early youth march. While the 2 March gathering did not devolve into the kind of violence that the city beheld on 28 March, local merchants did call in Memphis police to disperse the primarily black crowd.[34]

Frich qualified her criticisms of the young participants in this march by claiming she did not believe that all young black Memphians embraced the philosophy and tactics of the Invaders. However, she did fear the emergence of problems later in the strike as black student supporters of striking workers grew more enamored of the message of Black Power as interpreted by the Invaders. Many activists, black and white, shared Frich's concern over the growing impulse of Black Power within the civil rights movement. Ann Geary, an early member of the SLG, expressed enormous disdain for the rising militant impulse in the civil rights movement. She did distinguish, however, between the younger generation of "militants" and the more established, older generation of religious leaders. Geary also demonstrated some of the paternalism of southern white activists by labeling the militancy inappropriate since white reformers like herself had done so much for the "race cause."[35]

King articulated his concern about the negative press generated by "militants," fearing that the militant impulse jeopardized a potential alliance with white activists and exacerbated underlying racial tensions between the white and African American communities.[36] However, not all white activists feared the power of the militant faction within the civil rights movement. In the February 1968 newsletter of the SSOC, Anne Braden praised adherents to Black Power, calling that wing of the movement the only contingent "with the strength to spark real change." In fact, Braden chastised those white activists who criticized and feared the militant branch of the movement. Braden also reiterated her belief in the absolute necessity of a coalition between black and white activists in order to focus on the plight of America's poor. Braden argued, along with many of her contemporaries, that white southerners had to reach out to those white southerners resistant to change and integration as the only way for any movement for economic change to triumph at that point in American history. She argued that building coalitions with black groups involved in civil rights solved the tough economic conditions for poor whites; indeed, the goal of student reformers committed to economic reform change must be to work with black groups, regardless of each organization's political persuasion.[37]

Memphis's white activist community heeded Braden's call to reach out to white southerners committed to segregation. On 10 March, Marty Frich distributed informational leaflets at Shady Grove Presbyterian

Church, in an attempt to alert the white community to the racial tone of the strike.[38] Frich and a male student, Jim Hayes, stood near the entrance to the church distributing their leaflets until ordered to stop by a male church member. After the service ended, however, Reverend Paul Fountain asked Frich and Hayes to return the following Sunday to share their message with some of the church's adult classes. Fountain also invited the duo to discuss their material with the Community Action Committee of Shady Grove Presbyterian Church in order to determine if the group sanctioned the material's distribution at future church events. Although Frich and Hayes summoned an additional thirty-three students to join them on 17 March, their messages fell on deaf ears. The congregants who listened to the students considered them "beatniks and rebels" more interested in bucking the status quo than transmitting any messages—or information—about racial injustice in Memphis. Frich also noted that the members with whom they talked viewed themselves as progressive in matters of race, since the church had invited an unnamed black woman to speak at a service several years earlier.[39] The irony did not deter Frich from her endeavors.

Marty Frich and several of her fellow students continued their efforts at bridge building within Memphis's white community when they spearheaded a predominantly white march in support of the strikers on 23 March. Organizers of the march, which began at the Poplar Plaza shopping mall, a facility catering to Memphis's white elite, intended to demonstrate to city officials that support for striking sanitation workers did not center exclusively within the African American community. Carrying signs condemning Loeb for his handling of the strike and criticizing him for allowing his racist ideas to cloud his judgment in resolving the strike, Southwestern students encountered an unexpected appearance of several black high school students. According to Frich and Dale Worsley, a fellow SSOC member and student, these students wanted to create chaos more than they wanted to participate in the march.[40]

As the strike progressed, Southwestern's chapter of the SSOC experienced a groundswell in membership numbers. The SSOC, founded in 1964 and intended to be the white southern counterpart to the Student Nonviolent Coordinating Committee (SNCC), initially focused its primary attention and activities on civil rights work. The civil rights movement did not witness a mass participation by southern white students until the Birmingham movement of 1963, and there remained no single group to organize white southern students at that point. What organizations did exist stayed isolated, localized, and unconnected to one another. Meanwhile, by 1964, SNCC had begun questioning the place of white members within its organization, and finally expelled white members in 1966. SSOC did see an initial membership of approximately 5 percent African American delegates, but due to the fact that the SSOC specifically targeted white students and held more moderate views than SNCC, African American membership quickly dwindled to nearly 0 percent by 1967.[41]

The SSOC sought to identify the extent to which white southern students participated in the civil rights movement and discern whether delegates had interest in other reform movements of that time. Students did express interest and involvement in the antiwar movement, activism against the death penalty, labor organization, and activities related to student rights on campus. At the group's founding meeting, held in Nashville, Tennessee, the weekend of April 3 through April 5, 1964, SSOC delegates constructed their platform, which, paraphrasing the southern Agrarians, was entitled "We'll Take Our Stand."[42]

SSOC members chose Nashville as the site for this organizational meeting due to the role of that city's SNCC members in the early sit-ins of the 1960s, along with the fact that white students had staged a sit-in of their own at the beginning of the 1963 school year, working closely with local SNCC members. Aimed at building a coalition of southern students dedicated to reform issues that involved many student activists at this point, SSOC resisted aligning itself with SNCC, as well as SNCC's white contemporaries, the Students for a Democratic Society (SDS). Forty-five students from fifteen southern colleges in ten southern states sent black and white representatives to this initial planning meeting.[43]

Several influential female activists played an important role in this first meeting, among them Constance Curry and Sue Thrasher, the first executive secretary and a native of Savannah, Tennessee.[44] Thrasher's involvement in civil rights work began shortly after the sit-ins of February 1960, when the nineteen-year-old attended a meeting of the Nashville chapter of the SCLC. She wrote that it was "the first time I heard black people speak for themselves" and pointed to this moment as an essential one on her journey into a full-time career in activism. While Thrasher held deep-seated religious beliefs that she felt had called her to missionary work in Nashville, she soon moved into working with the SSOC shortly after its founding, remaining cautious and acutely aware of the perils involved in an all-white southern group attempting to mobilize southern whites who, historically, had remained staunchly segregationist. The first large-scale activity of SSOC, the "White Folks Project," which occurred in the summer of 1964 and coincided with SNCC's and COFO's Freedom Summer project of voter registration, reinforced Thrasher's trepidation. While the project largely failed to bring more southern whites into the movement, it also drew heavy criticism from within the movement that organizing whites apart from blacks might not be the most effective tactic and could lead to a younger version of the South's infamous Citizens' Councils. Members of SSOC's chapter at Southwestern echoed Thrasher's concerns regarding the potential problems created by white activists mobilizing other white southerners. Nonetheless, the sanitation strike revealed deep racial divisions between Memphis's black and white communities, and any course of action was in order.[45]

In the wake of King's assassination, a group of black and white civic and religious leaders organized a mass meeting entitled "Memphis Cares" in the football stadium of Memphis's Central High School for 7 April 1968. In the meeting's published program, organizers eloquently exposed the city's divisive racial attitudes, accusing Memphians of ignoring these problems prior to King's death. Organizers intended for the meeting to begin the healing process so desperately needed in the aftermath of the violence of the strike and the death of the nation's most well-known civil rights leader.

The seven thousand attendees of "Memphis Cares," more than two-thirds of whom were white, called for an end to the strike as soon as possible, alleging that racism caused city officials' failure to recognize the union.[46] In addition to concern that further postponement of the strike's settlement would foment racial tension in the city, calls emanated from numerous segments of the Memphis community to end the strike in order to avoid further violence.

Critics of "Memphis Cares" abounded, claiming it was nothing more than a public relations stunt intended to improve Memphis's reputation nationally, and had little to do with an attempt to transcend the growing estrangement between Memphis's black and white communities. Joan Beifuss called the event a "white man's ceremony," illustrating her assumption that organizers structured the event to help Memphis's white community more than its African American one. The city divided itself between those who categorized the strike as primarily a racial issue and those who labeled it primarily a labor matter. Peggy Jemison admitted to initial skepticism toward those who categorized the strike as a racial, and not a labor, issue. She even feared King's entrance into the city, on the grounds that his arrival would foment violence, regardless of his stated intentions to keep his appearances in support of striking workers utterly nonviolent.[47]

Yet "Memphis Cares" changed Jemison's attitude dramatically. After hearing the emotional outpouring from several of the speakers, she actively sought out the company of black women she knew casually. Specifically, she targeted Mattie Sengstacke and Mary Collier. Upon enquiring, Jemison discovered the Saturday Luncheon Group; she attended her first meeting of the group in April 1968. For Jemison, King's death placed her on a path from which she could not veer. Her work with the Junior League and the Shelby United Neighbors shifted into a focus primarily on Memphis's African American community. Both Jemison and her friend Linda Allen began to exert energy in reform activities specifically targeting the African American population following King's death. Linda Allen sent a financial memorial to Coretta Scott King, compelled to donate money because she felt complicit in Memphis's racism.[48]

While many attendees articulated an intense feeling of solidarity with others present in the audience at "Memphis Cares," other activists pointed to the words of the meeting's speakers as motivations to activism. Perhaps the most riveting speech came from Mary Collier, an African American teacher from Melrose High School, a school with a primarily African American student body. Her speech highlighted the depth of racial tensions in Memphis since before King's death, and warned of the potential for serious problems in Memphis's race relations if citizens did not reach out to one another and learn about their neighbors. Collier encouraged harmony and cooperation between the black and white communities, calling on each audience member to take the initiative within her/his own community to reach out to someone of a different religious faith, social class, and skin color to continue the work that King had started, and, perhaps more important, avoid the violence that had caused King's assassination.[49]

Collier's speech that day had an immense impact on Jocelyn Maurie Dan Wurzburg, who later called King's death "probably the most transforming event of my life." Born in Memphis in 1940, Wurzburg attended Southwestern College, receiving a bachelor's degree in sociology in 1965. After marrying Richard Wurzburg in 1960, Jocelyn Wurzburg settled into domestic life, raising her three children and participating in local Republican Party functions and campaigns. Her traditional life as a well-to-do southern housewife took a dramatic turn that chilly April day in 1968.[50]

Shortly after the "Memphis Cares" program, Wurzburg invited Collier to her home to speak to approximately twenty friends, to explain to them, as she had to Wurzburg, why the strike was not simply a matter of labor, but one of race.[51] When Collier sent Elizabeth Phillips, a white professor from Memphis State University in her place, Wurzburg expressed dismay. Phillips began her talk with the assertion that the date of King's assassination was the worst and most sorrowful day in her life. Wurzburg called Phillips "high on hyperbole," since the majority of the women in attendance, including Wurzburg, were Jewish, and articulated their belief that the tragedy of the Holocaust represented a greater example of human evil than the murder of one individual leader. That meeting greatly altered Wurzburg's consciousness, awakening her to an understanding of institutionalized racism, yet it alienated many of those in attendance who disagreed with Phillips's characterization of racism as central to the strike and the larger socioeconomic problems in Memphis and throughout the southern U.S.[52]

Wurzburg had worked for Loeb's 1958 campaign for mayor, and had gone so far as to write Loeb a letter of support during the strike, encouraging him to "stay the course." Prior to King's assassination, however, Wurzburg began educating herself on the issues she deemed relevant to the strike —particularly the relationship between racism and economic inequity—by participating in lectures and events connected to settlement of the strike and to the racial problems in the city. On 20 March 1968, Wurzburg attended a meeting of the NCCJ. The literature circulated at this meeting included a pamphlet that highlighted the primary conflicts between Loeb and striking sanitation workers; it served as an early wake-up call to Wurzburg that an inextricable link existed between economics and race. Wurzburg credited her Republican Party allegiances to her belief that if any citizen suffered economically, such suffering would negatively affect the economy. If that economic handicap was based on an individual's race, it still was a handicap, according to Wurzburg, and thus must be addressed.[53]

Wurzburg believed she needed to uncover what truth there was to these revelations, especially in light of the fact that she was a mother to a six-year-old child who would grow up indoctrinated in these racial attitudes. Her concern for the city her children would inherit led her into participation in the Rearing Children of Goodwill Workshops, which led directly into her central role in the formation of Memphis's chapter of the Panel of American Women in 1969.[54]

While the sanitation strike and King's death led to the formation of some new women's groups in Memphis, it also led to the growth of certain existing organizations. The SLG, for instance, saw its membership numbers increase after King's death. The group's activities during the strike, however, remained minimal at best. After the successful integration of the city's restaurants in 1964, SLG members shifted their meetings to focus on strengthening the lines of communication between Memphis's black and white communities. The February 1968 meeting was just such a gathering. That month, SLG members sought to raise money to provide soap and washing powder for striking sanitation workers, since the federal assistance strikers received during the strike did not provide such items. Mary Collier even brought photographs documenting the remarkable attendance at the weekly mass meetings to drum up additional support for the striking sanitation workers. Unfortunately, attendance by members at the February meeting was sparse.[55] The meeting's minutes revealed that a number of women gave money, yet failed to attend the meeting. The record exposed a conscious attempt on the part of SLG members to keep up the appearance of racial harmony and cooperation by sending one white woman, Kay Portman, and one African American woman, Mary Collier, to deliver the contribution to the 24 February mass meeting at the Mason Temple.

The March meeting proved equally uninspiring for SLG veterans. While there were several new members in attendance, including some of the students from Southwestern, the turnout was as abysmal as that of the February meeting. Perhaps due to an unusual snowstorm that postponed the meeting until the day after King's 28 March gathering, the SLG's March meeting did not draw the numbers organizers expected for such a tumultuous period in the city's history, and further contributed to members' frustration over the group's potential for effecting change in Memphis during the strike.[56]

While many of the white members of the SLG praised the group as a true bridge builder between Memphis's black and white communities, many black participants had a different take on the group, especially after the strike. Gwen Kyles, whose status as the wife of SCLC member Billy Kyles served as her central link to civil rights work prior to the sanitation strike, began attending SLG meetings sporadically between 1965 and 1967. Her motivation for attending stemmed from her belief in the necessity for people from different economic, political, and racial backgrounds to communicate with one another and begin to understand each other.

Kyles, born in Macon, Georgia, and raised in Chicago, Illinois, moved to Memphis in 1960. She categorized her involvement in civil rights work as minimal prior to the strike, simply due to the fact that work related to her home and family commandeered the majority of her time. She attended virtually all of the mass meetings throughout the strike and was preparing dinner for King the night he was killed on the balcony at the Lorraine Motel.

Prior to the sanitation strike Kyles grew increasingly disenchanted with the group and stopped attending SLG meetings, after she discovered that some of the women attending were doing so just to say they had dined with an African American. Since Kyles, understandably, did not consider herself to be a novelty simply due to her racial identity, and, in light of the serious racial problems in Memphis illuminated by the strike and King's death, a meeting with no overt political purpose simply wasted her time. However, she did recognize a change in the white community in the wake of King's assassination; she labeled it a sense of "urgency" that racial problems needed to be addressed sooner rather than later, or more violence and untold chaos could ensue.[57]

Many of the women involved in the SLG were cognizant of the controversy brewing among guests at the meetings. Marjorie Cherry maintained her conception of the SLG as more of a place for women to keep each other informed of community activities, yet she also considered the interracial membership to be a vital element in the group's survival and success. Cherry believed that the SLG, although its achievements waned in importance as the decade of the 1960s progressed, endured as an effective conduit for interracial communication among Memphis's female activist networks. Cherry noted that a group of women had attempted to start a similar group in Nashville in 1964, but the group dissolved in 1967 after virtually all of the black women left for precisely the same reasons Kyles discussed: the notion that lunching with black women was more of a novelty than an attempt to contribute concretely to the activities of the civil rights movement. Minutes from SLG meetings in March and April 1968 corroborated Kyles's suspicions. The 22 March meeting had between thirty and thirty-five participants, half of whom were white. The meeting of 27 April, promoted as the "Unitarian-Universalist Evening Alliance at the Church of the River," consisted of over one hundred women in attendance, with more than half of them white.[58]

The tremors that gripped the SLG during the 1968 strike mimicked the history of earlier groups dedicated to interracial cooperation in the quest for racial equality. The Women's Council of the Commission on Interracial Cooperation (CIC) experienced many of the same problems as the SLG in fomenting and consolidating a biracial coalition that could work together to effect change. One of the earliest examples of southern white women's involvement in such biracial associations of the twentieth century emerged in 1920 with the CIC's convening of its Women's Council. The CIC formed in 1919 in an attempt to encourage conversation and empathy between black and white participants, while also working to end lynching and repeated violence against African Americans. The Women's Council took that agenda one step further, by including in its list of goals one of the primary concerns of the black women's club movement, the elimination of the sexual exploitation of African American women. Carrie Parks Johnson, the first leader of the Women's Council, verbalized many of the same observations put forward by white veterans of Memphis's SLG. Johnson marveled at the versatile cultural interests, high levels of education, and refined nature of the African American attendees. Black women who participated in the Women's Council also shared many of the sentiments Gwen Kyles articulated, namely, that white attendees pointed to their mere presence as evidence of the depth of their racial sensitivity. While the two groups differed greatly in their ideological goals, it is interesting to note that many of the same roadblocks to open communication and trust persisted throughout the decades. The inability to transcend years of skepticism and mistrust between black and white women continued to plague Memphis's activists, black and white, in the modern civil rights movement.[59]

The end of the strike came two weeks after King's 4 April death, in the wake of racial violence that gripped Memphis and other cities throughout the nation.[60] Many local and national organizations saw King's death as a wake-up call for action.[61] City officials also felt unbearable pressure from local and national leaders to end the strike immediately. President Johnson demanded that Loeb meet with James Reynolds, undersecretary of labor, and utilize him as a mediator in strike negotiations.[62] Local religious leaders also stepped up their entreaties to Loeb to end the strike. Hoping finally to persuade Mayor Loeb to end the strike by appealing to his Christian conscience and compassion for humankind, a group consisting largely of religious leaders from Memphis's white community launched a hunger strike on 5 April. The all-white group of hunger strikers stated publicly that they intended to force Memphis's white community to become involved in persuading Loeb to settle the sanitation strike. Participants feared that continuation of the strike after King's death would eventually polarize the community to such an extent that the two races could never find their way back to cooperation.

While the majority of the participants in this eight-day hunger strike were white men, four white women joined in the protest from its inception: Jane Dickson, Camilla Queener, Katherine Roop, and Sister Adrian Marie Hofstetter.[63] Sister Adrian Marie taught biology at the Catholic Church–affiliated Siena College and was a member of the Catholic laity. She also worked in the Community on the Move for Equality (COME), an organization formed on 24 February by Memphis's African American religious and civic leadership in an attempt to mobilize Memphis's white and black activist communities to band together to force a resolution of the strike. Her role in the hunger strike signified the beginning of a larger career in reform that continued long after the strike ended.[64]

King's assassination permanently tarnished the reputation that Memphis leaders had hoped to nurture for their community in the 1960s: Memphis as a progressive, racially sensitive southern city. However, King's entrée into the labor dispute in the city was not inevitable. Instead of escalating the strike into a national dispute over civil rights, Mayor Loeb could have circumvented this unwanted opprobrium by negotiating with the strikers and their union representatives from the beginning of the work stoppage.[65] Many members of Memphis's activist community blamed white Memphians for not dealing with the city's race problems before the beginning of the sanitation strike and thus held them guilty of complicity in King's death. These criticisms targeted not only those white Memphians who stood on the sidelines in the civil rights struggle, but those activists, such as the ones who participated in the organizations discussed in this chapter, who were late to join the movement or guilty of not doing enough to remedy the racial injustice of Memphis and the South in general.

The mass meetings and marches, Rearing Children of Goodwill, "Memphis Cares," and the Saturday Luncheon Group were the four primary outlets for those Memphis women who became involved in movements for racial and economic justice in the strike's wake. Some of these activists decreased their involvement in reform work after King's death and the strike's end. Whether afraid for the fate of Memphis after the violent nature of the strike or concerned about their families and their own lives, several women abandoned their activism after the strike, and returned to lives devoid of reform work of any kind. For other white women, these experiences translated into a move into larger forms of reform work, ranging from continued work within the quest for racial equality at the grassroots level to allying with organized labor to address the impact of racism on the socioeconomic status of city employees.

Chapter 5

"LITTLE OLD LADIES WITH TENNIS SHOES"
The Relationship Between White Women and Racial Reform in a Post-King Memphis

The Memphis chapter of the Panel of American Women (Panel), Concerned Women of Memphis (CWM), New Attitude-Memphis Encounter (NAME), and the Fund for Needy Schoolchildren (Fund) were the central organizations of Memphis's white female activist community in the aftermath of King's assassination and the resolution of the 1968 sanitation workers' strike. Many of their programs operated in concert at various times, and the groups shared personnel, tactics, and meeting space on occasion. Membership within these organizations often overlapped, yet their focuses varied from 1968 to 1971. The majority of Panel members identified as full-time housewives and mothers. The Memphis Panel seemed to be yet another example of the traditional, supposedly apolitical reform efforts that characterized this generation of Memphis's white activists. The "safe" endeavor of assisting impoverished children and enlightening the next generation of young people posed no threat to Memphis's racial hierarchy or conservative political structure.[1] Yet these organizations did just that. The seemingly benign intentions of the Panel, CWM, the Fund, and NAME led to concrete civil rights activism for many of their participants.

The first organization that resulted from this coalition of reformers became the Rearing Children of Goodwill (RCG). Sponsored by the National Conference of Christians and Jews (NCCJ), RCG launched its program of weekly workshops on 28 February 1968, at the height of tensions between the city government, national civil rights and labor leaders, and sanitation workers. The first workshop's title, "We Can't Afford Another Generation of Hate," revealed the group's chief goal: to eliminate the cycle of racism by changing the mindset of its members' own children. Attendees believed the racial climate that precipitated the sanitation strike and King's death, coupled with the racial segregation that continued to be the hallmark of the Memphis city school system and local neighborhoods, inevitably would transfer over to their children's generation. As wives and mothers, these women considered the education of their children to be the first—and in many women's opinions, the most—important step in eliminating the gulf between black and white Memphians.[2]

Meeting at the Evergreen Presbyterian Church, with representatives from the NCCJ, Catholic Council on Human Relations, and the Anti-Defamation League of B'nai B'rith, organizers designed a workshop that focused primarily on discussion. Joan Beifuss, chairperson of the RCG during the strike, modeled RCG on a Chicago meeting she had attended that sought solutions for successful, peaceful integration. She selected both African American and white speakers to facilitate discussion in an attempt to illuminate what "influenced" the children in these separate communities.[3]

Beifuss selected the three speakers at this first workshop, Paul Schwartz, Robert Vidulich, and Justin Adler, specifically for their credentials. Schwartz, director of the Memphis Jewish Community Center, asked the seventy-five attendees to encourage their children to continually question their environment, from the activities on the playground to the war in Vietnam. Schwartz contended that teaching a child to question everything within the first five years of life instilled that positive habit within her/him, thus creating independent, sophisticated thinkers who never accepted society's rigid boundaries of right/wrong, black/white. Vidulich and Adler, chair of the University of Memphis's psychology department and practicing psychiatrist, respectively, gave clinical definitions of prejudice prior to Schwartz's featured speech. All speakers agreed that mothers needed to train their children in this fashion, since "institutions" ranging from school to churches worked to discourage children's questions incessantly.[4]

The RCG workshops stood behind their "children-friendly" nature by offering child care providers for children aged five and younger. The attendees who took advantage of the service paid a fee for the child care. Organizers planned lecture series that would span a five-week period and take place in four different neighborhood churches throughout the city. Each individual series featured a wide range of topics, from civil rights to the role of religion in Memphis's black and white communities. While discussion was the RCG's primary activity, members also launched other endeavors aimed at relaxing racial tensions in Memphis. Members received a great amount of training from various Memphis State faculty members who volunteered their time facilitating workshops in cultural and racial sensitivity, as well as conflict resolution.[5] Ranging from tours of day care facilities in poor neighborhoods to a "Rumor Clinic" that attempted to mimic the ways in which rumors began and spread, RCG members put their ideas into action within the first six months of its existence.[6]

Claudia Davis replaced Joan Beifuss as chairperson of RCG in April 1968. A native of Little Rock, Arkansas, and an alumna of Little Rock Central High School, Davis expressed outrage over Governor Orville Faubus's handling of the school's 1957 integration. She deemed it a purely political move, aimed at engendering support for Faubus from Arkansas segregationists.[7] The year 1957 signified Davis's personal crucible of race. Her vocal public opposition to segregation began with the integration of Central High. Davis admitted to sharing the indoctrinated racism all southerners of her generation experienced. However, her religious beliefs led her to question the southern racial status quo, albeit silently, prior to this seminal event in civil rights history.

The birth of Davis's first child occurred in Conway, Arkansas, a small town of approximately nine thousand in the 1940s. Davis lived in Little Rock at the time, but she and her husband, Milton, consciously decided to have their daughter in a hospital without the latest medical technology, for the simple fact that the community's size mandated integration of the hospital. Davis understood that instilling racism in a child, even if that instilling occurred covertly or subconsciously, handicapped a child. Davis deemed this indoctrination a disservice to the holistic development of any child. She refused to subject any of her four children to such infestation, and she strove throughout the early years of the modern civil rights movement to avoid limiting her children's social exposure to people from a variety of socioeconomic, racial, ethnic, and religious backgrounds. Davis's children served as the catalyst to her engagement in religious groups like the Church Women United whose members increasingly devoted their resources to antiracist activism as the 1960s progressed.[8]

Davis encountered some resistance in planning meetings for the month of April when an unnamed Methodist minister refused to open his church for their workshops. Davis refused to name the church or the minister, who eventually allowed the women to use his church, although the church forced Davis to sign a release agreeing to pay for any damages incurred to the church during the workshops. Davis selected this church due to the fact that it was located in one of Memphis's integrated neighborhoods, yet she noted that congregants too shared some disdain for the RCG's use of the church.[9]

Davis's protégée and fellow RCG member, Donna Sue Shannon, recounted the difficulties RCG members encountered with congregants by relating the problems the RCG faced in locating child care personnel. Shannon also did not name the church where these problems occurred, stating only that the church, "now defunct," faltered in extending the space to the RCG participants. Nursery attendants, who were church members and not affiliated with RCG, refused to watch integrated groups of children, thus forcing the women to hire workers from outside the church to assist. In addition, use of the nursery hinged upon RCG members' bleaching the sheets, cribs, mats, and toys after each workshop; Davis and Shannon did so weekly throughout the month of April.[10]

Donna Sue Shannon entered Memphis's activist network through the final RCG workshop of March at Davis's invitation. A Memphis native, Shannon graduated from Whitehaven High School in 1957, fully cognizant of the turmoil occurring that year in Little Rock's Central High School. Shannon located that event as an early one in her personal awakening to racism's pernicious effects. While her family remained divided on the efficacy of integrating southern schools, Shannon's mother served as her "ally" in an antiracist ethos. She acknowledged an awareness of the name-calling, racial epithet–hurling white protesters' identity as "children of God," a startling contradiction for a young woman who grew up in a Christian household. In Shannon's words, this epiphany "planted the seeds."[11]

Shannon attended college at the all-white University of Tennessee from 1957 until 1960. She remembered only one student of color enrolled in the university's graduate program, a fact known to the entire campus due to its novelty. While Shannon remained on the sidelines of antiracist activism at this point, she recognized this realization as another step along her journey to discovery and mobilization to involvement in the civil rights movement. Upon returning to her hometown, Shannon immersed herself in caring for her husband, Wayne, and their two children, supplementing the family income through her work as a clerk at a local Memphis insurance company while her husband fulfilled his responsibilities with the Marine Corps.[12]

Shannon described herself as a "late bloomer" to both the civil rights and feminist movements, yet she situated her mundane activities in the early 1960s as key to her later activism. Reflecting on her experiences working full time while her husband finished his education through the GI bill, Shannon later realized that these early experiences created the potential for a feminist consciousness she developed later in her life. Shannon worked to help her family, not to further her own career in the insurance business. Indeed, when her employer asked her to begin traveling for business, she resigned, stating that the prospect of moving up through the ranks "scared [her] to death."[13]

Shannon spent the middle years of the 1960s completing her bachelor's and master's degrees at the University of Memphis in the school's communications department. That experience served as Shannon's linchpin for antiracist activism. Shannon grew "enlightened" by her professors, coursework, and the environment on campus. This environment exposed Shannon to an entirely new viewpoint that her childhood in a working-class suburb of Memphis had not.[14]

Although Shannon began engaging in educating herself on the timely social and political issues of the day, ranging from the Vietnam War to African American nationalism, her traditionally southern religious beliefs ultimately pulled her into political activism. Shannon met Claudia and Milton Davis prior to the sanitation strike through their involvement in Memphis's Methodist Church community, and Claudia Davis paved the way for Shannon's antiracist activism. Shannon's participation in this initial RCG workshop signaled the beginning of a new direction in her life.[15]

RCG continued holding workshops and public lectures for two months before being absorbed by the Memphis chapter of the Panel of American Women (Panel) in April 1968. Indeed, the two organizations adopted many similar philosophies, projects, and tactics. Jocelyn Wurzburg attended the first RCG workshop in February 1968 and recognized its format immediately as that of the Panel, a group she first encountered in Little Rock, Arkansas, in 1966.[16] The Panel began in 1955 in Kansas City, Missouri, as an avenue for women from a variety of religious, economic, and political backgrounds to engage in a dialogue about prejudice in all its incarnations and aid in the process of school desegregation. Esther Brown, the creator of that first chapter of the Panel, invited four acquaintances, three white women—one Catholic, one Jewish, and one Protestant—and one Protestant African American woman to speak before the Panel and discuss the ways in which prejudice had affected their individual lives, both positively and negatively. White women, for instance, gave examples of ways in which "white privilege" favored them, such as their being able to cash a check without providing identification or test-driving a car without leaving any collateral.[17] The rousing success of this first meeting led to seventy groups spreading throughout the Midwest and the southern United States by March 1968. The first chapter of the Panel in the South formed in 1963 in Little Rock. Jocelyn Wurzburg chaired Memphis's first chapter.[18]

For the African American panelists at each meeting, the effects of prejudice on their lives did not surprise those in attendance. Catholic women often discussed the prejudice they felt from living in a community where Protestants occasionally viewed Catholics with distrust, hearkening back to the nativism of the nineteenth and early twentieth centuries as proof of these archaic notions.[19] For many Jewish panelists, painful memories and discussions of the Holocaust dominated their dialogue. This common experience elucidated why Jewish women made up the primary organizers of the South's chapters of the Panel.[20] Bert Wolff, a leader of the National Council of Jewish Women (NCJW) in the early 1970s and a participant in the Panel from 1968 onward, categorized the memories of the Holocaust as vivid for her generation.[21] Like many of her white contemporaries in the civil rights movement of the 1960s, Wolff saw her role in the struggle for racial justice as essential to her identity as a Jewish woman. Discrimination that targeted a particular group, due to that group's race, ethnicity, or religious belief, caused many American Jews in the post–World War II era to remain vigilant; memories of the Holocaust motivated many Jewish activists to remain dedicated to eliminating racism and prejudice in all its forms.[22]

At the beginning of Panel meetings, the four chosen facilitators summarized their personal histories in five minutes, and followed up these introductions with a question and answer period. The rigidity of the Panel meeting's organization lent a credence and validity to individual participants' stories. Wolff remembered facilitators' attempts to make a powerful point by asking that the African American panelist only discuss racism, the Jewish panelist discuss anti-Semitism, and so forth.[23] According to Paula Barnes's examination of the Little Rock Panel, these questions were rarely spontaneous, but stemmed from a questionnaire distributed to Panel members upon joining the group. Consisting of over 150 questions, the questionnaire was divided up into sections that addressed specific social issues such as school and neighborhood integration, prayer in school, and women's liberation. Another segment of the questionnaire directed queries at specific groups of women, namely, "white majority" women, Jewish women, Mexican American women, Italian American women, and Catholic women.[24] The diversity of the questionnaire's subject matter served Memphis's purpose well. Dialogue between disparate groups of Memphians was essential, many white activists believed, if Memphis were to eliminate the racial gulf exposed by the sanitation strike and the assassination of Dr. Martin Luther King, Jr.

For many members of Memphis's Panel branch, King's death served as a wake-up call regarding the racial problems in their city. Jeanne Varnell, one of the early leaders of Memphis's Panel, categorized her stand on race as one of being "on the fence." Varnell considered herself to be politically and socially progressive, yet she never felt compelled to speak up and articulate her beliefs on any issues prior to King's assassination.[25] A native of Memphis, Varnell graduated from Memphis's East High School in 1955, attended Southwestern College at Memphis and received her master's degree in behavioral sciences from Washington State University.

Following King's death, Varnell soon immersed herself in any community project she could find, including a series of workshops held at Memphis State University in late 1969/early 1970. In what amounted to extensions of discussions at Panel meetings, faculty members from Memphis State facilitated discussion in the private homes of Memphis activists, encouraging attendees to share their personal histories and be open to criticism from the group. Varnell likened her experience at these sessions to Rip van Winkle's slow awakening from a long and deep slumber, and she moved into work with the Panel itself.[26]

Both Claudia Davis and Donna Sue Shannon expressed feelings similar to those of Varnell. Shannon described an "inner conflict" between what she heard from her neighbors and in her home and what she read in the newspapers and saw on television: these two sets of facts were like two "different universes."[27] Much like Varnell, Jones, Wurzburg, and countless other white Memphians, Shannon realized that the problems facing the sanitation workers were more than simply economic issues: the strikers' race was inextricably tied to their socioeconomic status. This realization proved so life altering that she had no choice but to become a "part of the solution."

Two other organizations of note formed in the midst of the sanitation strike were Save Our City (SOC) and the Memphis Search for Meaning Committee (MSM). SOC, founded in March 1968 by Mary Doughty and Pat Gilliam, veterans of the RCG workshops, touted itself as a "nonorganization" united in its support for the striking sanitation workers, and sought as its primary goal the compilation of a mailing list that would connect activists from Memphis's white and black communities into a network to effect political change and racial harmony. Consisting of many familiar names from Memphis's white activist community, male and female, Save Our City envisioned itself as a nonorganization due to the fact that none of the members ever spoke on behalf of one another or the organization itself.[28] News of this "nonorganization" organization spread rapidly: twenty-five people attended the first meeting on 14 March 1968; the second meeting one week later drew another eighty participants. Although primarily an information-gathering and -dissemination body, members also petitioned the city council and Mayor Loeb to end the strike in a timely fashion, even offering their own solutions to the problems and the negotiations' stalemate.[29]

The Memphis Search for Meaning Committee (MSM) began its career three days following King's death and extended, in membership and construction, from Save Our City. Memphis State University journalism professor David Yellin and his wife, author and activist Carol Lynn Yellin, created MSM as a way to capture and preserve the sanitation strike story. A native of New York City, Carol Lynn Yellin relocated to Memphis in 1964, whereupon she joined Memphis's activist community. At the time of the sanitation strike, Yellin was active with the Saturday Luncheon Group (SLG), and her work with this group, coupled with her occupation as an editor of the *Reader's Digest Condensed Books* series, stimulated her interest in preserving archival material for posterity. MSM also compiled the 1968 Sanitation Workers' Strike Collection in the University of Memphis's Mississippi Valley Collection.[30]

While some reformers focused only on the aspects of King's program that emphasized dialogue and interracial discussion, others seized upon the rhetoric of the Southern Christian Leadership Conference's (SCLC) Poor People's Campaign (PPC), thus putting King's ideas into action through projects targeting Memphis's poor community.[31] Yet another group that emerged during this period, the biracial Metropolitan Inter-Faith Association (MIFA), which formed on 15 September 1968, aimed to include members of every religious faith in Memphis to "help our city heal" in the wake of King's death. Originally focused on giving financial assistance, food, and clothing to Memphis's poor residents, white and black, young and old, MIFA eventually branched out into job placement for Memphis teenagers, mentoring projects aimed at assisting welfare recipients in finding adequate jobs, and providing temporary housing for individuals and families unable to afford rent payments.[32]

Memphis activists influenced by techniques pioneered by King in the Poor People's Campaign also proposed a strike among Memphis public employees in spring 1969. Although employees of Memphis's public hospitals began agitating for union representation even before settlement of the sanitation strike, these efforts gained momentum with the successful organizing of Memphis's sanitation workers by AFSCME in April 1968. Although threats of a strike did not materialize until 1969, Odell Horton, director of the City of Memphis Hospitals, stated at this early juncture that AFSCME representatives also targeted local hospitals, seeking an immediate implementation of a formal grievance procedure, as well as improved working conditions and equitable hiring policies for the hospitals' black and white employees. The racial composition of Memphis city hospitals' employees made an attempt at unionizing its workers a natural companion to the fight for unionization among sanitation workers: over 50 percent of its employees were African American.[33]

Numerous civil rights organizations in Memphis supported the struggle for union representation among all Memphis city employees. The Community on the Move for Equality (COME) released official statements in both daily newspapers calling for labor organization within the city government. In addition, COME urged the city council to enforce integration of the Memphis city school board and the city's public utilities division, Memphis Light, Gas, and Water, and called for the city council to allocate money earmarked for local implementation of national War on Poverty programs, such as the free school lunch programs.[34]

Women featured prominently on both sides of the threatened 1969 strike. Sister Marie Rita, chief administrator for St. Joseph's Hospital, opposed unionization of hospital employees, utilizing many of the same excuses Mayor Henry Loeb promoted during his negotiations with union representatives during the 1968 sanitation strike. Claiming that the presence of a union would jeopardize the "welfare of patients" by creating potential logjams in staffing issues, the sister argued that AFSCME, represented in Memphis by Jesse Epps, did not negotiate in good faith. Epps responded to the sister's allegations with accusations that racist hospital administrators had more interest in fomenting racial tensions between black and white employees than in granting employees basic benefits and addressing legitimate grievances. Save Our City also issued press releases condemning the labor problems at "St. Joe's" as impeded by racial bias, noting the similarities between the resistance of hospital administrators to allow union representation and the intractable stand of Mayor Loeb and city officials during the strike. The ill will present in the ranks of employees at St. Joe's manifested in the repeated circulation throughout the month of April 1969 of racist pamphlets containing threats to kill Epps and other black union representatives if talks of unions and strikes did not end.[35]

In response to a stalemate in negotiations between hospital management and union representatives, Epps suggested that the city appoint a committee consisting of persons unconnected, and who could presumably be objective, to either side of the debate to conduct a study on poverty levels among Memphis city employees. Among those handpicked by Epps was Myra Dreifus, one of only two women—one white, one black—chosen for the committee. In Epps's opinion, Dreifus's extensive work with feeding area schoolchildren qualified her for this position.[36]

At a grassroots level, Concerned Women of Memphis (CWM) weighed in early and decisively on the threatened strike at St. Joe's. A group with ties to the Memphis chapter of the Panel, CWM formed in the wake of a request by the Tennessee Human Relations Committee to enlist the help of the Panel in averting a strike—and the potential for violence that erupted during the 1968 sanitation strike.[37] Dorothy "Happy" Jones, president of CWM, sent numerous telegrams to Mayor Loeb, Memphis city council members, and AFCSME, requesting that all parties seek an immediate settlement in order to avoid the tragedy of the last strike of city employees in 1968.[38] Jones and her fellow cofounders of CWM, Anne Shafer, Jocelyn Wurzburg, and Sister Adrian Marie Hofstetter, maintained in this telegram that their group was "for the city." Their categorization of the problems between the city and union officials as a problem for all Memphians, black and white, was a popular refrain among political observers. Even the politically conservative Memphis newspapers characterized the strike as a problem for the city as a whole. Editorials emerged immediately after strike threats materialized claiming that a strike would destroy the city's cohesion, prove detrimental to the city's African American population, and "stifle city growth."[39]

Born in Memphis in the interwar years, Happy Jones grew up shuttling between Memphis, the small resort town of Horseshoe Lake, Arkansas, and the elite Miss Porter's school in Farmington, Connecticut, the site of her "liberal" education. Jones enrolled briefly in Southwestern College before leaving to marry Harry Jones and raise their three daughters. A sojourn in involvement with Memphis's Republican Party catapulted Jones into her activism in the early 1960s.[40]

As was the case with several other women involved in Memphis's civil rights struggle, including two original participants in the SLG, Linda Allen and Peggy Jemison, it was Jones's volunteer work with national political parties that piqued her interest in politics and civil rights work.[41] In 1962, Jones escorted a representative of the Washington, D.C., branch of the NAACP around Memphis, much to the chagrin of her husband, who claimed such excursions were "not done."[42] Throughout the 1960s, Jones continued her reform work under the auspices of the Republican Party, as well as within the Junior League–sponsored Florida

Street School Project, but, by the 1964 campaign of Barry Goldwater, the conservative element within Memphis's Republican Party had replaced moderate voices such as Jones's. Although Jones categorized her dedication to civil rights in its nascent stages as lukewarm, in that she did not publicly demonstrate against segregated facilities, she did note that "segregation did not feel right to" her.[43]

Jones recalled one of her first epiphanies regarding race relations during a monthly shopping trip into Hartford while a student at Miss Porter's. When her companion remarked on the physical beauty of African American people in general, Jones characterized the comment as a new idea for one steeped in the racist indoctrination of the pre–civil rights South: "Coming from the South, you don't think that way. I didn't reject it. I was fascinated with someone who would say that."[44] While this exchange mirrored the experience of Virginia Durr—and her moment of clarity dining with African American students in her college cafeteria—Jones's catalyst paled in comparison to the majority of African American activists moved to antiracist activism from direct, often violent personal attacks motivated by race. Nonetheless, the historical record must include the stories of those individuals like Durr, Jones, and others, who shifted from an unquestioned acceptance of a racist ideology instilled in them from birth to a refutation of racial prejudice and commitment to activism. Their accounts added an important dimension to the story of the modern civil rights movement by illuminating the cracks in the wall of racism and segregation from within the very communities that perpetuated them: the white South.

By the time of the sanitation strike of 1968, Jones was publicly speaking out and demonstrating her allegiance with striking sanitation workers while continuing to identify herself as a Republican Party member. Jones categorized her opinion about the strike as apathetic; she believed that neither union nor city officials were "negotiating in good faith." Unlike those who held to the traditional Republican Party line, however, Jones did not oppose unionization; she believed the strikers had a right to union representation if they so desired. However, like many other supporters of Mayor Loeb, Jones did not see a racial element to the strike; she perceived it solely as a labor dispute. Since such a stand was in opposition to the majority of Memphis's Republican Party membership, Jones found herself immediately ostracized by the Republican Party after

King's April 1968 death.⁴⁵ With King's assassination, Jones threw herself into the civil rights struggle full tilt. As it was for many other white Memphians, male and female, King's assassination was a turning point in her life, a wake-up call that Memphis's racial problems posed a severe and significant threat to the welfare of the city and its inhabitants.⁴⁶

As a cofounder of the Panel, Happy Jones characterized her experiences in Panel workshops as "humanizing" ones that motivated her to greater involvement. Her initial commitment to the group occurred while she was working at Memphis's Republican Party headquarters in early April 1968. Calling the moment one in which she landed "in the right place at the right time," Jones accepted an invitation to lunch with Jocelyn Wurzburg to discuss early plans for the Panel. Upon listening to Wurzburg's description of the Panel's national efforts, Jones pledged her full devotion to the Memphis chapter. The realization that racial discrimination had a tangible impact on the lives of black Memphians, rendering their economic position inferior to that of their white neighbors, spurred Jones to action.⁴⁷

While the group defined itself as a newly formed coalition, CWM members had worked on a variety of projects with existing organizations prior to 1969. The group adopted an eleven-point platform during the 1969 labor dispute that included some new and some familiar concerns of white female activists in Memphis. CWM's demands included calls for open and fair negotiations between the city and union representatives, the distribution of free lunches to schoolchildren, family planning education through community institutions and churches, a "living wage" for domestic workers, and a formal request that the Memphis city council solicit the national government to include Memphis in the federal free lunch program.⁴⁸

CWM participated in AFSCME's "Spread the Misery" campaign, intended to familiarize Memphis's white community with the poverty that plagued Memphis's black residents. Jesse Epps hoped such a campaign would encourage Memphis's white elite to assist in a fair redistribution of the city's wealth across racial lines, particularly if repeated demonstrations at the city's predominantly white shopping centers disrupted daily business operations.⁴⁹ Lester A. Rozen, chairperson of the Memphis and Shelby County Human Relations Commission, spurred on Memphis's white female community to action. Rozen agreed with Epps's idea that a boycott of Memphis's suburban shopping areas was an effective tactic, but Rozen also maintained that additional moves necessitated the shoring up of support in areas where apathy prevailed.

Rozen suggested to Jones, Wurzburg, and Shafer that the CWM host a neighborhood tour of Memphis's poorest residential areas in June of that year. CWM members planned to meet at one of the boycott centers, charter a bus, and tour neighborhoods where city employees threatening to strike lived. These women believed if they brought one companion with them who did not share their progressive ideas about race and class, they could have an impact on the bettering of race relations in the city. While Jocelyn Wurzburg, public spokesperson for CWM at the time of the "Spread the Misery" campaign, desired at least five non-CWM members to accompany each member on the tour, members met the more realistic expectation of one guest per member.[50]

Happy Jones commented on the demographics of the CWM members who attended the union-sponsored tour of neighborhoods in which sanitation workers lived. She credited the largely white, elite, Republican membership of the group with being among the few who could motivate the city government to action. Jones believed that government officials would only listen to the voices of those who were not black or poor, although she also speculated that the group may have "bitten off more than [they] could chew" by challenging the city's racial, economic, and social mores. Jones maintained, however, that the fact that CWM issued few public statements throughout their involvement in the 1969 strike controversy contributed to the city's acquiescing to labor's demands in the end and allowing AFSCME to represent all city employees in July 1969.[51]

Happy Jones also represented CWM at the 17 June 1969 city council meeting, where the group reported its findings on the "Spread the Misery" tour and attempted to persuade the council to resolve the economic inequity between Memphis's black and white communities.[52] These women publicly and privately persisted in their calls for fair negotiation between labor officials and the city, pointing to the three primary problems of Memphis's African American community—poverty, hunger, and racism—as being at the center of the grievances of city employees during the 1969 strike threat.[53] By August 1969, the CWM mailing list exceeded two hundred names; Jones attributed this quick growth to the success of the group in persuading the council to recognize AFSCME that summer.

Another key player in CWM who participated in these early campaigns, Sister Adrian Marie Hofstetter of the Dominican of St. Catherine, Wisconsin, contributed significantly to Memphis's reform community. Born Harriet Hofstetter in Nashville, Tennessee, in 1919, Sister Adrian Marie's journey into the Catholic order had a circuitous route. She entered Memphis's Siena College in 1937, pursuing a bachelor's degree in mathematics. During her second year of study, Sister Adrian Marie encountered Dorothy Day, whose involvement with the Catholic Worker Movement inspired Sister Adrian Marie to shift her focus away from teaching and education and toward social activism. A project in conjunction with Day's organization in Manhattan proved to be too difficult for the sister; the poverty she witnessed there weighed too heavily on her mind. Opting instead for a life of fellowship and service, and inspired by an aunt who was also a nun, Sister Adrian Marie decided to become a nun.[54] Although she entered the Catholic sisterhood prior to her graduation, the sister continued with her studies, ultimately earning a master of science degree from Notre Dame in 1952 and a doctorate in zoology four years later.[55] Yet her interest in science did not conflict with her passion for social justice, as evidenced by her extensive involvement in Memphis's civil rights community.

While Sister Adrian Marie's work outside her teaching and the Catholic Church focused primarily on civil rights, she also attended workshops and meetings in Memphis's nascent feminist community during the early 1970s. An experience Sister Adrian Marie had with male administrators at the Christian college Creighton, where she worked as a chaplain for a short time, emboldened her to include feminism in her reform agenda. She believed her dismissal from that position stemmed directly from the administrators' discomfort with women in positions of leadership in ministry.[56]

The sister focused the majority of her work with women's liberation on the campaign to allow ordination of women priests in the Catholic Church. In 1969 she formed the Memphis chapter of the National Coalition of American Nuns, which attempted to build upon the liberalization of the Catholic Church begun by Vatican II. She inextricably linked the liberation of women to that of all humanity, black and white, poor and wealthy, yet she acknowledged that the importance of rectifying Memphis's racial problems presented a more immediate concern for her.[57] Numerous historians have correctly identified the interconnectedness between movements for racial justice in the nineteenth and twentieth centuries and the first and second waves of feminism. However, an analysis of white female involvement in Memphis's civil rights movement revealed that the focus of activists remained on civil rights and desegregation of the Memphis city school system until 1972. While many of the subjects of this study did move into work focusing on women's liberation, only Sister Adrian Marie articulated her conception of feminism as inextricably linked to the struggle for racial justice.[58]

Not only was Sister Adrian Marie a cofounder of Memphis's chapter of the Panel, but she also drove the group New Attitude-Memphis Encounter (NAME). NAME planned to canvass nearly five thousand residents and twenty thousand homes located in three of Memphis's predominantly white suburbs—Frayser, Whitehaven, and East Memphis—on their ideas about race and its relationship to economic status. This would be done from 23 June through 8 August 1969. NAME's inspiration stemmed from the strike of sanitation workers, as well as the abortive 1969 strike of municipal employees; organizers hoped to "enlighten [residents] to the urgency of the racial and urban crisis."[59] While volunteers poured in from Memphis's activist community, including a large proportion of Memphis's Catholic sisterhood and such luminaries as Myra Dreifus and James Lawson, local businesses and the Memphis Chamber of Commerce also contributed financial support. All told, on 19 April 1969, nuns from seventeen states and Canada, along with fifty Memphis women, officially embarked upon what was initially called the "Siena College Summer Project." Project organizers who hoped to bridge the racial gap discovered this rift did not disappear with the resolution of the sanitation strike and the dialogue that ensued in the wake of King's death.[60]

NAME members sought not only to survey Memphis's racial attitudes for their own edification, but also to utilize the information they gleaned from their study to force city leaders to address the real problems of poverty and racial inequality in Memphis. Volunteers participated in a one-week orientation from 16 June through 22 June, in which they received instruction on how best to approach their subjects and encourage them to speak frankly about their racial attitudes without alienating them. While certainly the most publicized project of the group, the racial survey was not the sole task of the organization. NAME's other activities included plans for economic boycotts and direct action protests of businesses that failed to offer equal opportunity in hiring practices and promotion, as well as educational workshops on the relationship between poverty and race.[61]

Although the 1968 sanitation strike comprised one motivation for NAME organizers, another came from the recently published *Report of the National Advisory Commission on Civil Disorders* (or Kerner Report). Memphians grew more anxious about the urban violence spreading throughout the country in 1968, correctly locating Memphis in that spectrum of cities identified as susceptible to violence as the result of urban decay, unemployment, and racial discrimination—all characteristics of an unending cycle of poverty perpetuated by white racism.[62] The Kerner Report, so named due to the role of Illinois governor Otto Kerner in establishing the commission to investigate why the nation's cities had erupted in violence, addressed a variety of problems facing America's cities at this time, but activists in Memphis repeatedly pointed to the report's findings as corroboration of their belief that the violence following King's death merely portended more unrest to come.

Not every Memphian lived in fear of riots breaking out at the whim of a mob. While CWM cofounder Happy Jones articulated concern that King's death would trigger a violent reaction across the country, she did not fear such a response in Memphis; she claimed Memphians were too "apathetic to put on a riot." Although violence did break out across Memphis after King's assassination—prompting city officials to implement a dusk until dawn curfew—Jones's comment on the apathy of Memphis residents was an offhanded remark intended to symbolize the difficulty activists like herself had in mobilizing the general public, white and black, to action during the strike and immediately afterward.[63] In the end, perhaps coming as no surprise to activists like Jones, NAME failed to exert much influence on city officials to resolve the economic problems facing Memphis's black community. What began as an auspicious project targeting thousands of white Memphians ended with approximately six hundred residents agreeing to participate in the questionnaire, and even fewer, approximately eighty, expressing an interest in volunteering for racial and/or economic reform groups.[64]

Another group that garnered attention in the wake of the 1968 sanitation strike was Myra Dreifus's Fund for Needy Schoolchildren. Although in existence since the early 1960s, the Fund broadened the scope of its volunteer work by the latter part of the decade, both in the diversity of its projects and in the amount of public assistance the group received from local and national sources.[65] The Fund capitalized on an increase in public contributions primarily from the Department of Agriculture, which had taken the rhetoric of the Poor People's Campaign to heart and increased the amount of money allocated to the national school meal program, expanded the availability and number of food stamps in circulation, and broadened the distribution system of the nation's surplus food supply.[66]

The Fund's work with the Panel on the free lunch program for Memphis schoolchildren illustrated the expansion of the Fund's volunteer network during the latter years of the 1960s. Motivated by the national organization's campaign for the free lunch program, the Memphis chapter of the Panel increased contributions to the Fund. Since the Panel had embarked upon assisting local free lunch programs nationally, the Memphis chapter's collaboration with the Fund's efforts in this arena occurred naturally. The combined efforts of these two organizations, propelled largely by Myra Dreifus herself, produced positive results for Memphis schoolchildren between 1968 and 1970. Dreifus routinely appeared before congressional and presidential commissions testifying to the nutritional problems facing millions of American schoolchildren since the federal government's first steps into free meals for children in 1946. In attendance at a 21 May 1968 meeting of the House Education and Labor Committee in Washington, where she was but one representative from a group that included members of the YWCA, Church Women United, and the NCCJ, Dreifus worked tirelessly to obtain matching federal and state funds for Memphis's free lunch programs, programs funded for years in Memphis by private donations from individuals, organizations, and religious groups. Although the federal government distributed aid throughout the country, many Panel and Fund members attributed the influx of additional aid into Memphis's program in the wake of Dreifus's lobbying in Washington to her tireless efforts.[67] By 1970, some fifty-seven schools around the city of Memphis reaped the benefits that over four hundred volunteers could bring, and prompted enrollment numbers in the free lunch program that steadily increased during this period, reaching a peak of 25,500 students in 1975.[68]

In 1967, the Fund also took control of the Florida Street School Project, a community outreach program that the Memphis Junior League had begun in 1965. Panel members took control of the reigns for the project in 1968, yet Panel members continued to work closely with Dreifus and the Fund. Generally regarded as an acceptable charitable association for elite white women, married and unmarried, the Junior League created a surprisingly fertile training ground for several key figures in Memphis's white civil rights community, including Happy Jones. Membership requirements called for a specific amount of volunteer work from individual members, and volunteering as teaching assistants in inner city elementary schools under the auspices of the Florida Street School Project proved to be a perfect match for white women interested in charity work that, on the surface, seemed noncontroversial and appeared to have no political importance.

The Junior League targeted the Florida Street School due to the fact that its student body and staff consisted of African Americans. While Jones reveled in her volunteer work with students, other participants in the program did not. Jones disclosed that the Junior League planned to terminate the program with the Florida Street School a few years prior to the strike—in 1966—due to numerous complaints from volunteers who feared for their safety in a predominantly black and poverty-stricken neighborhood. Jones refused to abandon her post, labeling the Junior League's practices racially "discriminatory" and "absurd."[69]

Not only did Jones work in the school as a tutor and classroom assistant, but she also took the initiative to work independently of the program and the school itself. Each Friday, she shuttled five or six children around Memphis to explore the city's landmarks and history. Armed with nothing more than a tank of gas, Jones handed her travel companions a map of the city and asked them to choose a destination and instruct her on how best to arrive at the designated spot. She discovered quickly that these elementary students knew very little about Memphis outside their own neighborhoods; many of the students failed to name the Mississippi River correctly. Jones pointed to this experience as an early catalyst for her career in reform work that predated her shock over the 1968 King assassination: "Learning that they knew nothing about their city or how it functioned or what was there for them awakened a social conscience in me."[70]

Jones certainly knew of the events taking place at the time across the South. Nonetheless, she echoed the experiences of many of her contemporaries in the region. Many white southern women of Jones's generation embarked upon systematic racial reform only after having come face to face with the realization that racial inequities did not emanate from something foreign nor imagined by rabble rousers in the streets. Systemic racism, rooted in economic and political problems, begot serious, local, and immediate problems that went far beyond mere social rights.[71]

Much of the rationale behind the Fund's expansion of its work during the late 1960s and early 1970s stemmed from the personal involvement of Fund personnel in the Memphis Area Project-South (MAP-South). MAP-South received funding from Memphis's War on Poverty Committee on 1 January 1967 that enabled the group to be fully staffed and funded by March 1967. With the leadership of James Lawson—a key figure in the sanitation strike as well as in the Student Nonviolent Coordinating Committee of the early 1960s—MAP-South's establishment of "block clubs" facilitated discussion groups where residents in poor neighborhoods assembled to share their problems and brainstorm on potential solutions. The ingenious plan of involving neighborhood residents in these projects emanated from organizers' concern that poverty led to crime and violence. By allowing schools to double as local community centers for use by students and their parents and implementing black history programs and additional summer educational opportunities for area teachers, MAP-South members hoped to eliminate violence and increase education and opportunity.[72]

MAP-South overlapped with the Junior League's Florida Street School Project by working in tandem with volunteers to staff and fund summer programs for inner city children. In addition, Fund and MAP-South representatives established "parent education" programs, which consisted of seminars on nutrition, sewing, knitting, and "charm classes," which imparted information on, for example, how to set a table, give the proper address for acquaintances upon first meeting, and what the secret was to maintaining good posture while standing and sitting.[73] The group also utilized its access to federal monies to provide food supplements to the area's impoverished residents and to pay volunteers for their work. Indeed, Happy Jones's work with the Florida Street School Project led to a change in the school board's structure of the free lunch program. After observing students unable to qualify for the federal program being forced to sit in the cafeteria while other children ate lunch, Jones collected data and presented it to the school board. Her diligence led to the board's applying for—and receiving—funds for lunches in a school hitherto overlooked in the program. Selma Lewis and Myra Dreifus also enlisted the support of volunteers in the federal program Volunteers in Service to America (VISTA) to assist in surveying Memphis residents on their support of free lunch programs. Lewis and Dreifus agreed with Jones's recognition of the connection between poverty and race in this country, pointing to that perception as justification for their programs.[74]

Peggy Jemison, president of Memphis's Junior League during the 1968 sanitation workers' strike, and Linda Allen also participated in Head Start programs during the summer of 1968, but their specific goal centered on increasing the number of white students in the program. The women credited school board member and fellow member of CWM Frances Coe with informing them of the perilous state of the program if white enrollment did not increase in Memphis. Jemison and Allen believed that African American students needed the program more than white students, but they also feared the absence of such a program in Memphis's black communities. Their fear of what could happen if black schoolchildren had little to occupy their time when not in school propelled their involvement following King's death.[75] While this motivation may seem paternalistic, Myra Dreifus maintained that her involvement in MAP-South programs in African American school districts also came at the request of individual school administrators who sought an end to problems with vandalism at their schools while students were on vacation.[76]

While the period immediately following King's death marked neither the beginning nor the end of civil rights activism in Memphis, the visibility and effectiveness of female-led volunteer organizations dedicated to racial harmony peaked at this time. Within three years, the attention of the entire Memphis community, black and white, city official and private citizen, turned to busing and forced integration of Memphis city schools. For many veterans of Memphis's civil rights movement, the language of the PPC and the realization that black Memphians represented an inordinate number of Memphis's poorest citizens propelled them into a variety of projects. Working with such groups as the Tennessee Human Relations Committee and Memphis's Maternal Welfare League, activists broadened the scope of their reform work, branching out into campaigns for equal employment, expansion of child care facilities, and the inclusion of more women in state and federal government.

A number of activists continued working beyond the late 1960s with the groups discussed in this chapter. The Memphis chapter of the Panel continued its work until 1979, tapping into a network of approximately a thousand volunteers to continue exposing an estimated one hundred thousand individuals to the problems of racism and prejudice through their public workshops and meetings. Speaking to Parent-Teacher Associations, civic organizations, church groups, garden clubs, and even the Memphis Police Department, the Panel managed to offer an alternative voice to the conservative tone that dominated Memphis city politics and white society throughout the 1970s.[77]

The Panel enjoyed a unique longevity among the subjects of this chapter. For example, CWM was defunct by 1971. Perhaps due to the fact that CWM limited and expressly specified its goals, with its assistance in facilitating the end to the sanitation workers' strike as well as the successful aversion of the strike at St. Joseph's, members drifted into many of the other groups mentioned in this study. Although CWM spent the majority of its time and money in 1969 on attempting to convince the mayor and city council to allow unionization of the city's hospital employees, CWM also included on its agenda a state income tax and the redistricting of the Memphis school board to allow for a more appropriate racial representation of school board members. CWM did succeed in obtaining the school board amendment, perhaps a precursor to the next crisis in Memphis's racial history, the integration of the Memphis school system through busing.[78]

A key to the Panel's longevity stemmed from the fact that it did not form in reaction to one specific short-term event, such as the strike or King's assassination, and that it belonged to a network of Panel chapters across the nation. The Panel's focus on the elimination of racism and bigotry across generations and regions, instead of addressing one specific, localized event, contributed to its enduring legacy. According to Happy Jones, Memphis's white female activists needed to move into other endeavors in political and social reform. She feared that groups like CWM, who expended the majority of their energies on isolated projects, ended up looking like "little old ladies with tennis shoes," whose concern with the fashionable aspect of activism trumped concern for the tangible, productive potential for change within this activist network.[79]

Many women expressed optimism over the future of race relations in the wake of the 1968 sanitation strike, believing that the mobilization of Memphis's white activist community illustrated the brightness of this future. While many of the white female participants in Memphis's civil rights struggle moved into "race work" from religious and civic organizations, many others, particularly those women involved with Rearing Children of Goodwill and the Panel, came into the struggle motivated by personal reasons. These activists viewed King's death as a turning point in their lives, forcing them to choose between continuing to ignore Memphis's racial problems—thus rendering them complicit in the problem—or beginning to work for change.

Chapter 6

"Be Thankful It Was Only Sand"
Community Reaction to White Women in a Movement for Black Civil Rights

Histories of the civil rights movement highlight the contributions of white northern women, yet few detail the experiences of white southern women, who, in many instances, faced an enormous amount of resistance from their friends and family members, as well as other activists in the struggle for racial justice. While the backlash experienced by white southern women paled in comparison to that faced by black southern activists, male and female, opposition to their work existed, and the repercussions of their actions continued for years to come. Unlike their northern counterparts, southern workers did not return home after a particular project or action ended; the South was their home. Southern activists felt as though they had much more to lose than northern reformers because of this fact. For many of the subjects of this study, involvement in civil rights work symbolized a shirking of their responsibilities as southern, white, middle- and upper-class wives and mothers. Resistance to their activism varied in its sources and severity, and it grew in intensity throughout the decade of the 1960s. Animosity toward these women peaked in the wake of the sanitation strike.

Hostility toward civil rights activists did not emanate solely from segregationist quarters. Many southern natives harbored animosity toward northern activists who "came south" for a period, exacerbated racial tensions in a particular community, then returned home to their lives in the northern United States. Lillian Smith, a long-time activist whose credentials included working with the Congress of Racial Equality, the Southern Regional Council on Race Relations, the YWCA, and the Southern Conference for Human Welfare, noted that with the violence that characterized Selma, including the death of white activists James Reeb and Violet Liuzzo, the movement had turned a dangerous corner, and was "out of hand." Smith placed the brunt of the blame for this reckless and violent shift in the movement's tone to the influx of activists, white and black, from the northern U. S.; she argued that northerners lacked the knowledge and experience to effect decisive change since those who lived outside the South returned home upon completion of their project.[1]

For individuals who transplanted themselves from the North to the South, this bias remained. Joyce Palmer, a Minnesota native who relocated to Memphis in December 1967, immersed herself in Memphis's civil rights struggle during the sanitation strike of 1968. It was during one of the weekly mass meetings that she encountered a degree of hostility from black leaders of the 28 March meeting that followed a King-led march that had turned violent. While attempting to reach the front of Clayborne Temple to share with the event's organizer, Reverend James Lawson, her thoughts on how better to organize the meeting, another member of the Community on the Move for Equality (COME) stopped her. Palmer maintained that his reticence in listening to her suggestions came from the fact that she was an outside agitator and could offer no assistance in a southern movement.[2]

Many northern activists who "came south" to work in the movement for racial reform encountered resistance due to their designation as "outside agitators." Although on their home turf, southern activists also often erroneously received the same label if they dared to cross the South's racial line to work for civil rights. Enmity toward the "outside agitator" was not a new phenomenon in southern politics. Dating back to the Civil War and Reconstruction, southerners clung to a belief that the federal government had only nefarious plans for the South, and intended to render the South nothing more than a colony of the North.[3] John Dittmer's work on the civil rights movement in Mississippi articulated the theory that the animosity and violence met by freedom riders and voter registration workers affiliated with the Student Nonviolent Coordinating Committee (SNCC) in 1961 and 1962 resulted directly from the participants' hailing from states other than Mississippi.[4] When looking at the ways in which Memphians responded to "outside agitators," one must initially address the reaction to Dr. Martin Luther King, Jr., upon his arrival in the city in March 1968. Local newspapers saturated their coverage of King's visit with inflammatory articles about King and the Southern Christian Leadership Conference (SCLC), many of which bore no relevance to King's opinions of the strike or the SCLC's political philosophy.[5]

Opponents of the civil rights movement, at the local and federal levels, also enjoyed labeling a reformer a Communist as a deterrent. The effects of these accusations ranged in severity from mildly irritating and easily overcome to severely disruptive and capable of evoking criminal charges and incarceration. Sara Patton Boyle faced an enormous amount of resistance to her work in racial reform, and she, too, endured an onslaught of red-baiting when she began publishing letters to the editors of local Virginia papers. However, these accusations, Boyle asserted, paled in comparison to the rejection she faced from black civil rights workers and the isolation she encountered within the white community.[6] Among the multitude of groups targeted for dissolution by the FBI due to their alleged "Communist" ties were the National Committee to Abolish the Poll Tax, the Southern Conference for Human Welfare, and the Southern Conference and Educational Fund (SCEF); Virginia Durr and Anne Braden did extensive work with these allegedly subversive organizations.[7]

Although Virginia Durr faced accusations of being a Communist, her unflagging optimism prevented these accusations from slowing down her devotion to civil rights work. While living in Washington, D.C., in the late 1940s, Durr's husband, Clifford, a lawyer, constantly endured red-baiting for his work with labor movement clients. When Clifford Durr grew increasingly disillusioned with the roadblocks such allegations placed in his path while he was trying to defend clients and wished to return to Alabama, Virginia Durr convinced him to stay. She feared the community reprisals undoubtedly awaiting her family and herself if they returned home to Alabama after Durr's high-profile, public involvement with groups such as the National Committee to Abolish the Poll Tax.[8]

Ever true to her droll nature, Durr ridiculed attempts by opponents of the civil rights movement to discount its motives and effectiveness through red-baiting. She pointed to the fact that the majority of the major political leaders of the movement, as well as the younger students working with SNCC, took their initial forays into activism through their churches as evidence of the inability of Communist labels to stick. According to Durr, enemies of the movement found it too difficult a chore to paint Jesus Christ as a Communist.[9]

Anne Braden also endured accusations of holding sympathy for the Communist Party; however, for her these allegations carried a stiffer penalty. A native of Anniston, Alabama, Braden became involved in work for racial reform in the late 1940s upon joining the NAACP in Louisville, Kentucky. She moved into union organizing shortly thereafter, in 1949.[10] On 10 May 1954, Braden completed the purchase of a house for an African American friend, Andrew Wade, in a predominantly white neighborhood in Louisville. Braden considered the purchase of Wade's home both a way to test a 1948 Supreme Court decision declaring restrictive covenants in real estate unconstitutional and a favor to a friend. Braden's purchase of the Wade home came after repeated and futile attempts by Wade to purchase the house himself. Wade financed the entire purchase; the Bradens merely signed the contract and turned the deed over to him upon completion of the sale. She anticipated hostility toward Wade and his family once they took possession of the home, and within weeks of purchase, a bomb partially destroyed the house.[11] As a result, in December 1954, Braden, along with five others, including her husband, journalist and activist Carl Braden, faced federal charges of sedition. The sedition charges stemmed from the purchase of the Wade home, a transaction supposedly manipulated by the Communist Party. The conviction of all five defendants led to their incarceration, and Braden remained in jail for one week until a family friend paid her ten-thousand-dollar bond.[12]

Septima Clark, an activist and friend to both Durr and Braden after all three women worked with Myles Horton at the Highlander Folk School in Monteagle, Tennessee, encountered continual harassment from local officials and her employer while living in Charleston, South Carolina. Her experiences typified those of African American activists red-baited during the civil rights movement, yet they also served as a stark contrast to those of her white contemporaries. A member of the SCLC from its creation in 1956, Clark had an extensive history of civil rights work by 1956, the year she moved to Monteagle to train activists full-time. After refusing to "disavow" her membership in the NAACP, due to that group's supposedly Communist connections, Clark lost her teaching job in Charleston.[13]

Memphian Anne Shafer also received the label of Communist, due, she believed, to her support of "mixing the races."[14] Unlike Braden, however, Shafer did not face physical incarceration for her opposition to racism; yet the result of her alleged ties to the Communist Party cost her something more precious—her church. Shafer encountered a considerable amount of resistance to her commitment to civil rights while working under the auspices of the Council of Catholic Women (CCW) in the late 1950s and early 1960s. Although Memphis's Catholic clergy consisted of both black and white priests and nuns, individual parishes remained segregated, as did city-wide Catholic groups. In 1961, Shafer attempted to integrate the annual retreat of the CCW, but was unable to find support from any members. Shafer, nonetheless, invited all of Memphis's Catholic female population, black and white, but only one black woman accepted the invitation.[15] Shafer believed this event contributed to her eventual removal from the CCW executive board in 1963.

Shafer's problems with the Catholic clergy and laity in Memphis continued in 1963 when she assisted in the founding of the Catholic Human Relations Council (CHRC). An integrated organization, the CHRC suffered from the absence of a progressive leadership board. Bishop Joseph Durick, leader of the CHRC and a long-standing member of the John Birch Society, once again raised the specter of the "red menace" and attacked Shafer as a Communist due to her devotion to racial reform. While Durick approved of an integrated CHRC, he supported neither an agenda nor the allocation of financial resources that favored civil rights work over other projects not specifically targeting the black community.[16]

Animosity toward Shafer was not limited to the leadership of the Catholic Church in Memphis. For instance, upon her return to Memphis from Illinois, a rift developed between Joan Beifuss and Shafer. In 1968, Shafer formed a group called Women of the Church as a response to a "Call to Action" from the city of Chicago's Catholic diocese meeting early that year. The group's goals included mobilizing the female laity of Memphis's Catholic community to become involved in civil rights work at the grassroots level. Before the group could get off the ground, however, Beifuss took control and dissolved it. Shafer maintained that both Beifuss's and the Memphis Catholic leadership's hostility to her civil rights work were responsible for Women of the Church's failure to materialize as a cohesive unit. The group New Attitude-Memphis Encounter (NAME) formed shortly after Women of the Church disintegrated. Many of the personnel involved were identical, leading some observers to suggest that the group originally called Women of the Church continued, but under a different name and with different leadership.[17] Regardless of whether Shafer's alienation from Memphis's reform community and the Catholic Church was real or imagined, Shafer expressed deep despair over having "lost" her church due to her civil rights work. This characterization becomes especially poignant given the fact that Shafer's deep-seated religious faith is what brought her into the movement initially, and what gave her emotional strength in the face of hostility from others.[18]

Regardless of the repercussions, and aware of the potential destruction such activity wreaked, many activists took the chance to involve themselves in racial reform out of a sense of obligation to the South. What began as an attempt to improve their homeland evolved quickly into awareness that their homeland, the South, neither welcomed nor appreciated their work and designated them as "outside agitators." Activists spoke of a "homesickness," a feeling of isolation that increased along with their involvement in civil rights work. SNCC veterans Constance Curry, Joan Browning, Dorothy Burlage, and Casey Hayden all articulated a sense of loss that resulted from their involvement in the movement.[19] By stepping across the racial divide, what Anne Braden called "the wall between," these southern white women rendered themselves exiles in their own communities.[20] This wall between the races referred to the social, cultural, economic, and political differences between black and white southerners, the effects of living in a segregated society that alienated both races from each other, prevented each from communicating or interacting with the other, and fomented distrust between the two racial groups. Braden blamed this distrust for the animosity white southerners exhibited toward white southern civil rights workers as well as the reluctance of some black-led civil rights groups to work with white activists. Indeed, many white men and women born in the South faced rejection from their own white communities as well as from national civil rights organizations, who considered white southerners a liability in the movement.

The notion that the proper place for white activists in the civil rights movement was engaging in work within the southern white community was a common one among civil rights activists from 1965 onward. The increasing influence of the black separatist strain within the civil rights movement shifted the organizational structure of a number of the major civil rights groups, including SNCC, which expelled white members in 1966.[21] Yet, for many activists, this expulsion represented another rejection, perhaps more humiliating than that by the white community.

Sandra "Casey" Hayden revealed her ambivalence toward leaving SNCC. Hayden agreed with the SNCC leadership that by mid-decade, white activists in the civil rights movement serve as organizers within the white community. Yet, she also felt alone, isolated, and without a family, going so far as to call herself fortunate to have "survived" the trauma of expulsion from SNCC, primarily due to what she called her exile from the "beloved community."[22] Hayden spoke often of the "beloved community," a phrase used by both Dr. Martin Luther King, Jr., and SNCC to describe the unity of activists committed to nonviolence. Their steadfast reliance on nonviolence bonded them as closely as if they were born into the same family.[23]

The rationale behind the expulsion of white members from SNCC in 1966 emanated from the assumption among SNCC leadership that only fellow white southerners could effect any change in the mindset of white segregationists. This thinking lay behind the formation of the Southern Student Organizing Committee (SSOC), formed in 1964 by activists from a number of reform organizations in existence at the time. Organizers faced the burden of attempting to develop some type of southern consciousness/nationalism without romanticizing the Old South. Calls for the unity of white southerners in any fashion conjured up images of white-hooded Klansmen devoted to resurrecting segregation and rendering black southerners economically, politically, and socially inferior to white southerners. This public relations problem plagued SSOC throughout its life. In 1969, members launched a last-ditch effort to forge an alliance between impoverished white and black southerners, and to dispel stereotypes that all southerners were racists, by claiming that black and white southerners' shared economic oppression stemmed from the same source: the white elite power structure. In the end, the notion of a southern nationalism still reeked of racism, and perhaps contributed to the group's demise in 1969.[24] While these stereotypes were not insurmountable, the racial indoctrination imparted to white southerners from childhood on sometimes was.

Marjorie Cherry felt compelled to contribute to this campaign, and she began her quest of liberating white segregationists one individual at a time upon her arrival in Memphis in 1958. She recalled that when many of her friends from "up north" (New York State) learned of her plans to move to Memphis, they were appalled that she would dare to set foot in such a "hillbilly" town. However, Cherry and her husband both believed that their presence in Memphis would benefit the city's white inhabitants, since their plan was to enlighten the ignorant white masses upon arrival. Although James Cherry moved to Memphis for professional reasons—his work as a manager in the Memphis *Commercial Appeal*'s advertising department prompted their move from Virginia to Memphis in 1958—both he and his wife immediately embarked upon putting their paternalistic notions into practice. Marjorie Cherry joined the Memphis branch of the League of Women Voters, serving as its president in 1963, before turning her attention fully to civil rights work in 1964.[25]

Many white southern civil rights workers revealed a paternalistic attitude toward black southerners that compromised the integrity of their motivations and actions and created animosity among African American civil rights workers. Some white southern activists envisioned the southern black population as a stereotypical group of primitive, emotional, illiterate, violent, and helpless individuals. On occasion, black activists discounted the activities of southern white civil rights workers, pointing to this paternalism as casting a wider shadow over any individual's reform work.[26]

Sara Patton Boyle's journey into civil rights work and the resistance she faced from black leaders in Virginia illustrated this reluctance to include white southerners in a movement for African American racial equality. Although Boyle did not belong to any of the traditional national civil rights organizations, her deep religious faith led her to question the South's racial hierarchy. Her first public foray into speaking out against racial injustice came in 1950. Gregory Swanson, an African American student in Virginia, attempted to enter the University of Virginia law school in 1950, and Boyle wrote him a letter of support, claiming to speak for all of his white allies in Charlottesville. Swanson's response contained what Boyle described as "sophisticated" vocabulary, prompting Boyle to conclude Swanson had "forgotten his place."[27]

In the course of Swanson and Boyle's correspondence, Swanson shared some of Boyle's missives with T. J. Sellers, editor of the black-owned newspaper the *Richmond Times-Dispatch*, thus prompting Sellers to commence correspondence with Boyle. Sellers patiently and painstakingly exposed Boyle's own paternalism to her throughout their more than thirteen-year friendship, sending Boyle through repeated episodes of self-reflection over her place in the larger civil rights struggle. The alienation Boyle felt from the black civil rights community, combined with the ostracism she experienced within the white community in Charlottesville, led her away from work in racial reform and into a spiritual quest that began with her conversion to Orthodox Christianity in 1959 and abandonment of work for racial equality.[28]

Memphis's white activist community housed its share of female activists who considered their work underappreciated by the black community. This paternalism appeared most prevalent within the Saturday Luncheon Group. One of the initial participants in the SLG, Peggy Jemison, noted how upset she was upon discovering the depth of animosity within Memphis's black community following King's assassination, especially considering how Memphis had so gracefully acquiesced to integration in the wake of the Civil Rights Act of 1964. Ann Geary and Mary Kay Tolleson, SLG members in its early days, echoed Jemison's remarks made in the wake of King's death. Geary and Tolleson, two of a handful of white female participants in the infamous march of 28 March 1968 that disintegrated into violence, lamented the fact that the increase in militancy within the civil rights movement prevented interracial cooperation and illustrated the "sensitivity" and lack of appreciation evident among a section of Memphis's black population.[29]

Both Maxine Smith and Mattie Sengstacke illustrated the cynicism of many civil rights workers regarding white activists. Smith and Sengstacke believed white participants at SLG meetings viewed white attendance at integrated luncheons as a privilege for black attendees. According to

Smith and Sengstacke, some white members believed black members owed them a debt of gratitude for deigning to risk social ostracism for appearing in integrated groups at restaurants that catered to Memphis's white elite. Historical evidence corroborated Smith's suspicions.[30]

Yet another figure from the SLG's early years, Margaret Valiant, revealed a startling amount of paternalism in an interview regarding her tenure as the sole white inhabitant of a housing project in Memphis in the midst of the sanitation strike. Valiant labeled "integration as the thing" early in the civil rights movement, yet she decried the shift to "separatism" that generated the lion's share of publicity at the close of the 1960s. The ethos of black power in Memphis's civil rights community unnerved Valiant, and she pointed to several of her neighbors as illustrations of the problems "militancy" created. Valiant referred to Coby Smith, a leader of the Invaders, an organization that modeled itself on the Black Panthers and moved into the spotlight during the sanitation strike, as "one of these young bucks" who preferred relaxation to work. Her characterization of Smith arose from his friendship with several of Valiant's neighbors who refused to assist her in performing odd jobs around her apartment, such as lifting heavy objects and carrying the groceries to her residence. Valiant believed that Smith's "macho," pompous attitude came from his "African" ancestors, who made "women do all the work."[31]

Valiant continued to utilize the phrase "young bucks" throughout her narrative of the impact of King's death on her neighborhood and the vandalism that ensued in its immediate wake. She referred to the "young bucks loitering out front . . . [who] even broke a soul brother's window." These comments only scratched the surface of the language contained in this interview, ranging from her pronouncement that all African American men and women "were born with a sense of performance," to her belief that her inability to buy a television came from the fact that she "wasn't on welfare" like her neighbors, and, thus, could not afford the purchase.[32]

This language, although disturbing in its prejudice and ignorance, actually improved upon Valiant's notions about race she had as a child growing up in the rural Mississippi of the early 1920s. She remembered that her family instilled in her the notion that African American southerners, or "darkies," the term her family preferred, be treated with affection and considered no more human than a family pet. Valiant exhibited an attitude that typified many of her generation. Indeed, one of the enduring stereotypes, dating back to the 1930s and 1940s, of southern white liberals involved in "race work" remained that of the paternalistic reformer, whose racism resulted from living in a region with rigid racial lines, and whose inability to transcend racial indoctrination rendered him or her suspect.[33] Although Valiant's extensive career in reform work appeared contradictory to the stereotypes she accepted without question, her racism and paternalism highlight one of the contributing factors to the omission of this generation of civil rights workers from the movement's historiography.

While ostracism from national civil rights organizations and alienation from the South illustrated two negative reactions white women faced upon entering the civil rights fray, more immediate repercussions manifested themselves in the lives of these activists from within their own communities. Reprisals against Memphis's white female reformers varied in degree. Civil rights activists faced the destruction of personal relationships and ostracism from families while also enduring harassing phone calls and vandalism of property. Jeanne Varnell, for example, openly articulated her feelings of sorrow and pessimism on the future of race relations in Memphis following the death of King, although her friends and acquaintances did not share her sentiments. Varnell endeavored to organize a prayer vigil in her neighborhood shortly after the assassination, yet she failed to muster much enthusiasm within her community. Many invited guests expressed little remorse over King's death, only bitterness and resentment that the murder had occurred in Memphis. While this lack of compassion disheartened Varnell, the exclusion of her children from the neighborhood carpool compounded her fear over how her activism affected her family. Varnell repeatedly spoke of her concern about the ways in which her involvement in the Panel affected her children. After the forced integration of Memphis city schools began in 1971, and Varnell's daughter Ruth attended one of the "most perfectly integrated schools in Memphis," Varnell reluctantly allowed her to accompany an African American classmate to the senior prom. Her struggle and fear came not from any archaic ideas she herself harbored about black men, but from how white community members might respond to seeing an African American man arrive at the Varnell home to escort their daughter out for the evening.[34]

Donna Sue Shannon also expressed disgust and shock to learn that some of her friends and acquaintances rejoiced at the news of King's death, viewing his assassination as a welcome reprieve from the turmoil the strike and the civil rights movement had brought to Memphis. While Shannon's consciousness did not awaken upon King's death, her career in activism began at that point. These displays of hate and intolerance from neighbors shocked Shannon into putting her ideas into action by contributing whatever time and energy were available to the movement for racial justice. Indeed, a number of Shannon's contemporaries recounted similarly abhorrent comments from friends and family members upon hearing of King's death but noted that the comments simply drove them into a deeper commitment to civil rights work.[35]

Shannon hesitated to move into activist work, but she joined the Rearing Children of Goodwill (RCG) workshops during the 1968 sanitation strike—an act she considered a "bold, radical step." She gave up the values instilled in her from an early age, and created a level of discord and tension in her own home; Shannon's husband frowned upon her activism, and exerted enough pressure on her that she never publicly marched in solidarity with striking sanitation workers. Shannon also cited family responsibilities as another influence upon her decision not to become involved during the strike itself. Her fear for the lives of her children, and the danger her activism might place them in at school or among neighborhood children, kept her public activities at bay until resolution of the strike.[36]

For Anne Shafer, the problems she experienced due to her work with Concerned Women of Memphis (CWM) not only created a physical inconvenience but also garnered much publicity in Memphis's daily newspapers. After attending an initial meeting of CWM's NAME at Siena College in June 1969, Shafer returned to her home to find sand dumped in her front yard, covering the driveway and front door, blocking all but the rear entrance to the house. For four days following this incident, Shafer endured an endless stream of obscene phone calls, in which anonymous male voices declared, "It shoulda been nigger shit."[37] Although Shafer never discovered who ordered the sand, she did receive a bill of sale from the company who delivered it. When the now-defunct company refused to name the individual who ordered the sand, Shafer refused to pay the bill, telling company managers she was delighted to return the sand to them. The sand issue resolved itself when the Memphis *Commercial Appeal* ran a story on Shafer's predicament and advertised free sand to anyone who was interested. Within one week, friends and strangers brought trucks and wheelbarrows and removed the sand from the Shafers' front yard. CWM members went so far as to formally solicit assistance from a significant number of their spouses in cleaning up Shafer's yard; the group also suggested a resolution for submission to the Memphis Chamber of Commerce asking that body to attempt to quell the amount of hate mail targeting CWM members.[38]

Jocelyn Wurzburg recalled similarly detestable incidents after she became an active participant in CWM. Much like Shafer, Wurzurg endured countless threatening phone calls demanding that she end her involvement with the labor dispute, while another antagonist shuttled door-to-door salesmen to her home at thirty-minute intervals on a single day. Perhaps more detrimental to Wurzburg's life than these irritating episodes was the backlash from her husband's family, who made accusations that her activities were hurting the family's office supply business. Although instructions to "shut her up" failed, dissension sown by the different worldviews of Wurzburg and her in-laws took root.[39]

Wurzburg's post–sanitation strike work represented a continued commitment to race and class issues. Yet her work in the 1970s with the Tennessee Fair Employment Practices Commission (TFEPC) in constructing a law that prohibited discrimination in hiring practices represented both a professional triumph and a personal defeat. In discussing her endeavor, she observed, "I could frame each page [of the law] and put it on the wall, and put 'reasons for divorce.'"[40] Although Wurzburg insisted that the time she devoted to her work with the TFEPC constituted only one of the factors that contributed to the dissolution of her marriage, her work in racial reform from 1968 onward greatly displeased her in-laws and undoubtedly factored into her marital problems.

Ostracism from one's family appeared as a recurring theme for many white southern veterans of the civil rights movement. Marty Frich recounted the reluctance of many of her classmates to become involved in any form of activism, due to fear of the potential backlash from their parents. Frich came from an activist background, something of an anomaly among the subjects of this study; both of her parents volunteered their time and energy toward assisting in the integration of Central High in 1957.⁴¹ She credited her own family's background in "liberal" politics for sparing her that familial humiliation; however, she did acknowledge a degree of hostility from a few of her professors. Frich chalked up that hostility to what she considered her "outside agitator" status, since she was not a native of Memphis. Yet she wore the label as a badge of honor. The public criticism she endured from professors inside and out of the classroom legitimized her work, Frich believed, imbuing it with more importance than mere teenage rebellion.⁴²

College students did not occupy a lonely perch in their concern over the reaction their parents displayed upon discovering their civil rights work. Wives and mothers in their thirties and forties faced both approbation and support from their parents. For example, Jeanne Varnell's mother, a "woman of faith," contributed financially to the Panel every year of its ten-year existence, albeit anonymously. Her involvement with the YWCA and Church Women United created a welcoming environment for Varnell's later work; she represented a "model of compassion, simplicity, being who you truly are." Tacit support from one's family, especially from a mother, gave these women credibility. Varnell and Shannon both expressed gratitude and relief that their mothers buffered other family members' hostile responses—in Varnell's case, her grandparents vehemently opposed her activism—to white women involved in civil rights work.⁴³ Donna Sue Shannon credited her mother's support of the integration of Little Rock's Central High as pivotal to her own progressive racial consciousness later in life.⁴⁴

Former CWM chairperson Dorothy "Happy" Jones's experiences diverged somewhat from those of Varnell and Shannon. Jones's father, Bob Snowden, participated in the founding of the John Birch Society and shared a close friendship with Phyllis Schlafly; not surprisingly, his extremely conservative views clashed with Jones's. Jones gave her father credit for encouraging her outspoken nature, while she simultaneously attempted to hide the extent of her "volunteer work" from him. Jones's appearance on a Memphis newscast one evening speaking to the Memphis school board about reallocating unused school lunch funds to assist in other community projects, such as the Florida Street School, revealed the true nature of Jones's "volunteer" work. Her entire family expressed some displeasure about her public work, but Jones maintained they never created any problems for her because of her activism. Her father proclaimed he had no understanding of why she involved herself in these activities, but he admitted that she "certainly did it well."[45]

For younger civil rights workers, financial dependence necessitated parental acceptance of their civil rights work. Marty Frich astutely observed that parental acceptance in many instances differed based upon the gender of the worker. Speaking from the perspective of a young southern woman on a college campus, Frich distinguished between the reactions of parents of young men and those of young women active in the movement. Frich noted that parents of young women expressed more fear for their daughters' activities than those of young men. These different reactions referred to the stereotype and misconception that women lacked the ability to protect themselves physically, but Frich also alluded to the underlying fear of miscegenation that had permeated southern ideology since the Civil War.

The ghost of miscegenation haunted the civil rights movement, and for anyone who crossed the racial divide, black or white, male or female, serious, and in some instances, deadly consequences befell them. Many white women confronted roadblocks along their path placed in their way by workers who feared, and rightly so, that the presence of white women in a movement for racial justice carried dangerous undertones for black men. Memphis's white female activist community articulated an awareness of the danger their presence posed to black activists in public marches throughout the 1968 sanitation strike. Joan Beifuss and Ann Geary advised Carol Lynn Yellin against marching with King. Beifuss pointed out that her concern stemmed from her belief that black allies on the march would attempt to "protect" the white female participants, and, according to Beifuss, it was unfair to burden anyone with additional safety concerns.[46]

An understanding of the potentially volatile situation caused by the cooperative work of white women and black men permeated Memphis's activist community. The murder of Viola Liuzzo in 1965 brought home to civil rights workers the immediate reality that the archaic notions of the proper places for black men and white women in southern society were alive and well in the midcentury South.[47] Liuzzo's murder on a highway outside Montgomery, Alabama, by four members of the Ku Klux Klan on 25 March 1965 shocked the nation. Coming at the completion of King's march from Selma to Montgomery to protest the South's voting restrictions and push for a federal voting rights act, Liuzzo's death marked a turning point in the civil rights movement. Not only did support grow for federal legislation to eliminate restrictive practices such as poll taxes and literacy tests as prerequisites for voting in the South, but the specter of miscegenation moved front and center as a topic of debate within the movement itself. Liuzzo, a native of Detroit, drove a car with Michigan license plates throughout her activism in Alabama; some historians speculated that this fact alone caused her assailants to single out her vehicle for attack. Perhaps a more likely scenario explaining why the Klan targeted Liuzzo stemmed from the race and gender of her passenger, a nineteen-year-old male African American Alabama native named Leroy Moton.[48]

Accounts from participants at the Selma march revealed that Liuzzo shrugged off numerous warnings against her transporting a black man to his home after sunset. Liuzzo considered such warnings to be folly and the vestige of Old South ideas about the proper places for men and women.[49] Although Liuzzo's death illustrated an extreme example of community retaliation against civil rights activists, concern over interracial relationships emanating from cooperative endeavors between black and white activists manifested itself in lesser incidents on numerous occasions. Marty Frich recalled a frightening incident during the sanitation strike when two white police officers stopped the car in which she rode. The integrated carload of Southwestern students returning from one of the mass meetings escaped unscathed, although Frich remained convinced that the traffic stop resulted from the racial makeup of the passengers. Frich, the sole white female in the car, traveled with two white men and one black man.[50] The involvement of the CWM in attempting to uncover the true nature of poverty in Memphis elicited hostile responses from opponents of their work as well. An unidentified woman at a planning meeting of NAME on 18 June 1969 distributed a pamphlet filled with racial epithets and warning against the "race mixing" that project planners envisioned for the Memphis of the future. The pamphlet illustrated what project organizers discovered later that summer, namely, that instead of ameliorating racial tensions in the city, the project merely exacerbated those already in existence.[51]

Involvement in a movement for racial justice, particularly when that work earned a monetary wage, stirred up controversy as well.

Circumventing the traditional gender roles prescribed for them by southern society often wreaked havoc on activists' personal lives. When a woman did step outside traditional gender roles, opponents viewed her work as either frivolous and unimportant or as a method of avoiding some unnamed and hidden problem in her personal life. Jean Fisher grew more involved in civil rights work after the assassination of King; she helped her husband, John, organize Memphis Cares, a city-wide rally following King's death intended to heal the community's racial divide. Her activism prompted friends to question the health of her marriage and family, while acquaintances shied away from her, viewing her as "too pushy" and rude.[52]

Although Myra Dreifus's work on behalf of the Fund for Needy Schoolchildren (Fund) appeared noncontroversial on the surface, by the time the Fund began collaborating with the Panel in 1969 on projects aimed at accessing federal money to address serious problems in the city, such as poverty, a backlash against the group ensued. When Memphis faced the prospect of another racially divisive strike of municipal employees in the spring of 1969, the efforts of the Fund, CWM, and the Panel converged, and mean-spirited editorials appeared in the Memphis newspapers. One such editorial, published in the evening newspaper, suggested that members of Memphis's Local 1733 of AFSCME increase dues and supplement the Fund's coffers with the surplus. The editor included Dreifus's home address in the piece, and encouraged concerned citizens to send contributions at their earliest convenience.[53]

Jeanne Varnell's personal problems stemmed from her involvement in civil rights work as well as her desire to step outside traditional gender roles; her first marriage dissolved after her entrance into civil rights work and her moves to relinquish the traditional role of a southern wife and mother. Not only did Varnell's husband, a Methodist minister, frown upon her work in racial reform with the Panel, but he also disapproved of her ambition to become an ordained minister in the Methodist Church. Following her divorce in the early 1970s, Varnell successfully launched her own ministry in Memphis, remarried, and found unconditional support for her career choice and activism from her second husband, although her congregants did not always express support for her use of the pulpit as a place to discuss religion and politics.[54]

The majority of women active in civil rights work encountered hostility and resistance toward their efforts. Some, like Viola Liuzzo, lost their lives, yet a multitude of other female activists lost friends, acquaintances, jobs, and their "sense of place" within both the national civil rights movement and the South itself. Happy Jones correctly surmised that her status as a housewife and mother protected her from the more dire consequences faced by other activists. She assumed that had she stepped outside those traditional roles, a far worse fate would have awaited her.[55] Casey Hayden has spoken and written extensively on the isolation she felt both while she was involved in civil rights work and after she left the movement. She felt rejected by her family and fellow southerners because of her activism, yet the "beloved community" she embraced as her surrogate family ultimately abandoned her also.[56]

While the subjects of this study did not experience as profound a sense of alienation from the larger civil rights movement and their southern contemporaries as Hayden acknowledged, their losses did alter their lives in numerous ways. Many participants in Memphis's civil rights struggle came to the movement because of their environment and background, whether that background grounded itself in religion and interpreted Christianity as a revolutionary theology that favored the oppressed, or included an open-mindedness on the part of a family member or friend who sowed the first seeds of challenging the South's racial hierarchy. Such a journey became all the more ironic when examined alongside the ostracism these women faced from the very communities that nurtured their inquisitiveness and freedom of speech. Their decisions to participate in these movements created criticism and controversy within Memphis's larger community, as well as within the women's own families. Much like their contemporaries in the civil rights movement throughout the post-*Brown* South, many Memphis activists experienced a profound personal and professional backlash due to their involvement in racial reform, yet they remained undeterred. Their next project heralded the dawn of the 1970s, as the specter of forced integration through busing loomed on the horizon. Many of these women, such as those active in Rearing Children of Goodwill and the Fund, already cognizant of racism's effects on the young, would soon shift their attention to the bitter struggle over the racial composition of Memphis's public schools.

Chapter 7

"I Am Not Your Social Conscience"
Busing in the Memphis City Schools

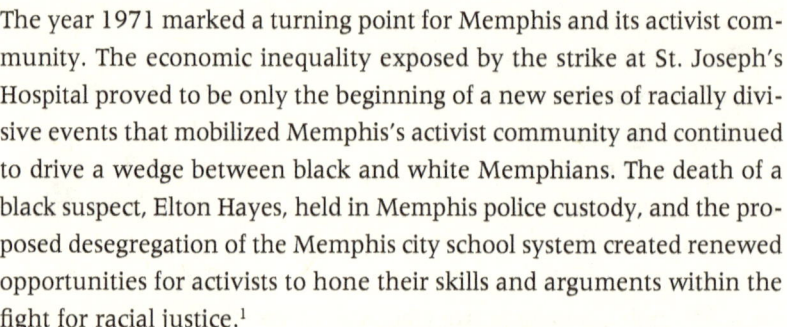

The year 1971 marked a turning point for Memphis and its activist community. The economic inequality exposed by the strike at St. Joseph's Hospital proved to be only the beginning of a new series of racially divisive events that mobilized Memphis's activist community and continued to drive a wedge between black and white Memphians. The death of a black suspect, Elton Hayes, held in Memphis police custody, and the proposed desegregation of the Memphis city school system created renewed opportunities for activists to hone their skills and arguments within the fight for racial justice.[1]

Dorothy "Happy" Jones met the horrors of seventeen-year-old Elton Hayes's October 1971 death with the formation of the Memphis Community Relations Commission (MCCR). Both the mayhem of the post–sanitation strike fallout of riots and violence and the black and white community outcry prompted the Memphis City Council to create the Memphis and Shelby County Human Relations Commission in May 1968. Memphis followed the model of cities like New Orleans and others, which had developed similar structures in the wake of the vestiges of racial tensions following the civil rights movement. Jones stood at the forefront of the group's creation at this early stage, writing a letter to the council criticizing the racial discrimination that permeated the city's housing and employment structures. Although the council publicly acknowledged the "city's seething racial problems and the need for a concerted effort . . . to correct the inequities brought on by years of racially prejudiced practices and racial discrimination," three years elapsed before the council allocated funds to the administration of the Memphis and Shelby County Human Relations Commission. Happy Jones served as the first chairperson of the MCCR in 1972, and she remained in that office three years.[2]

The MCCR built upon the model of multiracial discussion and communication initiated by the Panel of American Women, utilizing many of the same personnel in its projects and as administrators. Jones and Jocelyn Wurzburg both believed that the time had come to stop talking about the city's problems and start resolving them; the MCCR afforded them that opportunity. The MCCR functioned as an "ombudsman for city government," allowing citizens a forum from which to lodge complaints about racial discrimination. Jones admitted that the organization had no legal clout, but it did have a degree of political pull; the executive director of the MCCR at this time, James Netters, served simultaneously as a city council member. Jones herself served on the city's planning commission, working with Loeb's successor, Wyeth Chandler, a politician who believed no outside, federal agency had the power to force him to integrate. Jones recalled a verbal exchange she had with Chandler that illustrated this fact. While chairperson of the MCCR, Jones asked Chandler to expand African American representation in city hall. After he flatly refused, Jones reminded him that such a choice did not lie in the hands of a municipal official, but fell under the aegis of outside government agencies. Jones pointed to this conversation as illustrative of the recalcitrant climate in city hall. She lamented the fact that this unfortunate resistance characterized an administration that paid lip service to demands to alleviate Memphis's tense race relations. This attitude exposed the city's vital need for an organization like the MCCR.[3]

Along with assisting in the battle over busing, the MCCR made great strides in easing racial segregation in Memphis neighborhoods. From eliminating the unscrupulous practice of "blockbusting," in which realtors utilized "scare" tactics to sell an entire block of property quickly to ensure racial segregation, to forcing the city to suspend its annexation of surrounding areas before providing city services in efforts to facilitate "white flight" to the suburbs, the MCCR exercised its political muscle to influence city government to implement fair practices in administrating. Through the MCCR, Jones orchestrated a combined effort with the Department of Housing and Urban Development to informally investigate complaints filed with HUD regarding racial discrimination in rental properties. By tapping into her extensive network from the MCCR and the Panel, Jones trained and sent one African American potential "renter" to a property cited repeatedly by HUD for racial discrimination. A white "renter" followed the first, and tried to obtain the same apartment. Jones and her volunteers collected the data, and presented it to HUD to add to individual files. This type of activity was a hallmark of the MCCR, and it illustrated the manner in which Memphis's female activists moved their politics of discussion from the parlor into the halls of government.[4] Although the group's influence waned with Jones's departure, the structure itself remained, filling a vital vacancy in the space between city government and citizen relations.[5]

As Memphis reeled in the aftermath of King's death, the attempts at unionizing hospital workers at St. Joe's, and the death of Hayes, Memphis's activists shifted their attention to proposed busing of the city's schoolchildren. Those women dedicated to activities aimed at improving the lives of African American schoolchildren drew upon a wealth of experiences and networks already in place since their involvement in the 1968 sanitation strike. These women now had another organization whose resources they could tap, and one of their own at the helm.

With the end of Mayor Loeb's term in office in 1971, many Memphians hoped to put the turmoil of the three previous years behind them; indeed, several activists articulated as much. However, for other participants in Memphis's civil rights struggle of the 1950s and 1960s, debate over the effectiveness of forcing black and white children into school together cast a shadow over any relief they felt with Loeb's vacating of the mayor's office. A natural extension of civil rights work, the integration of Memphis city schools drew in a large number of white women who had spent the previous decade dedicated to working for racial equality in Memphis. For many of them, education paved the way for the elimination of racial prejudice, as evidenced by the work of Rearing Children of Goodwill (RCG) and the Panel of American Women (Panel). Memphis's schoolchildren needed not only an academic education, but also a cultural one, and busing seemed the obvious answer.

The emphasis on education as a tool of reform proved easy for many of the women whose entrance into social justice activism began with attempts to help children through such groups as Myra Dreifus's Fund for Needy Schoolchildren (Fund). The Fund's enduring history with the Memphis Board of Education—including support and involvement from long-standing board member Frances Coe—served its alumnae well when the fight over busing began. Coe's position as secretary of the Memphis Area War on Poverty Committee furthered strengthened this alliance.[6] The summer of 1969 witnessed increased involvement by the Fund in the effort to extend the school lunch program to include students deemed unworthy of assistance by the state and local welfare agencies. Memphis school board president Frances Coe certainly had the ear of Memphis's activist community when the plans surrounding forced busing emerged in the late 1960s/early 1970s. Her position as a member of the board of inquiry to investigate whether the Child Development Group of Mississippi deserved its funding cut in 1968/1969 rendered Coe a formidable ally of the Fund.[7]

Several Fund veterans went so far as to credit Myra Dreifus with single-handedly creating an open dialogue between Memphis reformers and the school board. Linda Allen, who worked with the Fund at the Florida Street School, praised Dreifus's accomplishments with the school board. Dreifus convinced the board to work with the Fund to finance school lunches, thereby avoiding the bureaucratic headaches associated with petitioning the state and/or federal government for additional resources to fund the project. Fund members even solicited money from within their own communities and filled the organization's coffers out of their own pockets when goals came up short.[8]

Although desegregation of Memphis's public school system theoretically began in 1965, it became clear as the decade progressed that busing was the only option if true integration were to occur.[9] An immediate and, at times, hostile resistance developed regarding forced busing as a remedy for the continued segregation of Memphis's school system. The historical intransigence on the part of white Memphians to educate their children within an integrated setting merely complicated matters. Debate over the efficacy of busing ranged from the concern that African American students faced too difficult a task in trying to compete with their white peers to a lack of municipal funds necessary in order to put the plan in motion. Fresh from the political catastrophe stemming from Mayor Loeb's handling of the sanitation strike, the mayor endeavored to postpone the end of his political career by adopting a hands-off policy toward busing. Loeb relinquished any city responsibility for the issue of busing by refusing to allow the city school board to submit its budget within the city's operating budget.[10] Officials—including the Memphis school board—opposed to forced busing repeatedly cited a lack of available financial resources as their justification for preventing such measures from taking effect.[11]

An October 15 school board meeting proved to be highly contentious. Not only did NAACP representatives, including executive secretary Maxine Smith, walk out of the meeting, but board member Frances Coe also abruptly left, citing her disgust with the "failure" of the school board to deal with the crisis in a responsible, thoughtful manner.[12] Coe's opposition to what she perceived to be the reluctance of the board to work in good faith with the demands of the NAACP and the greater African American community compounded the board's problems, deflating what white supporters of a segregated school system characterized as a problem that broke down along racial lines.[13] Perhaps indicative of the tensions between the African American and white communities, the controversies at this meeting focused more on African American representation on the school board than on concern over how to deal with integrating the city's school system. The school board acknowledged an existing problem with the segregated school system and agreed that further investigation and formal study were necessary.[14]

In the wake of the divisive school board meeting, Ezekial Bell organized, under the umbrella of the NAACP, the United Black Coalition (UBC), an association of groups concerned with a variety of problems related to white intransigence to integration and African American civil rights. The UBC included representatives from labor, politics, business, religion, and education; the group devised an organized, systematic protest that included a continuation of "Black Monday" protests, mass marches in the downtown area, and boycotting and picketing of white businesses, schools, and the city school board. The coalition mirrored other groups that developed in the wake of the sanitation strike in that they discerned an inherent connection between racial inequality in politics, education, economics, and residential segregation.[15]

Within two weeks, the board of education compromised with NAACP demands and announced the establishment of a biracial investigative body to study potential resolutions to the problem of segregation in the

Memphis city school system. The board did not publicly acknowledge the protest and pressure from the UBC and its allies as the impetus to establish the committee, but a separate action on the part of the city council revealed that community pressure caused political and educational leaders to reassess their policies. City councilwoman Gwen Awsumb announced on October 25 that the council itself crafted a plan to investigate how to resolve the school system's segregation without busing. One tactic involved an idea of Coe's from her early years on the school board: the consolidation of the city and county school systems.[16]

In April of 1971, a group of concerned parents and citizens organized a Memphis chapter of Citizens Against Busing, Incorporated (CAB), a national organization which included approximately one thousand families across the city of Memphis and held the support of numerous community leaders, including Henry Loeb. While the group consisted primarily of white members, some African American families did belong to the organization. All members united both in their belief that integration was an inevitable necessity and in their opposition to busing as a solution to segregated public school systems. By the end of the year, however, CAB fractured over the issue of how best to implement integration. One of the city's eight chapters formed its own group, the white-led Parents Against Clustering (PAC). PAC argued against tactical challenges through the legal system as the best way to deal with integration; public protest and picketing of school boards worked more effectively, it believed.[17]

PAC initially formed in response to plans to merge three city schools into one larger school as a way to racially integrate without busing. The resulting highly publicized three-day boycott of the schools, led by white students, saw 75 percent of the white student population voluntarily refuse to attend classes. CAB's split signaled a shift in leadership and ushered in a renewed momentum for those opponents of busing who believed direct, aggressive protest represented the only way to garner public support to resist future court decisions that demanded busing. Within days, the remaining seven chapters of CAB had committed themselves to the tactics and philosophies of PAC; CAB had also developed a new cadre of primarily female leaders and public liaisons.[18]

While these women identified themselves as mothers first and foremost, they believed, as did their male peers, that a commitment to CAB did not run counter to their traditional domestic roles; indeed, it was their duty as wives and mothers to stand up and speak out for the ways in which their children received an education. CAB avoided allying itself with any party or individual based purely on political affiliation; this nonpartisan nature mirrored such local groups as the Fund and Panel. Similarly, such national organizations as Women Strike for Peace and the League of Women Voters manipulated domestic rhetoric to justify their political action as legitimate. A familiar tactic utilized by female activists from the colonial era onward, the invoking of the "scepter of motherhood" in opposition to progressive political reform had never appeared on the reform landscape of Memphis, and it innovated this battle.

On 15 July 1971, tempers started to flare in the Memphis metropolitan area over the release of a Justice Department plan for immediate racial integration—accomplished through forced busing of schoolchildren—of the Shelby County school system. The plan prompted an outcry from county school board members and white parents of county schoolchildren, who saw the plan as yet another example of the federal government intruding upon a local community's private problems, as well as from the NAACP's Legal Defense and Education Fund, who thought the plan lacked realism and a thorough investigation into the impact of desegregating the county school system.[19] The Memphis city school system quickly responded by arranging a meeting to discuss volunteer participation in busing on an individual basis. The board intended to avoid court-ordered busing in the city school system in this manner.[20]

The decision regarding the Shelby County school system launched a well-organized grassroots resistance to busing throughout the city and county. Within days of the Justice Department decision, the Memphis Parent-Teacher Association (PTA) adopted a biracial, formal resolution that rejected busing as an option for integrating the school system, alternatively suggesting that the school board implement curriculum changes and school- and community-based programs that created racial harmony in each student's own neighborhood school. While PTA spokesperson Mrs. Bobby Montgomery argued that busing created an undue tax burden on local residents, she echoed the prevailing sentiment of opponents of busing that taking children away from their neighborhoods and families would lead to discipline problems, social isolation, and ultimately, juvenile delinquency.[21] An abundance of information existed documenting the inferiority of a segregated education to an integrated one by this point, and advocates for change in Memphis's segregated school system pointed to this data as justification for the complete racial integration of the Memphis city school system. Indeed, many of the arguments surrounding whether or not segregated schools rendered African American students inferior to their white peers swirled during this heated debate in Memphis. Frances Coe dove headlong into the literature on this controversy.[22]

While the Memphis school board acknowledged the problems with its segregated school system, it also proposed integration measures as alternatives to busing, primarily in the form of "socially oriented projects"; the board outlined these projects in a fifty-page document known as the "Memphis Plan."[23] The first of these workshops began on 6 February 1968 at selected high schools throughout the city. Faculty and administrative staff gathered to determine how they could amend the curriculum to assist "disadvantaged children, especially Negroes," preparing to move into the predominantly white-staffed and -attended schools. These initial workshops did nothing to develop an alternative curriculum; they merely aimed to determine the educational level of students coming from segregated schools.[24] These projects represented the school board's half-hearted attempt at avoiding the inevitable desegregation of the city schools. By 1971, however, the U.S. Supreme Court ruled in *Swann v. Charlotte-Mecklenburg County Board of Education* that busing offered one of the more plausible and economically sound solutions to the problem of the nation's racially segregated school systems. Memphis joined the more than one hundred school systems in the South that quickly followed suit by turning to the federal judiciary to end the segregation in their school systems.[25]

Although the school board articulated support in theory to integration, the court's suggested methods for desegregation rankled a school board averse to "outside" intrusion. However, by 1971, the board found itself in a period of transition. The 1971 election consisted of a slate of female candidates running on platforms that placed central importance on improving the elementary schools, "for the children's sake," and called for increased public access to the school board's weekly meetings and daily operations. Sixteen-year veteran Frances Coe filled the unique position as the sole member of the school board running for reelection in 1971. Her platform included a call for maintaining neighborhood schools, ensuring racial integration without necessarily turning to busing to accomplish that goal, increased assistance to teachers inside the classroom, and intensifying both literacy and vocational programs within the schools. Coe's moniker of the "calm voice of moderation" appealed to voters on either side of the busing fence.[26] Her fellow candidates took a similar approach.

Bert Wolff threw her hat into the ring of this 1971 school board campaign, lobbying for an improvement in the Memphis city school system as vital to the survival and success of area schoolchildren. Wolff's antiracist activism actually began with her work in the Memphis city schools, yet it predated this 1971 race. A native Memphian born in 1936, Bert Wolff lived her earliest years at the Tennessee Hotel, an establishment owned and managed by her father. She credited her experiences there, and her exposure to people from a variety of racial, religious, and socioeconomic backgrounds, as laying the basis for her later involvement in racial reform. Coupled with this unique upbringing was the stark reality of the Holocaust, an event that Wolff became aware of at a tender age. By the early 1930s, Wolff's German-born Jewish grandfather, who had migrated to the United States in the late nineteenth century, began bringing family members to live with him in the U.S.[27]

Wolff noted an awareness of inequality and social injustice at the age of seven or eight. At the behest of her mother, Wolff visited injured World War II veterans recovering at the regional medical facility in Memphis. She served as a surrogate sister for these men, offering them solace and comfort. On the heels of this endeavor, Wolff began visiting Memphis's Neighborhood House, a transitional residence where a number of recent German immigrants lived. Wolff befriended children her own age there, and in many instances, she became the first American friend of these young people. She positioned the beginning of her activism at this juncture of her life.[28]

Membership in a family of Jewish immigrants accelerated Wolff's awakening to racial inequality. Both her parents and grandparents engaged in social reform work, primarily among the Jewish community. However, Wolff's Jewish identity accompanied her southern one. Visits to her grandmother in Chicago in the 1940s exposed Wolff to an integrated world, yet she thought little of the separate water fountains perched in the lobbies of Memphis's movie theaters. A brief stint in 1953 at Sarah Lawrence College stimulated early questions regarding segregation. Wolff lived in an integrated dormitory and met her first African American friend across the hall. These experiences followed those of Wolff's peers throughout Memphis and the South. The women born between the two world wars experienced a catalyst before they launched into their civil rights work.[29]

Wolff left college shortly after her arrival there, marrying at the age of eighteen and focusing on domestic life. She acknowledged that she abided by the traditional domestic ideal of the postwar period, working as a volunteer and avoiding the wage-earning world until she faced the stark reality that those four children needed a college education. As many of her contemporaries did, Wolff found the motivation for her public work for racial equality in her role as a mother of four children. In 1961, Wolff accompanied her oldest child to first grade at Avon school, where six police cars, parked on the front lawn of the school, greeted Wolff, her son, and the five African American children attending the previously all-white Avon school for the first time. Wolff called the event "sad," due to the fact that these children endured such turmoil and hostility while merely attempting to enter their schoolrooms.[30] Within a few years, Wolff was president of the PTA at her children's school, Shady Grove Elementary, and on the cusp of her public and political involvement in the desegregation of the Memphis city schools.

In 1965, Wolff joined the Memphis branch of the Emergency School Assistance Program (ESAP), a program of the Health, Education, and Welfare Department devoted to aiding in local school districts' desegregation. Wolff took her concerns to the administrators at Shady Grove Elementary. She presciently recognized that Memphis doomed itself to the fate of judicial intervention in its own desegregation process. Wolff warned of the potential for legal involvement before the Memphis chapter of the Urban League, whose president, Herman Ewing, listened patiently as Wolff suggested a true, honest "cultural exchange" as the root of the solution. Communities such as Little Rock, Arkansas, had also endeavored to engage in such dialogues, but to no avail, and Ewing illuminated Wolff on the futility of her "naïve" proposal.[31]

Wolff continued her work within her children's schools as the sanitation strike heated up, and she also began work as a guidance counselor at Carver High School, an African American school targeted by Myra Dreifus in the Fund's mentoring programs. Assisting Carver graduates in finding financial and practical avenues through which they could enter college offered ample rewards for Wolff and her peers, yet Wolff yearned for the opportunity to effect greater change in the lives of Memphis's students.[32] By 1971, Wolff's commitment to integrating Memphis's schools had taken a decisive turn: she ran for a seat on the city school board that year. Her campaign came on the heels of a brutal fight for the redistricting of the Memphis school system in 1969–1970, and coincided with the school board's expansion from five members, with Memphis's African American community guaranteed three board members regardless of its numbers within the larger municipal population. Wolff lost the 1971 election in one of the newly formed school districts. She blamed her narrow loss in the runoff election on the Republican candidate, William Ray Ingram, and his stand against integration. Ingram's campaign emphasized his dedication to his Christian faith and his insistence that his opposition to forced integration of the schools stemmed from his particular interpretation of Christianity. The 1971 campaign marked Wolff's entrance into public service, and laid the foundation for a far more successful school board campaign in 1979, culminating in Wolff's election to school board president in 1983. In a departure from earlier tactics of her peers in Memphis's reform community, Wolff in her activism sought direct change through political agency. Influence over institutions and leadership failed to effect the necessary change, therefore, Wolff argued, electoral pressure and reform seemed the logical evolution of civil rights work for activist women.[33]

The fall 1971 elections ushered in a nine-member school board, including four women—Maxine Smith (simultaneously serving as executive secretary of the Memphis branch of the NAACP), Juanita Watkins, Barbara Sonnenburg, and Frances Coe.[34] Of the nine, three white members—Juanita Watkins, Neal Small, and William Ray Ingram—opposed integration of the school system, while the remaining three white board members, Coe, Sonnenburg, and Hunter Lane, Jr., and the three African American members, Smith, George H. Brown, Jr., and Carl Johnson, supported integration through the implementation of forced busing. In response to growing public concerns about matters related to the public school system, and to dispel conspiracy theories that the school board operated in collusion with federal legislative and judicial authorities, the board began scheduling weekly meetings open to the public.[35]

In the wake of the *Swann* case and the school board's response to it, CAB planned a protest march against the Federal Office Building in Memphis on 28 March 1972. CAB joined a chorus of voices throughout the city and state that called for federal intervention to prevent the school board from busing students, yet the Justice Department refused.[36] CAB's publicity chairperson, Ruth Saed, claimed her group's march served merely to demonstrate that the city government and school board utilized children as guinea pigs in their "experimentation" with desegregation. Characterized as the "motherhood arm" of CAB by local newspapers, the 202 female members of CAB walked over five miles—as promised—to the Federal Office Building, invoking the "scepter of motherhood" as justification for their opposition to busing.[37]

The controversy over how to fund the busing of between fourteen thousand students (roughly 10 percent of the student body as outlined in the school board's Plan A) and thirty-five thousand (as outlined in the board's Plan B) began with these March hearings.[38] With Judge McRae's April 20 decision to inaugurate Plan A in the 1972–1973 school year, the talk of how to finance this initial integration effort, as well as the eventual integration of the remaining twenty-five thousand students targeted for busing, escalated. The debate over how to implement Judge McRae's decision dominated contentious school board meetings in March 1972. A particular concern to proponents of integration focused on the efficacy of busing as a means to achieve those ends. Frances Coe voted consistently with Smith, Brown, and Johnson to opt for the accelerated pace of Plan B; she viewed continued segregation as a pernicious poison destined to destroy the city school system as more and more white students fled to the county schools in the ever-growing white suburbs.[39] Coe and her allies maintained there could be no cost too great for integration.

Nonetheless, pending legislation in the U.S. Congress gave hope to opponents of busing as McRae's ruling became public.[40] City councilwoman Gwen Awsumb, among the loudest voices opposing the decision, based her trepidation on the issue of fiscal accountability. Similarly, school board member Juanita Watkins believed politicians at both the state and federal levels shared her anxieties regarding the problems with funding; this government opposition, Watkins averred, solidified busing's eventual failure in Memphis. A decidedly nonpartisan voice emanated from the Memphis Education Association through its president, Peggy Pearson. She called for both calm and support of Judge McRae's decision out of a sense of civic duty and reverence for the law. Concomitantly, CAB, speaking through its two leading female figures, Ruth Saed and Kay Taylor, mobilized its forces.[41]

Leaders of CAB called upon concerned parents to boycott the Memphis public school system on April 27 and April 28; numerous civic and professional groups, including Frances Coe and other school board members, as well as the Memphis Area Chamber of Commerce denounced the call.[42] The first day of boycotts 39.4 percent of the student body, more than eight times the usual daily rate, failed to attend classes; the overwhelming majority of these students were white. Saed, therefore, called for an extension of the boycott to the predominantly white Shelby County school system, even though Judge McRae's ruling did not extend to the county schools. Saed hoped to create support in the suburban areas of the Memphis metropolitan area in order to propel community demands for an appeal of the decision.[43] Interestingly at this point in the struggle over busing, opposition to CAB's tactics—specifically the call for the school boycott—emanated from those organizations traditionally opposed to busing, such as the local newspapers. As with the opposition to the 1968 sanitation workers' strike, this opposition focused on the effect on innocent Memphians—in this case, children—due to the fact that parents, not their children, made the decision on whether or not the children would attend school. However, unlike the opposition to the 1968 strike, the opposition to using children as the shock troops of the movement crossed racial lines. Newspaper articles surfaced after the third "Black Monday" documenting black students' displeasure over abiding by a boycott they felt was forced upon them.[44]

Many of Memphis's female activists supported busing as a tool to integrate the city's schools and chose a variety of avenues to demonstrate their support. Judy Sullivan, for example, consciously placed her children in Idlewild Elementary School, one of the city schools targeted for busing. Sullivan also contributed to the movement by selling school supplies in the school itself, hoping that one "friendly white face" could disprove what she perceived as an assumption within Memphis's African American community that all white citizens opposed busing. Furthermore, Sullivan hoped to refute critics of busing who maintained that integration generated dangerously "wild" learning environments. Sullivan justified her activities by contending that she wanted her children to have an education in the physical realities of the world, an education unavailable to those who attended the sheltered—and racially homogeneous—private schools of Memphis and its suburbs. Sullivan believed that her presence in the school illustrated the fact that all children, regardless of skin color, could safely attend Idlewild.[45]

Like Sullivan, Jeanne Dreifus chose to keep her daughter in a school scheduled for integration, much to her child's chagrin. Dreifus's daughter, upon beginning the ninth grade as one of the few white students at Lester Junior High, informed Dreifus that she was "a victim of [her mother's] social conscience."[46] Dreifus's 1970–1972 tenure as the president of the National Council of Jewish Women and her involvement with the National Conference of Christians and Jews catapulted her into the center of the busing fray. Both organizations endorsed busing as a tool for integration, and Dreifus herself volunteered in the newly formed Creative Learning in a Unique Environment (CLUE) program for intellectually gifted students in the Memphis city school system.[47]

Members of the Panel also made the conscious decision to keep their children in Memphis's public school system to demonstrate their support of the school system's integration. Claudia Davis believed that her children would benefit from remaining in integrated schools through the broadening of their horizons and exposure to a multitude of disparate experiences and individuals.[48] Still other activists saw the discussion surrounding integration as indicative of the racial progress Memphis had made in the wake of Dr. King's death. Linda Allen pointed to the 1969 integration of a private school for women, St. Mary's Episcopal School, as a triumph for the larger civil rights movement. She displayed a mixed enthusiasm for the process, however, due to her belief that an organic integration process better served the school. Allen's husband, Newton, a board member at the school, recounted the integration struggle to her in detail, including the board's decision to integrate voluntarily in order to avoid any outside legal pressure.[49] While Allen's career within Memphis's reform community was well documented, her recollection of the integration of this elite school reminded one of the arguments put forward by opponents of busing who resented the intrusion on their daily affairs from outside judicial forces.

By October 1972, the question of how to pay for the buses slated for use during the 1972–1973 school year sharply divided the school board.[50] Frances Coe opposed the school board's plans to appeal McRae's decision, arguing that the need for racially diverse students to understand and grow acquainted with one another was an urgent one. In Coe's mind, the safe space of a school classroom created an ideal environment for students to challenge and question different ideas and cultures. Through her sixteen-year tenure on the Memphis city school board, Coe had made a priority out of investigating and developing new teaching methodology and curriculum. In repeated appeals to her adversaries on the school board, Coe referenced numerous studies refuting the assumption that bringing groups of students together from disparate educational backgrounds impaired the learning potential of the "better-educated" group of students. For Coe, the argument that African American children lacked the intellectual capability to learn at the same rate as their white counterparts was flawed, biased, and simply incorrect.[51]

The fight over the restructuring of the Memphis school system also mobilized other members of the activist community. Jocelyn Wurzburg took a keen interest in the debate over a redistricting program known as "clustering," whereby schools with a majority African American or white student body paired with another school in an attempt to balance the racial ratio. The Panel's reputation as an organization well qualified to educate the public on "sensitive" issues deemed it a likely ally to assist in the city schools' projects aimed at raising teacher and pupil awareness of members of other racial groups, specifically the position of African American students.[52] The Panel shuttled responsibility for educational programs to Wurzburg.

Both Jocelyn Wurzburg and Happy Jones worked through the Panel as busing began in the city schools. Between 1971 and 1973, both women solicited funds from ESAP to heighten diversity and cultural awareness throughout the community at the Panel's individual meetings. Basing their strategy on the state of Mississippi's use of posters displaying white and black children in school buses with the tag line "Maybe we'll all learn something" printed above, Panel members approached integration in a similar manner. Wurzburg served as the project director and Jones as the administrator of the Panel's ten-thousand-dollar grant. Jones stood at the forefront of this enterprise, not only through enlisting money from ESAP to assist in the integration of the school system through the purchase of additional buses and the hiring of supplemental personnel, but also in helping to establish optional schools that focused on the addition of art programs to the existing academic curriculum.[53] The Panel's management of the grant acted as one component to a larger chamber of commerce plan to quell fears of integrating black and white children in the city schools.

Another contribution to the chamber's plan emerged in 1971. An organization known as Involved Memphis Parents Assisting Children and Teachers (IMPACT), a biracial coalition of business, religious, and civic leaders, formed in November of that year. IMPACT sought educational exploration of the issues surrounding integration by warning against continued segregation as a guarantee of future problems educating all the children of Memphis. Supported by the Memphis newspapers, several city council and school board members, IMPACT served to counter CAB and that organization's fear of "race mixing" and substandard education for white students forced to assimilate to the inferior educational experiences of their black peers.[54]

While bickering persisted over the efficacy of busing and its financial feasibility, support emanating from the community level gained momentum. As Ruth Saed anticipated a prolonged court battle over busing, including an "expensive" trip to the U.S. Supreme Court, she announced in January 1973 CAB's new initiative, "Happiness Is Walking to Your Neighborhood School." This endeavor constituted both a protest against the projected integration of all city schools by the beginning of the 1973–1974 school year and a fund-raising effort to fuel the fight over desegregation.[55] During that same month a series of meetings between city and school board officials, Memphis police officials, and community leaders occurred. Those involved hoped to insure peace in the ensuing project. A biracial symposium of one hundred concerned citizens met in early January 1973 to investigate the proposal before the school board and pledge their commitment to integration at all costs.[56] Activists concerned about the welfare of their children's education took these CAB calls for school boycotts to heart and countered by refusing to take their children out of the public school system and placing their children on the first buses utilized to integrate the school system.[57]

On 24 January 1973 the first buses began their rounds of escorting students to Memphis city schools.[58] While busing met little resistance from fatalistic former opponents, staunch segregationists found new avenues to maintain racial separation. In January alone, some seventy-five hundred white students left the public school system for the suburban private schools, some attending existing institutions and others enrolling in makeshift "education centers" of CAB's creation.[59] The early 1974 exodus of the white student population from the public education system signaled both the demise of CAB and the end to rigid resistance to integration in the Memphis city schools. The shift in tactics of the anti-integrationists resulted in a demographic shift in the city's school enrollment. In each succeeding year, increased numbers of white children left the school system, so that by the end of the century the student body of Memphis city schools was 90 percent African American.[60]

The conflict over busing signified the end of an era for Memphis's white female activists. Radicalized into social reform through their immersion in the city's civil rights struggle, these women migrated into a diverse array of reform work. The recognition of the intersectionality of oppression, exposed by the plight of striking sanitation and hospital workers and recognized by Judge Robert McRae in his decision, proved to be of lasting significance to reformers involved in the struggle for racial equality in Memphis. Each woman focused on a different component of the interlocking hierarchy of oppression—be it race, class, physical ability, sexuality, or gender—in her future endeavors, yet all of these women found their voice and strength in the movements for racial equality.

Epilogue

An awareness of the interconnectedness of race, class, and gender motivated Memphis's female reformers into their work with civil rights organizations, and those connections evolved into work with groups dedicated to other reform efforts. All of the women in this study initially avoided characterizing their work as political activism, preferring instead to label it social reform work. Regardless of the moniker, these women effected tangible political change through such "innocuous" endeavors as assisting impoverished children receive free lunch and breakfast, teaching children Bible stories in ad hoc Sunday schools, and working to shift racist attitudes among the white power structure to which all of them belonged.

Jocelyn Wurzburg's connections through the Panel of American Women, for example, led to her work with the grant review committee of the Comprehensive Employment Training Act (CETA) Board that was in the process of allocating federal money to job training programs throughout the state of Tennessee. Wurzburg connected the problem of racial inequality to the lack of job opportunities, and she operated from that assumption while selecting which training programs received financial assistance in the late 1960s and early 1970s, as well as in her work in establishing the Tennessee State Human Relations Commission. Furthermore, Wurzburg's involvement with the creation of optional schools as an alternative to busing and the exodus of white students from the Memphis city school system led to her 1971 appointment to the

Tennessee Commission for Human Development, on which she served until 1977. In 2008, Wurzburg lives in Memphis, working as both a mediator in family law disputes and as an attorney.[1]

Dorothy "Happy" Jones continued her activism following the busing of students in the Memphis city schools. Her work with the Memphis Council on Community Relations included, in the wake of Elton Hayes's death in 1971, the creation of the Police-Community Relations Board as a moderating body dedicated to eliminating continuing harassment of African Americans by the Memphis Police Department. In the 1980s, Jones served as the first president of the Network of Memphis, continued her work with optional schools in the wake of busing, and contributed to such organizations as the National Conference for Community and Justice, the Urban League, and YWCA.[2]

Jones's earlier work with the Memphis planning commission, whose forerunner, the Human Relations Committee, listed a number of veterans of Memphis's civil rights struggle on its membership rolls, also catapulted her into reform work well after the close of the modern civil rights movement. In 2007, Jones was continuing to seek an end to rezoning attempts outside city limits that have resulted in a large number of retail establishments and entertainment complexes untouched by city taxes and laws. Indeed, the focus of Jones's activism in 2007 remained community development and the restoration of Memphis's city center in the face of increasing migration to the city's primarily white suburbs, along with an invigorated effort to raise the minimum wage and grant a living wage to all working Memphians.[3]

Still other activists, such as Donna Sue Shannon, motivated by their newly discovered awareness of the extent of racial inequality, continued to work with groups dedicated primarily to civil rights, including the Panel. The Memphis Police Department enlisted Panel staff and volunteers to train officers in race sensitivity workshops from 1973 until its demise in 1979. Jeanne Varnell, another participant in these workshops, carried on her work for racial justice throughout the interim years, serving on the board of the National Civil Rights Museum in 2003. As of 2007, Varnell belonged to the Memphis Interfaith Association and the Memphis Area Women's Council.[4]

Sara Evans pointed out in her work on the relationship between the civil rights and the feminist movements that many white female activists of the baby boom generation found the seeds of women's liberation planted during their tenure with organizations devoted primarily to civil rights work, and numerous Memphis women, including members of an older generation, followed that pattern. Unlike the subjects of Evans's study, however, these women were older and more traditionally married. This demographic difference complicates Evans's narrative by demonstrating that women of an earlier generation felt drawn to feminism in much the same way as their younger counterparts. Members of the Panel, including Jocelyn Wurzurg, assisted in the launch of the Women's Resource Center in 1974 in an attempt to create a network of activists from "women's groups" around Memphis and Shelby County. Based upon Save Our City, the Women's Resource Center strove to offer interested parties information on where to find other groups involved in women's liberation work, discussion circles, and lecture series. Among the groups working together to share mailing lists and personnel were Church Women United (CWU), the YWCA, the National Council of Jewish Women (NCJW), and Memphis Planned Parenthood.[5]

Memphis's chapter of the Panel of American Women endured until 1979.[6] While the Panel's efforts featured opening the lines of communication between disparate groups of women, many of those involved, including Donna Sue Shannon and Jocelyn Wurzburg, felt the first stirrings of Memphis's feminist movement growing within the city's chapter. Shannon observed that many Panel members identified nascent feminist issues under discussion at various moments in meetings, yet the overall consensus persisted, certainly during the sanitation strike, that the Panel needed to focus its activism on the elimination of racial inequality.[7]

Shannon continued her activism throughout the latter years of the twentieth century. In the wake of the sanitation strike, however, Shannon's focus resided in overcoming barriers between Memphis's black and white communities. She hosted coffees in her home for candidates for political offices in the early 1970s, encountering neighborhood ostracism for both deigning to engage in political organizing and for welcoming African American politicians into her home. Shannon continues to work as a community activist today, pointing to a sense of responsibility and duty as the impetus to work for social change. According to Shannon, she had no choice but to act. Indeed, she "had to do it."[8]

Jeanne Dreifus's reform work also shifted into work for women's issues, representing another divergence from the generational distinctions highlighted by Evans. Dreifus became president of the Memphis chapter of the NCJW in 1970. She worked extensively with the group ensuring that religious daycare facilities abide by the same licensing regulations as other daycare facilities unaffiliated with religious institutions. Dreifus also contributed to the NCJW's national endorsement campaign for the Equal Rights Amendment. This campaign evolved naturally from the NCJW's devotion to equality at every level, yet the ERA symbolized a chance to eliminate unequal pay and expand professional opportunities for women, two causes linked inextricably to racial and socioeconomic inequality, and a natural outgrowth of the NCJW's work for civil rights during the 1950s and 1960s. Having helped found the organization Women of Achievement in 1985, Dreifus continued her activism into the twenty-first century, working to foment racial tolerance and diversity in Memphis with the National Conference of Christians and Jews—now named the National Conference for Community and Justice (NCCJ).[9]

While some civil rights workers found inspiration from the language and ideology of the movement and moved into feminist work, other Memphis reformers discounted feminism as too "frivolous" an endeavor.[10] Much like the subjects of Evans's study, the majority of the Memphis women who moved into feminist work were younger than those who remained committed exclusively to racial reform. For example, both Selma Lewis and Myra Dreifus, cofounders of the Saturday Luncheon Group, continued to work with groups seeking an end to racial discrimination. Lewis played an integral role in the 1977 formation of the Memphis Coalition for the Homeless, and Dreifus stepped up her involvement in humanitarian groups such as CWU and the NCCJ, receiving one of the CWU's national designations of Woman of Courage in 1970, and becoming the first female recipient of the Memphis Catholic Relations Council's Human Relations Award earlier that year.[11] After an illustrious career in social activism, Myra Driefus died in January 1987. Prior to her death, the NCCJ named her Woman of the Year in 1980 and gave her its humanitarian award in 1984. Her unparalleled legacy in Memphis's reform community endures today through the work of her son, Jed, and his wife, Jeanne.[12]

Sister Adrian Marie Hofstetter continued her activism well after the end of the 1970s, enlarging her focus to include greater concerns with human rights on a global and spiritual level. Her first book, *Earth Friendly: Re-Visioning Science and Spirituality through Aristotle, Thomas Aquinas, and Rudolf Steiner*, formed a compendium of articles Hofstetter had written over the course of several decades. Her simple purpose in constructing this work emanated from her desire to encourage a shift in societal consciousness whereby humans began to think differently about the nexus of science and spirituality.[13]

Sister Adrian Marie relocated to the Hudson Valley of New York State in the early 1980s, coestablishing Boughton Place in Highland. This center for community activism, and the site of the Hudson Valley Psychodrama Institute, described itself as a place for people interested in working to end the human destruction of the earth and ensure the earth's rejuvenation and survival. She continued her work as an educator and activist throughout the 1980s and 1990s, engaging in peace activism by venturing to the Middle East and Israel on repeated mission trips.[14] In a May 2005 interview, the now-retired Sister Adrian Marie explained the ease with which she shifted her focus from science to philosophy and psychology: "The only thing that brings us to our humanity is the Word that we exchange with each other."[15] To Sister Adrian Marie, communication continued to be the key to human success, growth, and understanding, much as it had been for her during her earlier years in Memphis's New Attitude–Memphis Encounter.

Although Lewis, Myra Dreifus, and Sister Adrian Marie were Bert Wolff's elders, they also formed her contingent of peers during the 1960s and 1970s. These women kept the majority of their focus on improving the lives of Americans living in poverty, regardless of their location, racial composition, age, or gender. In other words, their activism did not follow the trajectory outlined by Sara Evans, and neither did Wolff's. Wolff's path illustrated the manner in which the nexus of race, class, gender, age, and religious affiliation structure systemic inequality.

Wolff continued her activism after her stint with the Memphis school board ended in the 1980s. Wolff's presidency of the school board in the early 1980s addressed a legacy of busing from a decade before when a small district in the suburban neighborhood of Raleigh faced forced integration through busing. The court order that mandated busing in

Memphis city schools in 1972 had different timetables and programs for those schools under the county system, which included the neighborhood of Raleigh. Wolff recalled a repeat of the protests, harassing phone calls, and police escorts that characterized the earlier attempts at school desegregation. She expressed great discouragement over the fact that race relations had improved little in the fifteen years since Martin Luther King, Jr.'s death. This setback in the movement for racial equality in Memphis's school system only fueled Wolff's activism. She assisted in the 2005 founding of Diversity Memphis, a human relations group funded through the city of Memphis to facilitate cooperation and tolerance across racial, ethnic, socioeconomic, and religious lines. She also continued her involvement with the NCCJ and Hadassah, the Women's Zionist Organization of America, into the twenty-first century, working with the Boy Scouts in Israel under the auspices of Hadassah, and serving as a member of the Memphis Area Women's Council in 2007.[16]

Panel member Claudia Davis continues to live in Conway, Arkansas, where she remains active with CWU in her state. Davis's work on behalf of children spanned most of her life, and her attempts at creating a better world for her children did not go unnoticed by them. Unlike the situation with several of the activists in this study, Davis's family, specifically her children, hold great pride in their mother's commitment to social justice. Her faith in a society's ability to change persists into the present day, as she noted her delight in the progressive political and social nature of her town—due primarily to its status as the home of Arkansas State University—as the Latino and African American populations grew at the dawn of the twenty-first century. Davis refused to rest on her laurels, reminded by the racism that lingers today in all regions of the U.S. that antiracist activists must remain vigilant and persistent in their efforts to eliminate racial inequality. Southerners, she said, did not corner the market on hate and racism.[17]

While Gwen Awswumb's position as Memphis's first female city council member represented a significant step forward for women in Memphis politics, she abandoned her public career following her second term on the council, during which she contemplated a brief run for city mayor in 1971.[18] The council accomplishments Awsumb treasured most moved women toward a more equitable place in Memphis's economic picture. She forced the Memphis police department to pay female detectives the same salary as their male counterparts, and she also implemented additional training for female police cadets, allowing them to serve as armed officers as well as "meter maids."[19]

Awsumb's role as the chairperson of the Memphis City Council also garnered her national attention. Richard Nixon appointed her to the National Council on Equality in Education in January 1973, specifically due to her role in city government at this critical time in Memphis's history. Although Awsumb resisted busing as an alternative due to what she perceived to be its fiscal irresponsibility, her support of issues deemed relevant to black Memphians while on the council—including her endorsement of the creation of a racially equitable school board at the height of the busing debate—earned her the position.[20]

Joan Beifuss took the wealth of information culled from her participation in and observance of the sanitation strike and transformed it into the first monograph of the event, *At the River I Stand*. From 1972 onward, Beifuss shuttled the culmination of the Memphis Search for Meaning's work from publisher to publisher and faced repeated rejections until St. Luke's Press published the work in 1990. Beifuss continued her career both as a freelance journalist, focusing on social justice in her reporting and writing, and as an activist, continuing to work as a member with such groups as the League of Women Voters, the Catholic Human Relations Council, and the Inter-Faculty Wives and Women of Memphis. As a tribute to her accomplishments in social reform, Memphis State University bestowed the Dr. Martin Luther King Jr. Human Rights Award on Beifuss in 1987. Although her death on 7 January 1994 cut short a life devoted to antiracist activism, Beifuss's legacy lived on in her written work and the vast catalogue of information collected for posterity within the 1968 Sanitation Workers' Strike Collection in the University of Memphis Special Collections.[21]

Margaret Valiant died on 12 April 1982 in the Rosewood Nursing Home in Memphis. Her move to the facility came at the urging of friends concerned about her ability to care for herself in LeMoyne Gardens, where she had remained for over twenty years. She continued to work for both women's and African Americans' civil rights after King's death, most notably through campaigning for Shirley Chisolm's run for the White House in 1972. Public activism took a back seat in Valiant's life during the second half of the 1970s as her health suffered, yet she phoned regularly to local radio talk shows to weigh in on community and national issues of the day.[22]

Conquering division created by difference provided the ideology behind Memphis's female activists, and it fueled the larger fight for integration in the city's public accommodations, neighborhoods, political offices, and schools. In the case of Memphis, Tennessee, communicating across racial, religious, and socioeconomic lines opened an essential dialogue between enemies on two fronts: the battle between African American and white communities in the modern civil rights movement, and that between white segregationists and white integrationists. Their legacy, however, remains mixed, if only due to the pernicious persistence of racism and racial inequality in Memphis today. While critics argued that Memphis's white activist community failed to reach out to its African American counterparts—as its biracial predecessors in Memphis and thoughout the South had before—one cannot ignore the complicated historical relationship between these two groups of women. The mistrust and skepticism exhibited by both black civil rights and black feminist activists toward white allies undoubtedly played a role in the two communities in Memphis; such scholars as Wini Breines, Lynne Olson, and Kimberly Springer have documented this complex relationship. Progress may continue to inch forward slowly, but the women of this study took an important step in contributing to a dialogue necessary for the achievement of racial equality. These women wanted to both contribute to and steer the movement's conversation, a distinction Lynne Olson makes between the two generations of white civil rights activists born before and after World War II.[23] As members of the white Memphis elite, these women had the ear of a political and business establishment that had historically resisted integration.

A fuller picture of the civil rights movement emerges with the inclusion of Memphis's white female activists in the history of both Memphis and the struggle for racial equality. Between 1955 and 1973 these women utilized their activities with volunteer and religious organizations as a springboard for political activism. They demonstrated the potential for success in white organizing within the white community, a goal of proponents of black self-determination. Groups such as SNCC consciously solicited white members from their inception, yet by 1964 they began encouraging white activists to seek allies for the struggle from among the white population. Through their contact with members of Memphis's white elite population and their engagement in activities that for the most part seemed deceptively "ladylike," these women helped to weaken the South's traditional racial hierarchy by persuading the white elite committed to racial inequality to broaden its conceptualization of tolerance and equality. While the work of established black civil rights organizations should not be overlooked in a study of Memphis's civil rights history, the story of Memphis's white female activists has the potential not only to expand an understanding of the ways in which women engaged in political and social reform in American history, but also to highlight the often neglected role that elite white women of the interwar generation specifically played in the history of the civil rights movement.

These women do not warrant the term "radical," because they did not seek an overhaul of the entire system that created a racial hierarchy in which white citizens enjoyed more privilege than their African American counterparts. However, their contributions to Memphis's race relations proved essential to the easing of racial tensions in danger of boiling over after the assassination of Dr. Martin Luther King, Jr. The work of white activists in the civil rights movement has always been secondary to that of African American participants, yet white southern activists had the ear of white segregationists, something that African Americans never had. In a country historically resistant to women's political agency, women have utilized their most effective political tool, influence and persuasion, to their advantage in a variety of endeavors. The white women of Memphis's civil rights movement overcame a lifetime of indoctrination into racism and white supremacy through what they witnessed in their backyards. This epiphany led them to begin changing the hearts and minds of their white peers, a necessary step in a region committed to racial injustice. Indeed, it was this ideological shift that could be considered their greatest success, and they did so without compromising the maternal characteristics assigned to wives and mothers. In fact, Memphis's white female activists capitalized on these identities with great aplomb.

Appendix

List of Organizations with Dates of Operation

Catholic Human Relations Council (1963–present)
Church Women United (Original Title: United Council of Church Women [1941–present])
    **Outpost Sunday School (1965–1970): Claudia Davis, organizer
Community on the Move for Equality (March 1968–December 1968)
Concerned Women of Memphis (1969–1971)
Council of Catholic Women (1920–present)
Fund for Needy Schoolchildren (Original Title: Food for Fitness [1964–1986])
Memphis Area Project-South (1967–present)
Memphis City Beautiful Commission (1930–present)
    **Anne Shafer, president (1964–1966)
Memphis Search for Meaning Committee (April 1968–May 1974)
Methodist Student Movement (1958–present)
    **Affiliated with Southern Student Organizing Committee (1964–1969)
New Attitude–Memphis Encounter (June 1969–September 1969)
Panel of American Women, Memphis Chapter (1968–1979)
    **National Organization (1955–present)
Rearing Children of Goodwill (February 1968–April 1968 [when absorbed under the auspices of the Panel of American Women])
    **Joan Beifuss, initial chairperson (Claudia Davis, first official chairwoman)
Saturday Morning Luncheon Group (1963–1975)

Notes

Introduction

1. Amended and Supplemental Bill in the Chancery Court of Memphis, Tennessee (1968) No. 69415-1 R.D., art. V, Box 12, Folder 100, 1968 Sanitation Workers' Strike Collection, Mississippi Valley Collection, McWherter Library, University of Memphis, Memphis, TN. Hereafter cited as Strike Collection. For the South's historical resistance to labor organizing, see Alan Draper, *Conflict of Interests: Organized Labor and the Civil Rights Movement in the South, 1954–1968* (Ithaca: Cornell University Press, 1994); Michael K. Honey, *Southern Labor and Black Civil Rights: Organizing Memphis Workers* (Urbana and Chicago: University of Illinois Press, 1993); Elizabeth Jacoway and David R. Cothburn, eds., *Southern Businessmen and Desegregation* (Baton Rouge and London: Louisiana State University Press, 1982); Robert Sigafoos, *Cotton Row to Beale Street: A Business History of Memphis* (Memphis: University of Memphis Press, 1999).
2. Maxine Smith, interview with Bill Thomas and Joan Beifuss, 13 June 1968, Box 24, Folder 217, Strike Collection.
3. Resolution Unanimously Adopted by the Board of Memphis Branch NAACP; Annual Report, 1968, of the Memphis Branch NAACP, both in Box 10, Folder 75, Strike Collection.
4. Jimmy Covington, "King Implored by Ministers To Come Here," Memphis *Commercial Appeal*, 14 March 1968, p. 1.
5. Fund-raising letter from King to "SCLC Supporter," 15 February 1968, Box 6, Folder 30, Strike Collection. See also "Dr. King Promises Housing for March of Poor People," *New York Times*, 24 March 1968, p. 56.
6. See Roundtable Discussion with Joan Beifuss, Edwin Hoover, Virginia Hoover, Joyce Palmer, Charles Palmer, Judy Shultz, Carol Lynn Yellin, David Yellin, 19 May 1968, Memphis, TN, Box 23, Folder 163, Strike Collection. For more information on the PPC and King's evolution in thinking at this point in his life, see Anne Braden, "Civil Rights: The New Target Is the Economy," *SCLC Newsletter*, vol. 11, no. 9 (Oct.–Nov. 1967): 10–12. For an exploration of the allegations that King, SCLC, and the PPC were FBI and COINTELPRO targets during this period, see Gerald D. McKnight, *The Last Crusade: Martin Luther King, Jr., the FBI, and the Poor People's Campaign* (Boulder and Oxford: Westview Press, 1998). McKnight argued that the FBI not only played a role in the destruction of King's credibility during this time, but the bureau also watched Memphis's black

"militant" community for opportunities to infiltrate and thwart King's efforts in resolving the strike.

7. Covington, "King Implored by Ministers To Come Here."
8. David L. Chappell, *Inside Agitators: White Southerners in the Civil Rights Movement*, with a foreword by Clayborne Carson (Baltimore and London: Johns Hopkins University Press, 1994); Mary Stanton, *Freedom Walk: Mississippi or Bust* (Jackson: University Press of Mississippi, 2003); Emilye Crosby, *A Little Taste of Freedom: The Black Freedom Struggle in Claiborne County, Mississippi*, The John Hope Franklin Series in African American History and Culture (Chapel Hill: University of North Carolina Press, 2005).
9. See Sherry L. Hoppe and Bruce W. Speck, *Maxine Smith's Unwilling Pupils: Lessons Learned in Memphis's Civil Rights Classroom* (Knoxville: University of Tennessee Press, 2007); Laurie B. Green, *Battling the Plantation Mentality: Memphis and the Black Freedom Struggle*, The John Hope Franklin Series in African American History and Culture (Chapel Hill: University of North Carolina Press, 2007).
10. Linda Allen and Peggy Jemison, interview by Joan Beifuss and Carol Lynn Yellin, 24 February 1969, Memphis, TN, Box 20, Folder 4, Strike Collection. For general discussion of the manner in which Memphis's white activist community responded to King's death, see Roundtable Discussion with David Yellin, Carol Lynn Yellin, Doug Yellin, Emily Yellin, John Beifuss, Joan Beifuss, Ted Hoover, Virginia Hoover, Jenka Hoover, Mike Hoover, Pat Swink, Jerry Viar, Midge Wade, Participants in 1969 Memorial March for Dr. King, 29 April 1969, Memphis, TN, Box 23, Folder 164, Strike Collection.
11. Happy Jones, "Statement of Organizations United for Reconciliation," 12 November 1969, Memphis, TN, Box 1, Folder 15, Jocelyn Dan Wurzburg Papers, Mississippi Valley Collection, McWherter Library, University of Memphis, Memphis, TN. Among the organizations included in this coalition in addition to the groups discussed in this chapter were the Memphis and Shelby County Human Relations Commission, the Council of Jewish Women, the Saturday Morning Luncheon Group, the Memphis chapter of the United Nations Association of the USA, the American Association of University Women, the Catholic Human Relations Council, and the YWCA.
12. *The Long Walk Home*, directed by Richard Pearce, 98 minutes, Miramax Films, 1990, videocassette. For additional information on the historical accuracy of the film's portrayal of the 1955 boycott and its participants, see Jacqueline Jones, "The Long Walk Home," in Mark C. Carnes, ed., *Past Imperfect* (New York: Henry Holt and Company, 1996), pp. 262–265; "'Older, Wiser, Stronger': Representation and Self-Representation, *The Long Walk Home* and *Daughters of the Dust*," in Margaret Miles, *Seeing and Believing: Religion and Values in the Movies* (Boston: Beacon Press, 1996), pp. 117–137.
13. See Sally Belfrage, *Freedom Summer*, with a foreword by Robert P. Moses (Charlottesville and London: University Press of Virginia, 1965); Sara Evans, *Personal Politics: The Roots of Women's Liberation in the Civil Rights Movement and the New Left* (New York: Vintage Books, 1979).
14. See Nancy Cott, *The Grounding of Modern Feminism* (New Haven and London: Yale University Press, 1987); Amy Swerdlow, *Women Strike for Peace: Traditional Motherhood and Radical Politics in the 1960s* (Chicago and London: University of

Chicago Press, 1993), p. 243; Louise A. Tilly and Patricia Gurin, eds., *Women, Politics, and Change* (New York: Russell Sage Foundation, 1990); Kathryn Kish Sklar, *Florence Kelley and the Nation's Work: The Rise of Political Culture, 1830–1900* (New Haven: Yale University Press, 1995).

Chapter 1

1. See Constance Curry et al., *Deep in Our Hearts: Nine White Women in the Freedom Movement* (Athens: University of Georgia Press, 2000); Sara Evans, *Personal Politics: The Roots of Women's Liberation in the Civil Rights Movement and the New Left* (New York: Random House, 1979); Mary King, *Freedom Song: A Personal Story of the 1960s Civil Rights Movement* (New York: William Morrow and Company, 1987); Sally Belfrage, *Freedom Summer* (Charlottesville: University Press of Virginia, 1990); Casey Hayden, "A Nurturing Movement: Nonviolence, SNCC, and Feminism," *Southern Exposure*, Summer 1988, p. 51.
2. See Sarah Patton Boyle, *The Desegregated Heart: A Virginian's Stand in Time of Transition* (Charlottesville: University Press of Virginia, 1962); Anne Braden, *The Wall Between* (New York: Monthly Review Press, 1958); Virginia Foster Durr, *Outside the Magic Circle: The Autobiography of Virginia Foster Durr*, ed. Hollinger F. Barnard (New York: Simon and Schuster, Inc., 1985).
3. "Mayor Plans Action on Trolley Incident," *Tri-State Defender*, 9 January 1954, pp. 1–2.
4. Ibid. See also "Plan Mass Meeting on Bus Boycott," 2 January 1954, *Tri-State Defender*, p. 1, Memphis, TN. For additional information on these initial efforts at desegregating Memphis's public transportation system, see "Bus Driver Pulls Gun in Dispute," *Tri-State Defender*, 16 January 1954, pp. 1–2, Memphis, TN.
5. Maxine Smith, interview with Bill Thomas and Joan Beifuss, 13 June 1968, Box 24, Folder 216, 1968 Sanitation Workers' Strike Collection, Mississippi Valley Collection, McWherter Library, University of Memphis, Memphis, TN. Hereafter cited as Strike Collection. See also Sherry L. Hoppe and Bruce W. Speck, *Maxine Smith's Unwilling Pupils: Lessons Learned in Memphis's Civil Rights Classroom* (Knoxville: University of Tennessee Press, 2007), pp. 28–39, 62, 68, 89.
6. "Miss Lacey Has New Plan for Zoo, Fairgrounds Use by Races—Hopes it Will Improve Relations," *Memphis Press-Scimitar*, 5 September 1958, p. 5. For more discussion of attempts to desegregate the Memphis zoo, see "Sues To End Park Bias," 10 January 1959, p. 1, and "Evers Criticizes City's Position on Parks, Zoo," 14 March 1959, pp. 1–2, both in *Tri-State Defender*, Memphis, TN.
7. "Supreme Court Says 10 Years is 'Too Slow,'" *Memphis Press-Scimitar*, 27 May 1963, pp. 1, 4; "City Orders All Pools Closed as Parks are Desegregated; 17 Playgrounds May Follow," Memphis *Commercial Appeal*, 31 May 1963, p. 1.
8. Smith interview.
9. "Loeb Threatens to Veto Mixing," Memphis *Commercial Appeal*, 29 January 1962, p. 15.
10. For detailed analyses of the Greensboro sit-in movement, see Clayborne Carson, *In Struggle: SNCC and the Black Awakening of the 1960s* (Cambridge: Harvard University Press, 1981); William Chafe, *Civilities and Civil Rights* (New York: Oxford University Press, 1980); Howell Raines, *My Soul Is Rested: Movement Days in the Deep South*

Remembered (New York: Penguin Books, 1977); Aldon D. Morris, *The Origins of the Civil Rights Movement* (New York: The Free Press, 1984); Howard Zinn, *SNCC: The New Abolitionists* (Boston: Beacon Press, 1964).

11. Wesley Pruden, Jr., "Dozen Negroes Stage Sit-In; McLellan's on Main Closes," Memphis *Commercial Appeal*, 19 March 1960, p. 1.
12. "All 23 Arrested Are at LeMoyne," p. 1; "Armour Hailed by Commission," p. 16; Wesley Pruden, Jr., "Negro Lawyers Agree to Truce on Sit-Ins Here," p. 1, all in Memphis *Commercial Appeal*, 23 March 1960; Bob Marks, "Segregation Will Continue in Libraries of Memphis," Memphis *Commercial Appeal*, 2 July 1958, p. 25. For more information on the sit-in movement in 1960, see Markham Stansbury, "Memphians Rally, Help Arrested in Sit-Downs," 26 March 1960, p. 2; "Negroes at Fever Pitch, Vow All-Out Support of Students," 26 March 1960, p. 1; "Three More Lawsuits Now in the Works: More Sit-In Arrests Made," 9 April 1960, pp. 1–2; Burley Hines, Jr., "9 Resume Sit-Ins," 21 May 1960, pp. 1–2; "Adults Join Pickets on Main Street," 28 May 1960, pp. 1–2; "Students Hit Churches and Lunch Counters," 27 August 1960, p. 1, all in *Tri-State Defender*, Memphis, TN.
13. Clark Porteous, "Negro Lawyers to Seek Two-Week Sit-In 'Truce,'" *Memphis Press-Scimitar*, 23 March 1960, pp. 1–2; "Ministers with Those Arrested," *Tri-State Defender*, 27 August 1960, pp. 1–2.
14. "White Youth Among Arrested in 'Sit-Ins,'" *Tri-State Defender*, 3 September 1960, p. 2; "Fine, Say Memphis State Students after Year," *Tri-State Defender*, 4 June 1960, p. 1. For more information regarding the integration of Memphis State College, see the following: "Four Negro Students Seek to Enter MSC," Memphis *Commercial Appeal*, 5 June 1954, p. 17; John Spence, "Five Negroes Want MSC to Admit Them Now—State Ruling Forbids," *Memphis Press-Scimitar*, 16 June 1955, p. 18; "Negroes Told 'No' by State Board," *Memphis Press-Scimitar*, 13 August 1954, p. 5; "Court of Appeals Puts 'Heat' on Judge Boyd in School Case," *Tri-State Defender*, 7 February 1959, pp. 1–2; "Negro Students Won't Bow to Bias at MSU," *Tri-State Defender*, 19 September 1959, pp. 1–2.
15. Southwestern students Marty Frich, Bill Casey, Dale Worsley, interview with Modine Thompson and David Yellin, 3 June 1968, Box 24, Folder 218, Strike Collection.
16. Art Gilliam, "Saturday Luncheon Group Serves Purpose," Memphis *Commercial Appeal*, 1 April 1974, p. 17. See also James and Marjorie Cherry, interview with David and Carol Lynn Yellin, 8 February 1968, Box 20, Folder 38, Strike Collection.
17. Cherry interview. Cherry, Johnston, and Margaret Valiant are all credited with having begun the luncheon group, but the majority of sources, including those from participants themselves, indicate that Cherry and Johnston were the pioneers of the group. Due to the informal organization of the group, as well as the lack of written records from meetings or discussions among the various members, such discrepancies are hardly surprising.
18. Ibid.
19. Ibid.
20. Ibid.
21. Ibid.
22. Ibid. See also Peter Cooper and Margaret Valiant, interview with Joan Beifuss and David Yellin, 12 September 1968, Box 24, Folder 240, Strike Collection.

23. Cherry interview.
24. Cherry interview.
25. Judith Schulz Sullivan, interview with Kimberly K. Little, Memphis, TN, 29 December 1999.
26. Gilliam, Memphis *Commercial Appeal*, 1 April 1974.
27. Sullivan interview. See also Amy Swerdlow, *Women Strike for Peace: Traditional Motherhood and Radical Politics in the 1960s* (Chicago and London: University of Chicago Press, 1993); Joanne Meyerowitz, ed., *Not June Cleaver: Women and Gender in Postwar America, 1945–1960* (Philadelphia: Temple University Press, 1994).
28. Cherry interview.
29. Sullivan interview.
30. Ibid.
31. Ibid.
32. Ibid. For an excellent discussion of black women and work, see Jacqueline Jones, *Labor of Love, Labor of Sorrow* (New York: Basic Books, Inc., 1985). For additional information on the nature of black women's political activism, see Paula Giddings, *When and Where I Enter: The Impact of Black Women on Race and Sex in America* (New York: Morrow, 1984); Gerda Lerner, *Black Women in White America: A Documentary History* (New York: Vintage Books, 1972). For information on white women's political and social reform activism throughout U.S. history, see also Carl Degler, *At Odds: Women and the Family in America from the Revolution to the Present* (New York: Oxford University Press, 1980).
33. Gilliam, Memphis *Commercial Appeal*, 1 April 1974.
34. Sullivan interview.
35. Ibid. See also Swerdlow, *Women Strike for Peace*, p. 243.
36. Linda Allen and Peggy Jemison, interview with Joan Beifuss and Carol Lynn Yellin, 24 February 1969, Box 20, Folder 5, Strike Collection.
37. Sullivan interview.
38. "Race Bar Drops in Restaurants," Memphis *Commercial Appeal*, 6 May 1964, p. 21.
39. Gilliam, Memphis *Commercial Appeal*, 1 April 1974.
40. Valiant and Cooper interview.
41. "Margaret Valiant, Activist, Dies at 81," *Memphis Press-Scimitar*, 13 April 1982, p. 19. See also Thomas BeVier, "A Glass of Sherry with Margaret Valiant," Memphis *Commercial Appeal*, 30 April 1972, pp. 7–8, 10; Valiant and Cooper interview.
42. Kay Pittman Black, "View from Housing Project Still as Rosy for Woman with Grandiose Memories," *Memphis Press-Scimitar*, 12 October 1977, p. 19.
43. Valiant and Cooper interview.
44. "Warned by Whites Not to Move In," 18 April 1953, pp. 1–2; "Door to Door Drive: Whites Suggest Negroes Get Out," 30 May 1953, pp. 1–2; "'Won't Tolerate Bombings'—Mayor," 4 July 1953, pp. 1–2; "Masonic Leader, Family Now in Fordhurst Home," 18 July 1953, pp. 1–2; "Deny Charge Made in Homes Row," 25 July 1953, pp. 1–2; "Trouble Flares Again Over Olive St. Homes," 29 August 1953, pp. 1–2; "Pressure Realtor for Selling 'Gray Area" Homes,' 11 July 1953, p. 2, all in *Tri-State Defender*.
45. Ibid.
46. Valiant and Cooper interview; Cherry interview.

Chapter 2

1. Nancy F. Cott, *The Grounding of Modern Feminism* (New Haven and London: Yale University Press, 1987), pp. 85–86. For more information regarding the role of volunteer associations in the lives of political activists, see also Susan Ware, "American Women in the 1950s: Nonpartisan Politics and Women's Politicization," in *Women, Politics, and Change*, ed. Louise A. Tilly and Patricia Gurin (New York: Russell Sage Foundation, 1990), pp. 281–299; Linda Gordon, "Black and White Visions of Welfare: Women's Welfare Activism, 1890–1945," *Journal of American History* 78 (2) (September 1991): 559–590. For additional information on the League of Women Voters's impact on forming political consciousness among its members, see Barbara Stuhler, *For the Public Record: A Documentary History of the League of Women Voters* (Westport, CT and London: Greenwood Press, 2000) and Louise M. Young, *In the Public Interest: The League of Women Voters, 1920–1970* (New York and London: Greenwood Press, 1989).
2. Virginia Foster Durr, *Outside the Magic Circle: The Autobiography of Virginia Foster Durr*, ed. Hollinger F. Barnard with a foreword by Studs Terkel (New York: Simon and Schuster, Inc., 1985), pp. 50–57.
3. Ibid., pp. 78, 99–102.
4. Ibid., pp. 78, 99–102, 120–121.
5. Ibid., pp. 142, 152–153, 186, 227–233. See also *The Highlander Fling*, November 1940, Monteagle, TN, 2: 7, in Freedom of Information Act Files, FBI, Part Three, www.foia.fbi.gov.
6. "Three Women: Dreifus, Awsumb, and Coe: Ahead of Their Times," *Memphis Magazine*, pp. 22–27. Contained in Myra Dreifus Papers, Clippings Box 2, Mississippi Valley Collection, McWherter Library, University of Memphis, Memphis TN. Hereafter cited as Dreifus Papers. See also *Memphis Press-Scimitar*, 6 November 1955, p. 12; *Memphis Press-Scimitar*, 2 January 1956; John Spence, "Calls for More School Money," *Memphis Press-Scimitar*, 7 January 1957, p. 12.
7. John Spence, "Mrs. Coe's Aims: Smaller Classes, Better Schools," *Memphis Press-Scimitar*, 14 October 1955, p. 19.
8. Mary Raymond, "Mrs. Coe Finds That 24 Hours a Day Aren't Enough for All Her Activities," *Memphis Press-Scimitar*, 4 June 1940, p. 19.
9. "Three Women: Dreifus, Awsumb, and Coe: Ahead of Their Times," *Memphis Magazine*, p. 25. See also *Memphis Press-Scimitar*, 18 October 1939; Deborah M. Clubb, comp. and ed., *A Legacy of Achievers: Women of Achievement—1985–1994* (Memphis: Women of Achievement, Inc., 1994), p. 79; David Tucker, *Memphis Since Crump: Bossism, Blacks, and Civic Reformers, 1948–1968* (Knoxville: University of Tennessee Press, 1980), pp. 45–52.
10. "Citizens Say Mrs. Cooper Dismissed Without Cause," "Mrs. Cooper's Dismissal Not Justified," both in *Memphis Press-Scimitar*, 2 November 1949; "McMahon Reply on Resignation," *Memphis Press-Scimitar*, 24 October 1949.
11. *Memphis Press-Scimitar*, 30 September 1941; *Memphis Press-Scimitar*, 24 January 1950.
12. *Memphis Press-Scimitar*, 24 June 1948; Carl Marsh, "Her First Political Talk Is a Plea for Kefauver," 4 August 1948, p. 8; John Spence, "Mrs. Coe Plays Waiting Game,"

12 June 1959, p. 8; John Spence, "Mrs. Coe to Run Again for School Board Post," 10 September 1963, p. 10; Paul Vanderwood, "Let's Stop Paying School Board Members, 2 of Members Urge," 7 August 1959, p. 7; "More Pay for Teachers, If—," 15 March 1962, p. 8, all in *Memphis Press-Scimitar*.
13. "Good Education Costs, Mrs. Coe Tells Mothers," *Memphis Press-Scimitar*, 4 March 1958.
14. Arch McKay, "Grant to Feed Needy Students," Memphis *Commercial Appeal*, 22 September 1964, p. 12.
15. Myra Dreifus, interview with Joan Beifuss and David Yellin, 30 October 1968, Box 21, Folder 61, 1968 Sanitation Workers' Strike Collection, Mississippi Valley Collection, McWherter Library, University of Memphis, Memphis, TN. Hereafter cited as Strike Collection.
16. Clubb, comp. and ed., *A Legacy of Achievers*, p. 147. See also Lawrence Buser, "Myra Dreifus, Friend of Needy Children, Dies at 82," Memphis *Commercial Appeal*, 9 January 1987, p. 16; "Three Women: Dreifus, Awsumb, and Coe: Ahead of Their Times," *Memphis Magazine*, p. 22; "Mrs. Dreifus Awarded as Top Volunteer," *Tri-State Defender*, 2 February 1971, p. 6; Dreifus interview.
17. Dreifus interview. For information on the history of federal policies regarding school nutrition, see Kimberly F. Stitzel, "Child Nutrition Programs Legislation: Past and Present," *Topics in Clinical Nutrition* 19 (January–March 2001): 9–19; Jill Quadagno, *The Color of Welfare: How Racism Undermined the War on Poverty* (New York: Oxford University Press, 1995).
18. Dreifus interview. See also Myra Dreifus and Selma Lewis, interview with David Yellin, 16 January 1969, Box 21, Folder 62, Strike Collection.
19. Dreifus interview. For the classic, yet problematic discussion of the relationship among race, politics, and the southern commitment to states' rights, see Wilbur J. Cash, *The Mind of the South* (New York: Alfred A. Knopf, 1941); Yasuhiro Katagiri, *The Mississippi State Sovereignty Commission: Civil Rights and States' Rights* (Jackson: University Press of Mississippi, 2001).
20. Clubb, comp. and ed., *A Legacy of Achievers*, p. 147.
21. Dreifus and Lewis interview.
22. Ibid.
23. Ibid.
24. Ibid. See also Clubb, comp. and ed., *A Legacy of Achievers*, p. 135.
25. Theda Skocpol, *Protecting Soldiers and Mothers: The Political Origins of Social Policy in the United States* (Cambridge, MA and London: Harvard University Press, 1992), pp. 2, 10; Alice O'Connor, *Poverty Knowledge: Social Science, Social Policy, and the Poor in Twentieth-Century U.S. History* (Princeton: Princeton University Press, 2001).
26. Dreifus interview. See also "Poverty Post Is Given to Mrs. Coe," *Memphis Press-Scimitar*, 14 June 1865.
27. Dreifus and Lewis interview. For additional information on types of educational programs begun by Fund volunteers, see also James Denley, "'Step Beyond' Food Stamps Urged," Memphis *Commercial Appeal*, 17 July 1969, p. 42.
28. Lynne Olson, *Freedom's Daughters: The Unsung Heroines of the Civil Rights Movement from 1830 to 1970* (New York: Scribner, 2001).
29. Dreifus and Lewis interview. See also David Vincent, "Clothes Lighten Burden of Learning," Memphis *Commercial Appeal*, 19 January 1968, p. 9.

30. Margaret McKee, "Needy School Children Profit from One Woman's Concern," *Memphis Press-Scimitar*, 13 May 1969, p. 17. See also "Food for Schoolchildren," Memphis *Commercial Appeal*, 4 September 1967, p. 6; "Health Clinic opens in South Memphis," *Memphis Press-Scimitar*, 14 November 1968, p. 12; Charles Thornton, "Hunger Stalks Needy Children," Memphis *Commercial Appeal*, 21 December 1968, p. 14; Kay Pittman Black, "Reporter Visits Poverty Areas, Finds Children Hungry, Stunted, Retarded" and "Lack of Pre–Natal Care Blamed for Deaths of 320 Infants," both in *Memphis Press-Scimitar*, 21 May 1969, p. 33.
31. Clubb, comp. and ed., *A Legacy of Achievers*, p. 149.
32. Ada Gilkey, "Lunch Program Hit By Minister Group," *Memphis Press-Scimitar*, 2 December 1968, p. 7.
33. Jerry Robbins, "Federal Lunch Program in Memphis Schools Defended," *Memphis Press-Scimitar*, 17 September 1969, p. 6. See also "School Lunch Complaints," Memphis *Commercial Appeal*, 29 September 1969, p. 6; Bill Evans, "'Clear, Definite Need' Cited in School Lunch Program," *Memphis Press-Scimitar*, 31 March 1970, p. 3; "A Resume of the Panel Presentation on the Memphis School Lunch from the Board of Education, Prepared by Mrs. Lawrence Coe," Box 1, Folder 14, Jocelyn Daniel Wurzburg Papers, Mississippi Valley Collection, McWherter Library, University of Memphis, Memphis, TN.
34. David Vincent, "New Official Efforts—And Debbie's Bazaar—Finance Lunch Program," Memphis *Commercial Appeal*, 1 October 1969, p. 24. See also David Vincent, "Fiscal Limitations Tangle Answers for Memphis's Hungry School Children," Memphis *Commercial Appeal*, 25 July 1969, p. 19; Jerry Robbins, "City School Board Planning Wider Free-Lunch Program," *Memphis Press-Scimitar*, 27 June 1969, p. 4; James Denley, "Church Aid Asked in Hunger Fight," Memphis *Commercial Appeal*, 26 August 1969, p. 7; Richard Lentz, "Schools Assured of Extra Funds," Memphis *Commercial Appeal*, 26 April 1969, p. 1.
35. "Citizen Group to Probe School Lunch Program," *Memphis Press-Scimitar*, 5 June 1969, p. 8. See also William Green, "A Doctor Is Angry As Infant Death Roll Swells," Memphis *Commercial Appeal*, 5 June 1969, p. 39; "Feeding the Children," Memphis *Commercial Appeal*, 25 June 1969, p. 6. A document dated 30 April 1969 stated the poverty study committee's purpose as being to "impartially and accurately describe the condition of the poor in Memphis and Shelby County," and to offer potential, "workable" solutions to governmental agencies involved. Box 1, Folder 7, Dreifus Papers.
36. Clubb, comp. and ed., *A Legacy of Achievers*, p. 135. See also "Lunch Program Helping 21,500 in City Schools," Memphis *Commercial Appeal*, 23 September 1969, p. 18.
37. Clubb, comp. and ed., *A Legacy of Achievers*, p. 147.
38. For discussion of "nonleadership" within Women Strike for Peace, see Amy Swerdlow, *Women Strike for Peace: Traditional Motherhood and Radical Politics in the 1960s* (Chicago and London: University of Chicago Press, 1993).
39. "The New Detroit: What Will It Demand of You?" Box 1, Folder 6, Dreifus Papers.
40. Box 1, Folder 2, Dreifus Papers.
41. Anne Shafer, telephone interview with Kimberly K. Little, 15 April 2002.
42. Anne Shafer, interview with Kimberly K. Little, 12 June 2002, Memphis, Tennessee. For an examination of the confluence of civil rights and unionization,

see John A. Salmond, *Southern Struggles: The Southern Labor Movement and the Civil Rights Struggle* (Gainesville: University Press of Florida, 2004).
43. Shafer interview, 12 June 2002.
44. Anne Whalen Shafer, *History of the Memphis City Beautiful Commission and Its Impact on Our Lives* (Memphis: Published by the author, 1996), p. 77. See also Shafer, telephone interview; Mary Frederickson, "'Each One Is Dependent on the Other': Southern Churchwomen, Racial Reform, and the Process of Transformation, 1880–1940," in *Visible Women*, ed. Nancy Hewitt and Suzanne Lebsock (Urbana: University of Illinois Press, 1993), p. 297.
45. Shafer, *History*, pp. 15–17. See also Louise Nolan, "Women Taking Lead in Beautifying City," Memphis *Commercial Appeal*, 1 January 1940, p. 12; Al Capley, "The City Beautiful," Memphis *Commercial Appeal*, 13 April 1952, p. 19.
46. Shafer, *History*, p. 81. For additional information on Mayor Crump's domination of Memphis politics from his first election in 1909 until his death in 1954, see William D. Miller, *Mr. Crump of Memphis* (Baton Rouge: Louisiana State University Press, 1964). For his reliance on black voters, see Sharon D. Wright, *Race, Power, and Political Emergence in Memphis* (New York: Garland, 2000), chapter 3.
47. Shafer telephone interview. See also Shafer, *History*, pp. 14, 80.
48. Shafer telephone interview. See also "Women of Achievement: United for the Purpose of Advancing Women," *Memphis Woman*, 9:3, March 2001, p. 18.
49. Shafer, *History*, p. 41.
50. Shafer interview, 12 June 2002. See also Shafer, *History*, pp. 37, 74.

Chapter 3

1. Anne Firor Scott, *The Southern Lady: From Pedestal to Politics, 1830–1930* (Chicago and London: University of Chicago Press, 1970), p. 143. See also Mary E. Frederickson, "'Each One Is Dependent on the Other': Southern Churchwomen, Racial Reform, and the Process of Transformation, 1880–1940," in *Visible Women: New Essays on American Activism*, ed. Nancy A. Hewitt and Suzanne Lebsock (Urbana and Chicago: University of Illinois Press, 1993), pp. 296–324.
2. Anne Braden, *The Wall Between* (New York: Monthly Review Press, 1958), pp. 19, 37.
3. Ibid., pp. 22, 34, 229–230.
4. Lillian Smith, *Killers of the Dream*, rev. ed. (New York: W.W. Norton and Company, Inc., 1949, 1961), pp. 28, 32, 85, 99. For additional discussion of white southern awakening to racial injustice, see Fred Hobson, *But Now I See: The White Southern Racial Conversion Narrative* (Baton Rouge: Louisiana State University Press, 1999).
5. For additional information on Smith's opinions on the race problem in the South as well as numerous items of correspondence between herself and the leaders of groups she worked with over the years, including the NAACP, the Southern Regional Council, CORE, YWCA, and the Southern Conference for Human Welfare, see Margaret Rose Gladney, ed., *How Am I To Be Heard? The Letters of Lillian Smith* (Chapel Hill and London: University of North Carolina Press, 1993). Sara Patton Boyle, a contemporary of Smith's, also found herself involved in civil rights due to her religious beliefs. For her journey from segregationist to activist, see her autobiography, Sara Patton Boyle, *The Desegregated Heart: A Virginian's Stand*

in Time of Transition, with an introduction by Jennifer Ritterhouse (Charlottesville and London: University Press of Virginia, 2001). For more general information regarding the radicalizing potential of Christianity for individual civil rights activists, see Charles W. Eagles, *Outside Agitator: Jon Daniels and the Civil Rights Movement in Alabama* (Tuscaloosa and London: University of Alabama Press, 2000); Alan Scot Willis, *All According to God's Plan: Southern Baptist Missions and Race, 1945–1970*, Religion in the South Series (Lexington: University Press of Kentucky, 2005); Ernest Trice Thompson, *Presbyterians in the South, Volume 3: 1890–1972* (Richmond, VA: John Knox Press, 1973); Robert Wuthnow, Virginia A. Hogkinson and Associates, eds., *Faith and Philanthropy in America: Exploring the Role of Religion in America's Voluntary Sector* (San Francisco: Jossey-Bass Publishers, 1990); Mark Newman, *Divine Agitators: The Delta Ministry and Civil Rights in Mississippi* (Athens and London: University of Georgia Press, 2004); Mark Newman, *Getting Right with God: Southern Baptists and Desegregation, 1945–1995*, Religion and American Culture Series, ed. David Edwin Harrell, Jr., Wayne Flynt, and Edith L. Blumhoffer (Tuscaloosa and London: University of Alabama Press, 2001); William R. Hutchison, ed., *Between the Times: The Travail of the Protestant Establishment in America, 1900–1960*, Cambridge Studies in Religion and American Life Series, ed. Robin W. Lovin (Cambridge: Cambridge University Press, 1989); James F. Findlay, Jr., *Church People in the Struggle: The National Council of Churches and the Black Freedom Movement, 1950–1970* (New York and Oxford: Oxford University Press, 1993); Michael B. Friedland, *Lift Up Your Voice Like a Trumpet: White Clergy and the Civil Rights and Antiwar Movements, 1954–1973* (Chapel Hill: University of North Carolina Press, 1998); James B. Bennett, *Religion and the Rise of Jim Crow in New Orleans* (Princeton: Princeton University Press, 2005); Charles Marsh, *God's Long Summer: Stories of Faith and Civil Rights* (Princeton: Princeton University Press, 1997).

6. An abundance of secondary material exists on the connection between the black church and liberation struggles of African Americans from slavery through the modern civil rights movement. See, for example, C. Eric Lincoln and Lawrence H. Mamiya, *The Black Church in the African American Experience* (Durham and London: Duke University Press, 1990); Taylor Branch, *Parting the Waters: America in the King Years, 1954–1963* (New York: Simon and Schuster, 1985); Taylor Branch, *Pillar of Fire: America in the King Years, 1963–1965* (New York: Simon and Schuster, 1998); Albert J. Raboteau, *Slave Religion: The "Invisible Institution" in the Antebellum South* (Oxford: Oxford University Press, 1980).

7. Margaret Valiant and Peter Cooper, interview with Joan Beifuss and David Yellin, 12 September 1968, Box 24, Folder 240, 1968 Sanitation Workers' Strike Collection, Mississippi Valley Collection, McWherter Library, University of Memphis, Memphis, TN. Hereafter cited as Strike Collection.

8. James and Margorie Cherry, interview with David and Carol Yellin, 8 February 1968, Box 20, Folder 38, Strike Collection. For more information on the role of church groups in the civil rights struggle, see K. L. Billingsley, *From Mainline to Sideline: The Social Witness of the National Council of Churches* (Washington, D.C.: Ethics and Public Policy Center, 1990); Mark Newman, *Getting Right with God: Southern Baptists and Desegregation, 1945–1995*, Religion and American Culture Series, ed. David Edwin Harrell, Jr., Wayne Flynt, and Edith L. Blumhoffer (Tuscaloosa and London: University of Alabama Press, 2001).

9. Sara Evans, *Personal Politics: The Roots of Women's Liberation in the Civil Rights Movement and the New Left* (New York: Vintage Books, 1979), pp. 35–36.
10. Elinor Kelley, "Church Group Breaks Away," Memphis *Commercial Appeal*, 11 March 1965, p. 12.
11. See "Three Churches Reject Negro Worshipers," Memphis *Commercial Appeal*, 29 August 1960, p. 4; "Negro's Plea: Open Churches To All," *Memphis Press-Scimitar*, 29 August 1960, p. A-16; "Judge Terms Negro Action 'A New Low,'" *Memphis Press-Scimitar*, 1 September 1960, p. 20; "Two Negroes, White Arrested at Church," *Tri-State Defender*, 3 September 1960, p. 2; "14 Arrested at 'Public' Meeting," *Tri-State Defender*, 10 September 1960, p. 1. For further analysis of the impact of the civil rights movement on the Presbyterian Church in the South, see Joel L. Alvis., Jr., *Religion and Race: Southern Presbyterians, 1946–1983* (Tuscaloosa and London: University of Alabama Press, 1994); Virginia Foster Durr, *Outside the Magic Circle: The Autobiography of Virginia Foster Durr*, ed. Hollinger F. Barnard with a foreword by Studs Terkel (New York: Simon and Schuster, Inc., 1985), p. 295; Ernest Trice Thompson, *Presbyterians in the South, Volume 3: 1890–1972* (Richmond, VA: John Knox Press, 1973); James F. Findlay, Jr., *Church People in the Struggle: The National Council of Churches and the Black Freedom Movement, 1950–1970* (New York and Oxford: Oxford University Press, 1993); William R. Hutchison, ed., *Between the Times: The Travail of the Protestant Establishment in America, 1900–1960*, Cambridge Studies in Religion and American Public Life Series, ed. Robin W. Lovin (Cambridge: Cambridge University Press, 1989).
12. Margaret Shannon, *Just Because: The Story of the National Movement of Church Women United in the USA, 1941 through 1975* (Corte Madera, CA: Omega Books, 1977), pp. 14, 21, 23. The author of this source wrote her history of CWU while executive director of the group in 1977. Shannon had been a member of the different incarnations of CWU since 1941, and, although the work is presented as a straightforward history, one should not lose sight of the relationship of the author to her subject. The work utilizes the official records of CWU as the primary sources for the analysis, which the reader should also be mindful of when examining Shannon's work. For more information on the actions of Protestant church groups during the civil rights movement, see Lois A Boyd and R. Douglas Brackenridge, *Presbyterian Women in America: Two Centuries of a Quest for Status*, 2nd ed. (Westport, CT and London: Greenwood Press, 1996); Margaret Lamberts Bendroth and Virginia Brereton, *Women and Twentieth Century Protestantism* (Urbana and Chicago: University of Illinois Press, 2002).
13. Shannon, *Just Because*, pp. 14, 139, 252, 271.
14. Ibid., pp. 109–110, 119–120.
15. Claudia Davis, telephone interview with Kimberly K. Little, 15 April 2002.
16. Ibid.
17. Ibid.
18. Ibid.
19. Jeanne Varnell, telephone interview with Kimberly K. Little, 9 May 2002.
20. Anne Shafer, interview with Kimberly K. Little, 12 June 2002, Memphis, Tennessee.
21. Ibid.
22. For additional discussion of the red-baiting of civil rights activists, see also Taylor Branch, *Parting the Waters: America in the King Years, 1954–1963*; John Egerton, *Speak

Now Against the Day: The Generation Before the Civil Rights Movement in the South (New York: Alfred A. Knopf, 1994); Howell Raines, *My Soul Is Rested: Movement Days in the Deep South Remembered* (New York: Penguin Books, 1977); Jo Ann Gibson Robinson, *The Montgomery Bus Boycott and the Women Who Started It: The Memoir of Jo Ann Gibson Robinson*, with a foreword by David J. Garrow (Knoxville: University of Tennessee Press, 1987); Virginia Foster Durr, *Outside the Magic Circle: The Autobiography of Virginia Foster Durr*; Anne Braden, *The Wall Between*; Lillian Smith, *Killers of the Dream*.

23. Anne W. Shafer, Memphis, to Bishop William L. Adrian, Nashville, 15 September 1964; Anne W. Shafer, Memphis, to Bishop Joseph Durick, Memphis, 28 May 1965. Contained in the private papers of Anne Whalen Shafer, Memphis, TN. See also David W. Southern, *John LeFarge and the Limits of Catholic Interracialism, 1911–1963* (Baton Rouge and London: Louisiana State University Press, 1996).
24. Bishop William L. Adrian, Nashville, to Monsignor Joseph Leppert, Memphis, 21 August 1963, Box 5, Folder 5, Strike Collection.
25. Shafer interview, 12 June 2002.
26. Evans, *Personal Politics*, p. 27. For more information on the connection between the YWCA and civil rights work, see also Marion W. Roydhouse, "Bridging Chasms: Community and the Southern YWCA," in Hewitt and Lebsock, eds., *Visible Women*, pp. 270–295.
27. Evans, *Personal Politics*, pp. 27, 29–30. See also Casey Hayden, "A Nurturing Movement: Nonviolence, SNCC, and Feminism," *Southern Exposure* 16 (Summer 1988): 48–53.
28. Evans, *Personal Politics*, pp. 31–32.
29. Southwestern students Marty Frich, Bill Casey, Dale Worsley, interview with Modine Thompson and David Yellin, 3 June 1968, Memphis, TN, Box 24, Folder 213, Strike Collection.
30. James M. Lawson, Jr., "From a Lunch Counter Stool," *Motive* XXVI (February 1965): 42–43. See also David Chappell, "A Stone of Hope: Prophetic Faith, Liberalism, and the Death of Jim Crow, "*Journal of the Historical Society* 3 (March 2003): 129–163.
31. Gayle Graham Yates, "Mississippi's Child," *Motive* XXV (February 1965): 39–40.
32. Ibid., pp. 33, 48. See also Casey Hayden, "Fields of Blue," in Constance Curry et al., *Deep In Our Hearts: Nine White Women in the Freedom Movement* (Athens and London: University of Georgia Press, 2000), pp. 333–375.
33. Evans, *Personal Politics*, p. 33.
34. Clubb, *A Legacy of Achievers*, pp. 76–77.
35. Arthur V. Murrell, Regional Director, Tennessee Region, "A Vision of Brotherhood: A Brief History of the National Conference of Christians and Jews." Contained in Box 1, Folder 12, Jocelyn Dan Wurzburg Papers, Mississippi Valley Collection, McWherter Library, University of Memphis, Memphis, TN.
36. See Clive Webb, *Fight Against Fear: Southern Jews and Black Civil Rights* (Athens and London: University of Georgia Press, 2001); Cheryl Greenberg, "The Southern Jewish Community and the Struggle for Civil Rights," in *African Americans and Jews in the Twentieth Century: Studies in Convergence and Conflict*, ed. V. P. Franklin, Nancy L. Grant, Harold M. Kletnick, and Genna Rae McNeil (Columbia and London: University of Missouri Press, 1998); Mark K. Bauman and Berkley Kalin, eds., *The*

Quiet Voices: Southern Rabbis and Black Civil Rights, 1880s to 1990s (Tuscaloosa and London: University of Alabama Press, 1997).
37. "Three Women: Dreifus, Awsumb, and Coe: Ahead of Their Times," *Memphis Magazine*, pp. 22–27. Contained in Myra Dreifus Papers, Clippings Box 2, Mississippi Valley Collection, McWherter Library, University of Memphis, Memphis, TN. See also Lawrence Buser, "Myra Dreifus, Friend of Needy Children, Dies at 82," Memphis *Commercial Appeal*, 9 January 1987, p. 16.
38. Clayton Braddock, "Gleam of Hope Shines Bright in Midst of Poverty," Memphis *Commercial Appeal*, 24 July 1966, p. 2.
39. Myra Dreifus and Selma Lewis, interview with David Yellin, 16 January 1969, Box 21, Folder 62, Strike Collection.
40. Jeanne Dreifus, interview with Kimberly K. Little, 21 January 2001, Memphis, Tennessee.
41. Ibid.
42. Ibid.
43. Ibid.
44. Evans, *Personal Politics*, p. 58.

Chapter 4

1. Myra Dreifus letter to Mayor Henry Loeb, 29 March 1968, Box 1, Folder 2, Myra Dreifus Papers, Mississippi Valley Collection, McWherter Library, University of Memphis, Memphis, TN. Hereafter cited as Dreifus Papers.
2. Roundtable Discussion with Joan Beifuss, Edwin Hoover, Virginia Hoover, Joyce Palmer, Charles Palmer, Judy Shultz, Carol Lynn Yellin, David Yellin, 19 May 1968, Memphis, TN, Box 23, Folder 163, 1968 Sanitation Workers' Strike Collection, Mississippi Valley Collection, McWherter Library, University of Memphis, Memphis, TN. Hereafter cited as Strike Collection.
3. "'Businessman's Council' Is Ready to do Business," Memphis *Commercial Appeal*, 7 January 1968, p. 16. For more information on Loeb's council, see David Tucker, *Memphis Since Crump*, pp. 152–161.
4. Biographical information on Gwen Awsumb, Box, 26, Envelope 4, Strike Collection.
5. Clark Porteous, "Mayor? No, Says Mrs. Awsumb," *Memphis Press-Scimitar*, 1 January 1971, p. 13.
6. Bonita Sparrow, "New Routine Gets Going For Mrs. Loeb," Memphis *Commercial Appeal*, 2 January 1968, p. B8. See also James G. Andrews, "Women with Power," *Mid-South Magazine* in Memphis *Commercial Appeal*, 16 June 1974, pp. 24–28, 30, 32.
7. Barney DuBois, "For God, Country, Motherhood—And Some Unexpected Things," *Mid-South Magazine* in Memphis *Commercial Appeal*, 11 May 1969, pp. 6, 8.
8. Gwen Awsumb, interview with David and Carol Lynn Yellin and Anne Trotter, 8 May 1968, Box 20, Folder 7, Strike Collection; James and Marjorie Cherry, interview with David and Carol Lynn Yellin, 8 February 1968, Box 20, Folder 40, Strike Collection. See also Joan Beifuss, "Three Women: Dreifus, Awsumb, and Coe: Ahead of Their Times," *Memphis Magazine*, pp. 22–27. Contained in Myra Dreifus Papers, Clippings File 2, Mississippi Valley Collection, McWherter Library, University of Memphis, Memphis, TN.

9. Awsumb interview, 26 April 1968. See also Joseph Sweat, "Negro Pastors Take Reins As Garbage Strike Leaders In Switch to Racial Pitch," Memphis *Commercial Appeal*, 12 March 1968, p. 17. For discussion of the city's early, unspoken recognition of the racial undertone within the strike, see also Norman Pearlstine, "Garbage Strike Piles Up Negro Unity," *Wall Street Journal*, 8 March 1968. Clippings file contained in Box 12, Folder 101, Strike Collection.
10. DuBois, "For God, Country, Motherhood," p. 9.
11. Awsumb interview, 8 May 1968. For comments on the gradual radicalization of Memphis's white female reformers prior to King's arrival, see Allen and Jemison interview, 24 February 1968. Carol Lynn Yellin, the interviewer of Linda Allen and Peggy Jemison and a central figure in the SLG, Fund for Needy Schoolchildren, and the Memphis Search for Meaning Committee, also commented in this transcript on her awakening to the true nature of the sanitation strike's ties to the civil rights movements.
12. Margaret Valiant and Peter Cooper, interview with Joan Beifuss and David Yellin, 12 September 1968, Box 24, Folder 240, Strike Collection. For other examples of white women who chose to remain uninvolved in civil rights activism, yet who felt compelled to express their disgust with Loeb's treatment of the strikers, see also letter from Carolyn Hurley to Mayor Henry Loeb, 26 February 1968; letter from Mrs. Clive Worth to Mayor Henry Loeb, 28 February 1968, both in Box 84, Folder 15, Loeb Papers.
13. Linda Allen and Peggy Jemison, interview with Joan Beifuss and Carol Lynn Yellin, 24 February 1968, Box 20, Folder 4, Strike Collection.
14. Ibid.
15. Smith interview, 13 June 1968.
16. Whittier Sengstacke family, interview with David and Carol Lynn Yellin, 25 June 1968, Box 24, Folder 211, Strike Collection.
17. Thomas Fox, "Marchers Draw Little Attention on Main Street," Memphis *Commercial Appeal*, 3 March 1968, p. 1.
18. Joseph Sweat, "Housewives Tell of Concern About Strike, Racial Tension," Memphis *Commercial Appeal*, 8 March 1968, p. 23. See also "Walkout Posing Financial Problem," Memphis *Commercial Appeal*, 12 March 1968, p. 17.
19. Roundtable Discussion with Joan Beifuss, Edwin Hoover, Virginia Hoover, Joyce Palmer, Charles Palmer, Judy Shultz, Carol Lynn Yellin, David Yellin, 19 May 1968, Memphis, TN, Box 23, Folder 163, Strike Collection.
20. Sengstacke interview.
21. Roundtable Discussion with Beifuss et al.
22. James and Marjorie Cherry interview.
23. Linda Allen and Peggy Jemison, interview with Joan Beifuss and Carol Lynn Yellin, 24 February 1968, Box 20, Folder 4, Strike Collection.
24. Roundtable Discussion with Beifuss et al.
25. Ibid.; *Dateline Democrat*, 15 April 1968, Box 7, Folder 42, Strike Collection.
26. Roundtable Discussion with Beifuss et al.
27. Ibid. See also curriculum vitae of Joan Turner Beifuss, Box 26, Envelope L, Strike Collection.
28. Linda Allen and Peggy Jemison, interview with Joan Beifuss and Carol Lynn Yellin, 24 February 1969, Memphis, TN, Box 20, Folder 4, Strike Collection. For

King's words condemning American involvement in Vietnam, see James Melvin Washington, ed., *A Testament of Hope: The Essential Writings of Martin Luther King, Jr.* (San Francisco: Harper and Row Publishers, 1986).

29. Roundtable Discussion with Beifuss et al. See also Joan Turner Beifuss, "So King Came to Memphis: Inquiries into the Sanitation Strike of 1968," address at the Memphis State University Liberal Arts Honor Society Banquet and Induction Ceremony, 23 April 1972, Memphis, TN, Box 26, Envelope L, Strike Collection.

30. Maxine Smith, interview with Bill Thomas and Joan Beifuss, 13 June 1968, Memphis, TN, Box 24, Folder 217, Strike Collection. For more information regarding the violence of this 28 March protest and the city's response to it, see Walter Rugaber, "A Negro Is Killed in Memphis March," *New York Times*, 29 March 1968, pp. 1, 29. See also "Wise Advice for Church Leaders," 1 April 1968, p. 6; "Curfew Is Lifted; Main Near Normal," 1 April 1968, pp. 1–2; "Council May Play Bigger Strike Role," 2 April 1968, pp. 1, 4; Clark Porteous, "Council Resolution Calling for Resumption of Strike Mediation Passes 10–1," 3 April 1968, p. 18; "U.S. Judge Forbids Big March Planned by King, Union Men," 3 April 1968, pp. 1, 4; Charles H. Schneider and W. Frank Ahlgren, "Wilkins and the 'March,'" 3 April 1968, p. 12; "Two Nationwide Forces Plan for March," 3 April 1968, p. 40, all in *Memphis Press-Scimitar*.

31. Roundtable Discussion with Joan Beifuss et al.

32. See Virginia Foster Durr, *Outside the Magic Circle: The Autobiography of Virginia Foster Durr*, ed. Hollinger F. Barnard, with a foreword by Studs Terkel (New York: Simon and Schuster, Inc., 1985); Anne Braden, *The Wall Between* (New York: Monthly Review Press, 1958); Sara Patton Boyle, *The Desegregated Heart: A Virginian's Stand in Time of Transition*, with an introduction by Jennifer Ritterhouse (Charlottesville and London: University Press of Virginia, 2001).

33. Roundtable Discussion with Beifuss et al. See also Rabbi James Wax, interview with Selma Lewis and William Sater, late May 1968, Memphis, TN, Box 24, Folder 243, Strike Collection.

34. Southwestern students interview.

35. Ann Geary and Mary Kay Tolleson, interview with Poppy Karchner, 30 March 1968, Memphis, TN, Box 21, Folder 73, Strike Collection.

36. Bert Wolff, interview with Kimberly K. Little, Memphis, TN, 30 April 2002.

37. Anne Braden, "A Continuing Quest," *New South Student*, February 1968, Vol. 5, No. 1, pp. 14–15.

38. Southwestern students interview. See also untitled document, circulated at Memphis area churches on 10 March 1968 by "Concerned Students of Southwestern," written by Bill Casey, Box 5, Folder 3, Strike Collection.

39. Southwestern students interview.

40. Ibid.

41. Jack Newfield, "SSOC: Bridging the Gap Between Bureaucracy and Anarchy," in *Motive*, vol. 26, no. 6, March 1966, pp. 13–15. See also Clayborne Carson, *In Struggle: SNCC and the Black Awakening of the 1960s* (Cambridge and London: Harvard University Press, 1981).

42. 1968 SSOC Handbook, University of Cincinnati Microfilm, reel 30, Underground Newspaper Collection. For information regarding other southern female activists

drawn to the message of the SSOC, see also Sara Evans, *Personal Politics: The Roots of Women's Liberation in the Civil Rights Movement and the New Left* (New York: Vintage Books, 1979); Jane Stembridge, *I Play Flute and Other Poems* (New York: The Seabury Press, 1966 and 1968).

43. Newfield, "SSOC," pp. 13–15.
44. For additional information on the role of both Thrasher and Curry in SSOC and the civil rights movement as a whole, see Constance Curry et al., *Deep In Our Hearts: Nine White Women in the Freedom Movement* (Athens and London: University of Georgia Press, 2000); Constance Curry, *Silver Rights*, introduction by Marian Wright Edelman (Chapel Hill, NC: Algonquin Books of Chapel Hill, 1995); Connie Curry, "White Girl," in Howell Raines, *My Soul Is Rested: Movement Days in the Deep South Remembered* (New York: Penguin Books, 1977), pp. 103–108.
45. Thrasher, in Curry et al., *Deep In Our Hearts*, pp. 222, 226, 229–233, 236.
46. Ray Wilson, "Memphians Rally in Search for Trust and Respect," *Memphis Press-Scimitar*, 8 April 1968, p. 13. For more discussion from participants of "Memphis Cares" about the necessity of a mass meeting to quell violence in the wake of King's assassination, see also John T. Fisher, interview with Tom Becker and David Yellin, 20 June 1968, Box 21, Folder 71, Strike Collection; Anne Shafer, telephone interview with Kimberly K. Little, 15 April 2002; Roundtable Discussion with Beifuss et al., 19 May 1968, Memphis, TN, Strike Collection. See also "Racial Peace Sought By Two Negro Pastors," *Memphis Press-Scimitar*, 4 April 1968, pp. 1, 2.
47. Linda Allen and Peggy Jemison, interview with Joan Beifuss and Carol Lynn Yellin, 24 February 1969, Memphis, TN, Box 20, Folder 4, Strike Collection. See also Roundtable Discussion with Beifuss et al., 19 May 1968, Memphis, TN, Strike Collection.
48. Allen and Jemison interview, 24 February 1969.
49. Mary Collier, "Presentation at 'Memphis Cares' Meeting, Sunday, April 7, 1968," Box 7, Folder 39, Strike Collection. See also "Program: Memphis Cares. . . ," Box 1, Folder 6, Myra Dreifus Papers, Mississippi Valley Collection, McWherter Library, University of Memphis, Memphis, TN.
50. Resume of Jocelyn Maurie Dan Wurzburg, Box 1, Folder 25, Jocelyn Dan Wurzburg Papers, Mississippi Valley Collection, McWherter Library, University of Memphis, Memphis, TN. Hereafter cited as Wurzburg Papers.
51. Jocelyn Wurzburg, interview with Kimberly K. Little, 2 August 2001, Memphis, TN.
52. Ibid.
53. Ibid. See also National Conference of Christians and Jews, "Some Facts About the Sanitation Strike," 20 March 1968, St. Louis Catholic Church, Memphis, TN, Box 5, Folder 3, Wurzburg Papers.
54. Wurzburg interview.
55. Notes from February 1968 meeting recorded by Carol Lynn Yellin, undated, Box 5, Folder 3, Strike Collection.
56. James and Marjorie Cherry, interview with David Yellin and Carol Lynn Yellin, 8 February 1968, Memphis, TN, Box 20, Folder 39, Strike Collection.
57. Gwen Kyles, interview with Jerry Viar, Joan Beifuss, and Carol Lynn Yellin, 28 May 1968, Memphis, TN, Box 22, Folder 123, Strike Collection.

58. James and Marjorie Cherry, interview with David Yellin and Carol Lynn Yellin, 8 February 1968, Box 20, Folder 39, Strike Collection.
59. Lynne Olson, *Freedom's Daughters: The Unsung Heroines of the Civil Rights Movement from 1830 to 1970* (New York: Scribner, 2001), pp. 46–47. See also Clayton McClure Brooks, "Unlikely Allies: Southern Women, Interracial Cooperation, and the Making of Segregation in Virginia, 1910–1920," in *Women Shaping the South: Creating and Confronting Change*, ed. Angela Boswell and Judith N. McArthur (Columbia and London: University of Missouri Press, 2006), pp. 120–151; Jacquelyn Dowd Hall, *Revolt Against Chivalry: Jessie Daniel Ames and the Women's Campaign Against Lynching* (New York: Columbia University Press, 1979); Winifred Breines, *The Trouble Between Us: An Uneasy History of Black and White Women in the Feminist Movement* (Oxford: Oxford University Press, 2006).
60. For more information on anticipated and actual violence in Memphis after King's assassination, as well as city officials' attempts at quelling and preventing said violence, see "Curfew Advice: 'Stay At Home,'" 6 April 1968, p. 1; "Daylight Violence Breaks Out After Busy Night for Police," 5 April 1968, p. 13; "Curfew Tonight Relaxed in Both City and County," 9 April 1968, pp. 1, 5; "Council Plans Penalties for Curfew Law," 12 April 1968, p. 1, all in *Memphis Press-Scimitar*.
61. Arthur Waskow, "Reconstruction of the Cities," *New South Student* 5 (December 1968): 5–7. See also "Telegrams Pouring in to Loeb," *Memphis Press-Scimitar*, 8 April 1968, p. 5; Earl Caldwell, "Abernathy in Memphis, Pledges 'Militant Action,'" *New York Times*, 16 April 1968, p. 32.
62. Charles Brown, "LBJ's Aide Taking Part," 6 April 1968, p. 1; "Mediators Rest, Resume at 4 p.m.," 8 April 1968, p. 20, both in *Memphis Press-Scimitar*.
63. Reverend Richard Wells, interview with David Yellin and Carol Lynn Yellin, 1 September 1972, Memphis, TN, Box 24, Folder 248, Strike Collection. See also "An Open Letter from the Hunger Strikers," dated 15 April 1968, Box 9, Folder 66, Strike Collection; Barnes Carr, "Four White Men Still Fasting in Support of Strikers," *Memphis Press-Scimitar*, 6 April 1968, p. 13; "'Settle Strike,' Ministers Urge," *Memphis Press-Scimitar*, 5 April 1968, p. 12.
64. For additional information on COME, see "C.O.M.E. Leaflet Appeal," 28 March 1968, Box 13, Folder 120; "Call for March 22 demonstration," COME document, Box 12, Folder 97; "C.O.M.E.: Call to Action from 'Save Our City,'" 18 March 1968, Box 12, Folder 97; *C.O.M.E. Appeal*, Vol. 1, No. 1, March 1968, Box 97, Folder 11, all in Strike Collection.
65. "Garbage Strike Ends: Both Sides O.K. Pact," 16 April 1968, pp. 1, 8; "Downtown Buzzes with Business as Giant City Cleanup Begins: Settlement Helps All," 17 April 1968, pp. 1, 4; "Victory for the Community," 17 April 1968, p. 12; "Some Have Recriminations Over Delay in Strike Pact," 17 April 1968, p. 33, all in *Memphis Press-Scimitar*.

Chapter 5

1. Jeanne Varnell, telephone interview with Kimberly K. Little, 9 May 2002.
2. Claudia Davis, telephone interview with Kimberly K. Little, 15 April 2002.

3. Fundraising/Informational Letter from Joan Beifuss, 5 February 1968, Memphis, TN, Box 5, Folder 2, Strike Collection.
4. Barney DuBois, "Issues Outnumber Answers at 'Child-Rearing' Seminar," Memphis *Commercial Appeal*, 29 February 1968, p. 9.
5. Varnell telephone interview.
6. "Rearing Children of Goodwill Announcement," Claudia Davis to Mailing List Members, 21 October 1968, Box 5, Folder 2, Strike Collection.
7. Davis telephone interview.
8. Ibid.
9. Ibid.
10. Ibid. See also Donna Sue Shannon, telephone interview with Kimberly K. Little, 9 April 2002.
11. Shannon telephone interview.
12. Ibid.
13. Ibid.
14. Ibid.
15. Ibid.
16. Jocelyn Wurzburg, interview with Kimberly K. Little, 2 August 2001.
17. See Varnell telephone interview; Shannon telephone interview. For more information on the ways in which "white privilege" manifests itself in American society, see Peggy McIntosh, *White Privilege and Male Privilege: A Personal Account of Coming to See Correspondences Through Work in Women's Studies* (Wellesley, MA: Wellesley College, Center for Research on Women, 1988).
18. Davis telephone interview; Wurzurg interview. An interesting consideration of the role of the Panel's Little Rock chapter in dealing with the aftermath of the Little Rock school desegregation crisis is Paula C. Barnes, "Sara Alderman Murphy and the Little Rock Panel of American Women: A Prescription to Heal the Wounds of the Little Rock School Crisis," in *The Southern Elite and Social Change: Essays in Honor of Willard B. Gatewood, Jr.*, ed. Randy Finley and Thomas A. DeBlack, with a foreword by James C. Cobb (Fayetteville, AR: University of Arkansas Press, 2002), pp. 164–176. See also Wurzburg interview.
19. For more information on the correlation between anti-Catholic sentiment in America as a catalyst for Catholic involvement in reform movements, see David W. Southern, *John LeFarge and the Limits of Catholic Interracialism, 1911–1963* (Baton Rouge and London: Louisiana State University Press, 1996); Robert Wuthnow, Virginia A. Hogkinson, and Associates, eds., *Faith and Philanthropy in America: Exploring the Role of Religion in America's Voluntary Sector* (San Francisco: Jossey-Bass Publishers, 1990); Benny Kraut, "A Wary Collaboration: Jews, Catholics, and the Protestant Goodwill Movement," in *Between the Times: The Travail of the Protestant Establishment in America, 1900–1960*, ed. William R. Hutchison (Cambridge: Cambridge University Press, 1989), pp. 193–230.
20. See *Voices: Women's Reflection of the Memphis Civil Rights Movement*, produced by Facing History and Ourselves, 35 minutes, 1999, videocassette.
21. Bert Wolff, interview with Kimberly K. Little, 30 April 2002.
22. A number of historical examinations exist on the role of Jewish activists in the struggle for civil rights. See Debra L. Schultz, *Going South: Jewish Women in the*

Civil Rights Movement, with a foreword by Blanche Wiesen Cook (New York and London: New York University Press, 2001); Clive Webb, *Fight Against Fear: Southern Jews and Black Civil Rights* (Athens and London: University of Georgia Press, 2001); Eli N. Evans, *The Provincials: A Personal History of Jews in the South* (New York: Atheneum, 1973); Eli N. Evans, *The Lonely Days Were Sundays: Reflections of a Jewish Southerner* (Jackson: University Press of Mississippi, 1993); Leonard Dinnerstein and Mary Dale Palsson, eds., *Jews in the South* (Baton Rouge: Louisiana State University Press, 1973). For more information on the philanthropic work of the NCJW, see Faith Rogow, *Gone to Another Meeting: The National Council of Jewish Women, 1893–1993*, with a foreword by Joan Bronk (Tuscaloosa and London: University of Alabama Press, 1993); Bernice Graziani, *Where There's A Woman: 75 Years of History as Lived by the National Council of Jewish Women*, with an introduction by Dore Schary (New York: National Council of Jewish Women, Inc., 1967).
23. Wolff interview.
24. "Questions," circulated in 1971 and 1972 by the Panel of American Women, Box 2, Folder 21, Wurzburg Papers. See also Paula Barnes, "Sara Alderman Murphy," in *The Southern Elite and Social Change*, ed. Finley and DeBlack, pp. 164–176.
25. Varnell telephone interview.
26. Ibid.
27. Shannon telephone interview. See also Davis telephone interview.
28. Reverend Richard Wells and Dodie Wells, interview with David Yellin and Carol Lynn Yellin, 1 September 1972, Memphis, TN, Box 24, Folder 249, Strike Collection.
29. "Save Our City," *Memphis Press-Scimitar*, 14 March 1968, p. 8. See also Deborah M. Clubb, comp. and ed., *A Legacy of Achievers: Women of Achievement—1985–1994* (Memphis: Women of Achievement, Inc., 1994), pp. 35, 105.
30. Curriculum vitae for Carol Lynn Gilmer Yellin, Box. 26, Envelope N, Strike Collection.
31. For information on the way in which King's successor, Ralph Abernathy, envisioned the SCLC after King's death, see Martin W. Aldron, "S.C.L.C. Will Drop Peacemaker Role," *New York Times*, 16 August 1968, p. 14. For the ways in which Memphis's black community interpreted King's message in their lives, see Kay Pittman Black, "Welfare Mothers Protest," *Memphis Press-Scimitar*, 29 November 1968, p. 17; Earl Caldwell, "Negroes To Seek More in Memphis," *New York Times*, 21 April 1968, p. 31.
32. "MIFA's Five Guiding Principles: 2003 Annual Report," Memphis *Commercial Appeal*, 16 November 2003, Special Supplement. See also Selma Lewis, *Diversification and Unity: MIFA, 1968–1988* (Memphis: MIFA, 1988).
33. Jefferson Riker, "Union in Sanitation Strike Wooing Hospital Employees," Memphis *Commercial Appeal*, 3 April 1968, p. 2; "U.S. Judge Forbids Big March Planned by King, Union Men," *Memphis Press-Scimitar*, 3 April 1968, pp. 1, 4.
34. "Goal of Community on the Move for Equality," undated statement 1969, Box 9, Folder 66, Strike Collection.
35. Jesse Epps, "An Open Letter to Sister Marie Rita," undated, Memphis, TN, Box 6, Folder 25; Save Our City Newsletter, November 1968, Memphis, TN, Box 9, Folder 66, both in Strike Collection.

36. "Union Will Push City for $2 Minimum Wage," Memphis *Commercial Appeal*, 24 April 1969, p. 8. See also "Statement of Purpose: Poverty Study Committee," 30 April 1969, Box 1, Folder 7, Myra Dreifus Papers, Mississippi Valley Collection, McWherter Library, University of Memphis, Memphis, TN. Hereafter cited as Dreifus Papers.
37. Wurzburg interview.
38. "Telegrams Ask for Settlement of Negotiations," Memphis *Commercial Appeal*, undated clipping, Box 2, Dreifus Papers.
39. Dorothy "Happy" Jones, interview with Kimberly K. Little, 3 May 2002, Memphis, TN. See also Gordon Hanna, "City's Time Is Short," Memphis *Commercial Appeal*, 5 June 1969, p. 6.
40. Jones interview with Little.
41. Selma Lewis and Myra Dreifus, interview with David Yellin, 16 January 1969, Memphis, TN, Box 21, Folder 62, Strike Collection.
42. Jones interview with Little.
43. Ibid.
44. Ibid.
45. For more information on the political realignment of the South following the 1964 election, see Numan V. Bartley and Hugh Graham, *Southern Politics and the Second Reconstruction* (Baltimore: Johns Hopkins University Press, 1975); Reg Murphy and Hal Gulliver, *The Southern Strategy* (New York: Scribner, 1971); Kari A. Frederickson, *The Dixiecrat Revolt and the End of the Solid South, 1932–1968* (Chapel Hill: University of North Carolina Press, 2001); Dan T. Carter, *From George Wallace to Newt Gingrich: Race in the Conservative Counterrevolution, 1963–1994* (Baton Rouge: Louisiana State University Press, 1996); Earl Black and Merle Black, *The Rise of Southern Republicans* (Cambridge, MA: Belknap Press of Harvard University Press, 2002).
46. Jones interview with Little.
47. Ibid.
48. "Concerned Women Plan Social Action," Memphis *Commercial Appeal*, 29 June 1969, p. 4.
49. "City Lays Plan for Stopgap Essential Services," Memphis *Commercial Appeal*, 4 June 1969, pp. 1, 4.
50. Jones interview with Little. See also Art Gilliam, "East Memphis Women Offer Hope," *Memphis Press-Scimitar*, 14 June 1969, page number not included, Box 2, Dreifus Papers.
51. Jones interview with Little. See also Anne Shafer, telephone interview with Kimberly K. Little, 15 April 2002.
52. Happy Jones, interview in *Voices: Women's Reflections of the Memphis Civil Rights Movement*.
53. Jones interview with Little. See also Joan Beifuss, "Poverty Tour," report submitted to the *Tennessee Register*, 15 June 1969, Box 2, Folder 9, Wurzburg Papers.
54. Bethany Saltman, "Humbly Sprouting Roses," www.chronogram.com/issue/2005/.
55. Lane Johnston, "Liberalized Heart Is Still Stubborn," Memphis *Commercial Appeal*, 20 June 1970, p. 19.
56. Saltman, www.chronogram.com/issue/2005/.
57. Nancy Abazoris, "Sister Adrian Marie Hopes For Peace Between the Races," Memphis *Commercial Appeal*, 17 November 1968, p. 14.

58. See Sara Evans, *Personal Politics: The Roots of Women's Liberation in the Civil Rights Movement and the New Left* (New York: Vintage Books, 1979).
59. Kay Morgan, "Nuns to Make Survey of Racial Attitudes in Memphis," *Memphis Press-Scimitar*, 21 May 1969, p. 33.
60. Fundraising Request from Sister Adrian Marie Hofstetter, 19 May 1969, Siena College, Memphis, TN, Box 7, Folder 41, Strike Collection. See also Virginia Wensler, Sister Shirley, Sister Diana, Sister Jane Michael, Sister Maureen, Sister Mercedes, Sister Benedicta, interview with Joan Beifuss, 24 July 1969, Memphis, TN, Box 23, Folder 183, 184, Strike Collection.
61. Margaret McKee, "NAME Is Told of Crisis—'A Lot of Hope in Memphis,'" *Memphis Press-Scimitar*, 18 April 1969, p. 21. See also letter from Sister Adrian Marie Hofstetter, 23 April 1969, Memphis, TN, Box 1, Folder 17; "Abstract: New Attitudes–Memphis Encounter," undated, Box 1, Folder 17, both in Wurzburg Papers.
62. The National Advisory Commission on Civil Disorders, *Report of the National Advisory Commission on Civil Disorders* (Washington, D.C.: General Publishing Office, 1968).
63. Jones interview. For an appeal aimed specifically at Memphians to "keep the peace," see Jeanne Dreifus, "Summary of the Findings of the Kerner Report," in *Agenda: The Newsletter of the Health and Welfare Planning Council of Memphis–Shelby County*, April 1968, Box 1, Folder 6, Dreifus Papers.
64. "NAME Will Request help for Project from Ministers," *Memphis Press-Scimitar*, 4 August 1969, p. 4.
65. Varnell telephone interview.
66. William Steif, "Poor Campaign Sparks Three Hunger Program Changes," *Memphis Press-Scimitar*, 17 June 1968, p. 5. See also Joseph A. Loftus, "Women's Panel Charges School Lunch Program Ignores Needy," *New York Times*, 17 April 1968, p. 33.
67. Don Kirkman, "Freeman Urges Congress to Put Heat on States for School Lunch Aid," *Memphis Press-Scimitar*, 22 May 1968, p. 19; Loftus, "Women's Panel Charges School Lunch Program Ignores Needy," p. 22.
68. "Mrs. Dreifus Awarded as Top Volunteer," *Tri-State Defender*, 2 February 1971, p. 18. See also Clubb, p. 149.
69. Jones interview.
70. Ibid.
71. Ibid.
72. "Suggestions from staff of Prospect Guidance Center for General Improvements in the Memphis City School System," presented to the Memphis Board of Education, 18 April 1968, Box 1, Folder 6, Dreifus Papers.
73. Form Letter to "Member" of Save Our City, 17 April 1968, Memphis, TN, Box 9, Folder 66, Strike Collection. See also Allen and Jemison interview; Dreifus and Lewis interview.
74. Kay Pittman Black, "Reporter Visits Poverty Areas, Finds Children Hungry, Stunted, Retarded," *Memphis Press-Scimitar*, 21 May 1969, p. 33. See also Nancy Abazoris, "'Woman('s) Power' Ignites Drive to Feed 40,000," Memphis *Commercial Appeal*, 11 July 1969, p. 2; Dreifus and Lewis interview; Clubb, comp. and ed., *A Legacy of Achievers*, p. 135; Jones interview with Little.

75. Linda Allen and Peggy Jemison, interview with Joan Beifuss and Carol Lynn Yellin, 24 February 1969, Memphis, TN, Box 20, Folder 4, Strike Collection.
76. Lewis and Dreifus interview. See also Member Roster of Concerned Women of Memphis and Shelby County, June 1969, Box 2, Folder 8, Wurzburg Papers.
77. Wurzburg interview. See also Anne Whalen Shafer, *History of the Memphis City Beautiful Commission and Its Impact on Our Lives* (Memphis: Published by author, 1996).
78. Jones interview with Little.
79. Ibid.

Chapter 6

1. See Margaret Rose Gladney, ed., *How Am I To Be Heard? Letters of Lillian Smith* (Chapel Hill and London: University of North Carolina Press, 1993), pp. 345–347.
2. Roundtable Discussion with Joan Beifuss, Edwin Hoover, Virginia Hoover, Joyce Palmer, Charles Palmer, Judy Schultz, Carol Lynn Yellin, David Yellin, 19 May 1968, Memphis, TN, Box 23, Folder 163, 1968 Sanitation Workers' Strike Collection, Mississippi Valley Collection, McWherter Library, University of Memphis, Memphis, TN. Hereafter cited as Strike Collection.
3. Several of the standard works articulating the uniquely ambiguous and enduring relationship between the North and the South are as follows: Wilbur J. Cash, *The Mind of the South* (New York: Alfred A. Knopf, 1941); Edward L. Ayers, *The Promise of the New South: Life After Reconstruction* (New York and Oxford: Oxford University Press, 1992); C. Vann Woodward, *Origins of the New South, 1877–1913* (Baton Rouge: Louisiana State University Press, 1951); Eric Foner, *Reconstruction: America's Unfinished Revolution, 1863–1877* (New York: Harper and Row Publishers, 1988).
4. John Dittmer, *Local People: The Struggle for Civil Rights in Mississippi* (Urbana: University of Illinois Press, 1994), p. 115. Dan Carter's work on southern politicians used Alabama governor George Wallace as an exemplary model of the southerner who considered himself victimized by the "godless" Communists. Carter used words from Wallace's 1963 inaugural address that lamented the federal government's actions to integrate to illustrate this phenomenon: "the 'basically ungodly government,' led by the United States Supreme Court, . . . fed and encouraged 'everything degenerate and base in our people' with its substitution of 'what it calls "human rights" for individual rights.'" Dan T. Carter, *From George Wallace to Newt Gingrich: Race in the Conservative Counterrevolution, 1963–1994* (Baton Rouge: Louisiana State University Press, 1996), p. 3. See also Charles W. Eagles, *Outside Agitator: Jon Daniels and the Civil Rights Movement in Alabama* (Chapel Hill and London: University of North Carolina Press, 1993); Frank T. Adams, *James A. Dombrowski: An American Heretic, 1897–1983*, with a foreword by Arthur Kinoy (Knoxville: University of Tennessee Press, 1992).
5. Powell Lindsay, "Tax Status of King's Group Hit," *Memphis Press-Scimitar*, 4 April 1968, p. 10.
6. See Sara Patton Boyle, *The Desegregated Heart: A Virginian's Stand in Time of Transition*, reprint edition (Charlottesville, VA: The University of Virginia Press, 2001), pp. 233–235.

7. "Communism and the NAACP," no date (post-1958), Georgia Commission on Education, Atlanta, GA, in Freedom of Information Act Files, FBI, Part Five, www.foia.fbi.gov.
8. Virginia Foster Durr, *Outside the Magic Circle: The Autobiography of Virginia Foster Durr*, ed. Hollinger F. Barnard, with a foreword by Studs Terkel (New York: Simon and Schuster, Inc., 1985), pp. 223–224.
9. Ibid., p. 284.
10. Anne Braden, *The Wall Between* (New York: Monthly Review Press, 1958), pp. 46–47.
11. Ibid.
12. Ibid., pp. 212, 222, 228, 279. For additional information on the campaign to discredit Anne Braden's work, see Catherine Fosl, *Subversive Southerner: Anne Braden and the Struggle for Racial Justice in the Cold War South*, with a foreword by Angela Davis (New York: Palgrave Macmillan, 2002).
13. For additional exploration of Clark's life, see her autobiography, Septima Clark, *Ready From Within: Septima Clark and the Civil Rights Movement*, edited and with an introduction by Cynthia Stokes Brown (Trenton, NJ: Africa World Press, 1990).
14. Anne Shafer, interview with Kimberly K. Little, 12 June 2002.
15. Anne Shafer, telephone interview with Kimberly K. Little, 15 April 2002.
16. Shafer telephone interview.
17. Shafer interview.
18. Shafer telephone interview.
19. Constance Curry et al., *Deep in Our Hearts: Nine White Women in the Freedom Movement* (Athens and London: The University of Georgia Press, 2000), pp. 34, 63, 127, 349.
20. Braden, *The Wall Between*, pp. 7, 300–301.
21. For analysis of SNCC's move to encourage white activists to focus their attention and work on the southern white population, see Clayborne Carson, *In Struggle: SNCC and the Black Awakening of the 1960s* (Cambridge: Harvard University Press, 1981), pp. 102–103, 229, 236–242.
22. Casey Hayden, "The Movement," *Witness: The 1960s* 11 (Summer/Fall 1988): 244. See also Casey Hayden, "A Nurturing Movement: Non-Violence, SNCC, and Feminism," *Southern Exposure* 16 (Summer 1988): 48–53; Curry et al., *Deep in Our Hearts*.
23. For a discussion of the use of the rhetorical tool of the "beloved community" in the civil rights movement, see Barbara Ransby, *Ella Baker and the Black Freedom Movement: A Radical Democratic Vision* (Chapel Hill and London: University of North Carolina Press, 2003); Joanne Grant, *Ella Baker: Freedom Bound*, with a foreword by Julian Bond (New York: John Wiley & Sons, Inc., 1998); Taylor Branch, *Parting the Waters: America in the King Years, 1954–1963* (New York: Simon and Schuster, Inc., 1988); Taylor Branch, *Pillar of Fire: America in the King Years, 1963–1965* (New York: Simon and Schuster, Inc., 1988); Stephen B. Oates, *Let the Trumpet Sound: The Life of Martin Luther King, Jr.* (New York: Harper & Row Publishers, 1982).
24. For additional information on the formation of SSOC, see Christina Greene, "'We'll Take Our Stand': Race, Class, and Gender in the Southern Student Organizing Committee, 1964–1969," in *Hidden Histories of Women in the New South*,

ed. Virginia Bernhard et al. (Columbia: University of Missouri Press, 1994), pp. 173–203; Curry et al., *Deep in Our Hearts*.
25. James and Marjorie Cherry, interview with David and Carol Lynn Yellin, 8 February 1968, Box 20, Folder 38, Strike Collection.
26. See Fred Hobson, *But Now I See: The White Southern Racial Conversion Narrative* (Baton Rouge: Louisiana State University Press, 1999); Evans, *Personal Politics*, p. 51.
27. Boyle, *The Desegregated Heart*, p. 58.
28. Ibid., pp. 105, 125.
29. Ann Geary and Mary Kay Tolleson, interview with Poppy Karchmer, 30 March 1969, Memphis, TN, Box 21, Folder 73, Strike Collection.
30. See Maxine Smith, interview with Bill Thomas and Joan Beifuss, 13 June 1968, Box 24, Folder 216, Strike Collection; Whittier Sengstacke Family, interview with David Yellin and Carol Lynn Yellin, 25 June 1968, Box 24, Folder 211, Strike Collection.
31. Margaret Valiant and Peter Cooper, interview with Joan Beifuss and David Yellin, 12 September 1968, Memphis, TN, Box 24, Folder 20, Strike Collection.
32. Ibid.
33. For additional information on paternalism and the debate over the motives of southern liberals, see Howard Zinn, *The Southern Mystique* (New York: Knopf, 1968); Numan V. Bartley, *The Rise of Massive Resistance: Race and Politics in the South during the 1950s* (Baton Rouge: Louisiana State University Press, 1969); David R. Goldfield, *Black, White and Southern: Race Relations and Southern Culture, 1940 to the Present* (Baton Rouge: Louisiana State University Press, 1990).
34. Jeanne Varnell, telephone interview with Kimberly K. Little, 9 May 2002.
35. Donna Sue Shannon, telephone interview with Kimberly K. Little, 9 April 2002. See also Linda Allen and Peggy Jemison, interview with Joan Beifuss and Carol Lynn Yellin, 24 February 1969, Memphis, TN, Box 20, Folder 4, Strike Collection.
36. Shannon telephone interview.
37. Anne Shafer, telephone interview with Kimberly K. Little, 15 April 2002, Memphis, TN. Virginia Durr, perhaps the most well known of the southern white women involved in civil rights, endured an experience similar to Shafer's. After writing a letter to the editor of the Montgomery morning paper condemning the city's decision to close the zoo and surrounding park instead of integrating the facilities, Durr returned to her home one day to find "obscene pamphlets" of a sexual nature littering her front lawn. See Durr, *Outside the Magic Circle*, p. 288.
38. See Letter to Steering Committee of Concerned Women of Memphis from Carol Lynn Yellin and Joan Beifuss, 20 July 1969, Memphis, TN, Box 2, Folder 10, Jocelyn Dan Wurzburg Papers, Mississippi Valley Collection, McWherter Library, University of Memphis, Memphis, TN.
39. Jocelyn Dan Wurzburg, interview with Kimberly K. Little, 2 August 2001, Memphis, TN.
40. Ibid.
41. Southwestern students Marty Frich, Bill Casey, Dale Worsley, interview with Modine Thompson and David Yellin, 3 June 1968, Memphis, TN, Box 24, Folder 218, Strike Collection.
42. Southwestern students, interview, 2 June 1968, Memphis, TN, Box 24, Folder 219, Strike Collection.

43. Varnell telephone interview.
44. Shannon telephone interview.
45. Dorothy "Happy" Jones, interview with Kimberly K. Little, 3 May 2002, Memphis, TN.
46. Interview with Beifuss, Hoover, et al., 19 May 1968, Box 23, Folder 163, Strike Collection. For more on the planned memorial march for Dr. King, see also "Memorial March Monday Approved," *Memphis Press-Scimitar*, 5 April 1968, p. 1; COME leaflet dated 8 April 1968, Box 12, Folder 120, Strike Collection. See also Casey Hayden, in Constance Curry et al., *Deep in Our Hearts*, p. 355.
47. For information regarding the utilization of miscegenation as the justification for segregation and the defense of white womanhood, see Vron Ware, *Beyond the Pale: White Women, Racism and History* (London and New York: Verso Books, 1992); Bertram Wyatt-Brown, *Honor and Violence in the Old South* (New York: Oxford University Press, 1986); Bertram Wyatt-Brown, *Southern Honor: Ethics and Behavior in the Old South* (New York: Oxford University Press, 1982); Jacquelyn Dowd Hall, *Revolt Against Chivalry: Jessie Daniel Ames and the Women's Campaign Against Lynching* (New York: Columbia University Press, 1979); Ida B. Wells Barnett, *Crusade for Justice: The Autobiography of Ida B. Wells*, ed. Alfreda M. Duster, Negro American Biographies and Autobiographies Series (Chicago and London: University of Chicago Press, 1970); Sara M. Evans, "Myth Against History: The Case of Southern Womanhood," in *Myth and Southern History*, vol. 2, *The New South*, 2nd ed., ed. Patrick Gerster and Nicholas Cords (Urbana and Chicago: University of Illinois Press, 1989), pp. 149–154; Smith, *Killers of the Dream*. Perhaps the most startling example of the rigidity of the racial divide in the civil rights–era South was the 1955 death of Emmett Till, who also crossed the wall between the races by referring to a white woman as "Baby." For a discussion of the varied interpretations of white and black womanhood and motherhood, see Ruth Feldstein, *Motherhood in Black and White: Race and Sex in American Liberalism, 1930–1965* (Ithaca and London: Cornell University Press, 2000).
48. For accounts of Liuzzo's death and Governor George Wallace's reaction to it, as well as the national attention heaped on the state of Alabama in the wake of the killing, see Mary Stanton, *From Selma to Sorrow: The Life and Death of Viola Liuzzo* (Athens and London: University of Georgia Press, 1998); Juan Williams, *Eyes On the Prize: America's Civil Rights Years, 1954–1965*, with an introduction by Julian Bond (New York: Penguin Books, 1987); Lynn Olson, *Freedom's Daughters: The Unsung Heroines of the Civil Rights Movement from 1830 to 1970* (New York: Scribner Publishers, 2001).
49. Nannie Washburn, interview in Howell Raines, *My Soul Is Rested: Movement Days in the Deep South Remembered* (New York: Penguin Books, 1977), p. 405. Washburn, an active worker for racial justice since the 1930s and the "Scottsboro boys" case, warned Liuzzo against taking Moton home that evening. Referring to Liuzzo's violation of the South's racial hierarchy, Washburn stated, "They'd a lot ruther [sic] kill you'n a black man." Many younger white female activists also articulated an awareness of the danger their presence posed to black male southerners. Sara Evans admitted that many SNCC members realized that "they, as white women, were walking symbols of racial domination," due to the fact that southern vigilantes often invoked the defense of white womanhood as the rationale behind their criminal activities. The "enemy within, the southern lady" confounded

women in the movement who struggled to contribute to the betterment of their homes by attempting to rectify the racial hierarchy that retarded the progress of black southerners. Evans, *Personal Politics*, p. 43.
50. Southwestern students interview, 2 June 1968.
51. Statement warning against "race mixing" at Concerned Women of Memphis Meeting, 18 June 1969, Siena College, Memphis, TN, Box 6, Folder 25, Strike Collection.
52. *Voices: Women's Reflection of the Memphis Civil Rights Movement*, produced by Facing History and Ourselves, 35 minutes, 1999, videocassette.
53. "How About Hungry Children?," *Memphis Press-Scimitar*, 27 June 1969, p. 6.
54. Varnell telephone interview.
55. Jones interview. See also Shannon telephone interview; Wurzburg interview; Lewis M. Killian, *White Southerners*, rev. ed. (Amherst: University of Massachusetts Press, 1985).
56. Casey Hayden, "Race, Feminism, and the New Left: An Artifactual Journey," lecture presented at the Baker Peace Committee conference, "1968 Revisited," Athens, OH, 24 April 1998.

Chapter 7

1. For information on the death of Elton Hayes, see Jefferson Riker, "9 Law Officers Are Indicted, 4 for First-Degree Murder, in Slaying of Negro Youth," 10 December 1971, p. 1; Joe M. Dove, "Higgs' Order Limits Hayes Case Statements," 11 December 1971, p. 23, both in Memphis *Commercial Appeal*; Clark Porteous, "Citizens Group Asks City Council Not to Approve Reinstatement," *Memphis Press-Scimitar*, 12 December 1973, p. 6. See also Ken Lawrence, "Police Terror Grips Memphis," *Southern Patriot* 29 (December 1971): 1, 4, Box 6, Folder 7; "Relieved Police in Memphis," *Race Relations Reporter* 2 (15 November 1971): 2, Box 4, Folder 1, both in Frances Coe Papers, Mississippi Valley Collection, McWherter Library, University of Memphis, Memphis, TN. Hereafter cited as Coe Papers.
2. City of Memphis Community Relations Commission Annual Report, 1971. Contained in the private papers of Dorothy Jones.
3. Ibid. See also Dorothy "Happy"Jones, interview with Kimberly K. Little, 3 May 2002, Memphis, TN.
4. Jones interview.
5. Ibid.
6. Frances Coe, "Interview with State School Lunch Director, Mr. Laurence Bartlett," State Department of Education, undated, Nashville, TN, Box 6, Coe Papers. See also "Mrs. Coe Resigns as Director of Human Relations Council," Memphis *Commercial Appeal*, 11 November 1967, p. 12.
7. Edgar S. and Jean Camper Cahn, "The New Sovereign Immunity," *Harvard Law Review*, Vol. 81, No. 5 (March 1968): 932.
8. Linda Allen and Peggy Jemison, interview with Joan Beifuss and Carol Lynn Yellin, 24 February 1969, Memphis, TN, Box 20, Folder 4, 1968 Sanitation Workers' Strike Collection, Mississippi Valley Collection, McWherter Library, University of Memphis, Memphis, TN. Hereafter cited as Strike Collection.

9. For information on the problems with the integration of American school systems after the *Brown* decision, see Charles T. Clotfelter, *After* Brown: *The Rise and Retreat of School Desegregation* (Princeton and Oxford: Princeton University Press, 2004); J. Anthony Lukas, *Common Ground: A Turbulent Decade in the Lives of Three American Families* (New York: Alfred A. Knopf, 1985); Ronald P. Formisano, *Boston Against Busing: Race, Class, and Ethnicity in the 1960s and 1970s* (Chapel Hill and London: University of North Carolina Press, 1991); Thomas J. Cottile, *Busing* (Boston: Beacon Press, 1976); Derrick Bell, ed., *Shades of Brown: New Perspectives on School Desegregation* (New York and London: Teachers College Press, 1980); Derrick Bell, *Silent Covenants:* Brown v. Board of Education *and the Unfulfilled Hopes for Racial Reform* (Oxford: Oxford University Press, 2004); Peter H. Irons, *Jim Crow's Children: The Broken Promise of the Brown Decision* (New York: Viking, 2002); Christopher Silver and John V. Moeser, *The Separate City: Black Communities in the Urban South, 1940–1968* (Lexington: University Press of Kentucky, 1995); Arnold Rose, *De Facto School Segregation* (New York: National Conference of Christians and Jews, 1964); J. Harvie Wilkinson III, *From* Brown *to* Bakke: *The Supreme Court and Integration, 1954–1978* (New York and Oxford: Oxford University Press, 1979).
10. "Mayor's Budget Message for the Fiscal Year July 1, 1968–June 30, 1969, City of Memphis, Presented to the Council on April 23, 1968," Box 13, Folder 113, Strike Collection.
11. For information regarding resistance to integration in communities surrounding Memphis, see "Construction Sparked by Desegregation Deadlines Dents School Budgets," Memphis *Commercial Appeal*, 24 August 1970, p. 17. President Richard Nixon also opposed forced busing as a strategy for desegregation shortly after his 1968 election. See Gary Orfield, "Congress, the President, and Anti-Busing Legislation, 1966–1974," *Journal of Law and Education* 4 (January 1975): 81–139.
12. For an extended discussion of Maxine Smith's role with both the NAACP and the Memphis city school board during this phase of busing, see Sherry L. Hoppe and Bruce W. Speck, *Maxine Smith's Unwilling Pupils: Lessons Learned in Memphis's Civil Rights Classroom* (Knoxville: University of Tennessee Press, 2007), chapters 2, 3.
13. David Vincent, "Events May Have Undercut School Board's Good Intentions," Memphis Commercial Appeal, 27 October 1969, p. 1.
14. David Vincent, "Threat of Negro Boycotts Looms As NAACP Bolts School Meeting," Memphis *Commercial Appeal*, 16 October 1969, pp. 1, 10. See also "Keep School Talks Open," Memphis *Commercial Appeal*, 17 October 1969, p. 6.
15. David Vincent, "New Coalition of Negro Groups Plan Mass March as First Step," Memphis *Commercial Appeal*, 17 October 1969, p. 1. See also David Vincent, "Two Roads Are Taken Seeking School Reform," 19 October 1969, p. 1; "Marchers Hear Endurance Call," 19 October 1969, p. 22; Calvin Taylor, Jr., "600 Teachers Vow to Skip School to Push NAACP's 'Black Monday,'" 20 October 1969, p. 1; David Vincent, "Old Humiliations Spur NAACP to New Strength, Prestige, Unity," 26 October 1969, pp. 1, 10, all in Memphis *Commercial Appeal*.
16. "Biracial School Advisers Promised by December 1 in Move to Cool Protests," Memphis *Commercial Appeal*, 25 October 1969, pp. 1, 15. See also "Mrs. Coe Opposes Early School Consolidation," *Memphis Press-Scimitar*, 1 February 1957, p. 12; "No Consolidation Until Fall, 1962, Says Mrs. Coe," *Memphis Press-Scimitar*,

1 April 1960, p. 4; "Solid School Progress," Memphis *Commercial Appeal*, 17 November 1969, p. 6.
17. William Bayne, "Leaders of CAB Resign in Flap over Goals of Organization," Memphis *Commercial Appeal*, 13 December 1971, p. 1.
18. James Chisum, "CAB Pledges Activist Role," Memphis *Commercial Appeal*, 15 December 1971, p. 29.
19. Michael Lollar, "County, NAACP Attack Plan," Memphis *Commercial Appeal*, 23 July 1971, p. 1.
20. Jerry L. Robbins, "School Board Set to Approve Busing for Transfer Students," *Memphis Press-Scimitar*, 21 July 1971, p. 1; "Absenteeism Delays Meeting on Busing," Memphis *Commercial Appeal*, 23 July 1971, p. 23.
21. Bonnie Ragland, "Busing Given 'F' by PTA Council," Memphis *Commercial Appeal*, 22 May 1971, p. 1.
22. Frances Coe, "Integration in Education in Memphis and Shelby County, 1954–1966," undated paper presented to the Memphis city school board, Box 4, Folder 1, Coe Papers; Mrs. A. Hunnicutt, "Programs in the City Schools," undated paper presented to the Memphis city school board, Box 4, Folder 1, Coe Papers.
23. Michael Lollar, "Two Plans Are Ordered on School Integration—Both Include Busing," Memphis *Commercial Appeal*, 11 December 1971, pp. 1, 12.
24. David Vincent, "Means to Reach All Pupils Will Be Goal of Workshop," Memphis *Commercial Appeal*, 30 January 1968, p. 17. For additional discussion on the "perils" of putting children from different racial groups into the same school, see "Busing Order Hit by Mayor," "Massive Move for City School Under Plan A Gets Underway," 19 January 1973, p. 10; "McRae Allows Minor Changes," 20 January 1973, p. 1, all in Memphis *Commercial Appeal*.
25. Bonnie Ragland, "'Reason' Urged as Solution of School Busing Problems," Memphis *Commercial Appeal*, 21 May 1971, p. 1. For more information on the impact of the *Swann* decision on Charlotte, see James T. Patterson, Brown v. Board of Education*: A Civil Rights Milestone and Its Troubled Legacy*, in Pivotal Moments in American History Series, ed. David Hackett Fischer and James M. McPherson (New York: Oxford University Press, 2001), pp. 155, 158; Frye Gaillard, *The Dream Long Deferred* (Chapel Hill and London: University of North Carolina Press, 1988); Bernard Schwartz, *Swann's Way: The School Busing Case and the Supreme Court* (New York and Oxford: Oxford University Press, 1986); Davison M. Douglas, *Reading, Writing, and Race: The Desegregation of the Charlotte Schools* (Chapel Hill and London: University of North Carolina Press, 1995). For more information on the impact of the *Swann* decision on other southern communities, see Richard A. Pride and J. David Woodard, *The Burden of Busing: The Politics of Desegregation in Nashville, Tennessee* (Knoxville: University of Tennessee Press, 1985); Robert F. Campbell, "Busing Decisions Provide Leeway," *Race Relations Reporter* 2 (7 September 1971): 4–6; "NAACP Challenges Quality of Schools," *Race Relations Reporter* 2 (4 October 1971): 1, both in Box 4, Folder 1, Coe Papers.
26. Marilyn Duncan, "Women Seek to Add New Dimensions," Memphis *Commercial Appeal*, 9 September 1971, p. 18; Campaign Pamphlet for Frances Coe, 1971, *Memphis Press-Scimitar*, Clippings Files of Frances Coe, Mississippi Valley Collection, McWherter Library, University of Memphis, Memphis, TN.
27. Bert Wolff, interview with Kimberly K. Little, Memphis, TN, 30 April 2002.

28. Ibid.
29. Ibid.
30. Ibid.
31. Ibid. For information of the impact of white women on ESAP's work in Little Rock, as well as the role of the Panel of American Women in the integration crisis in 1957, see Paula C. Barnes, "Sara Alderman Murphy and the Little Rock Panel of American Women: A Prescription to Heal the Wounds of the Little Rock Crisis," in *The Southern Elite and Social Change Essays in Honor of Willard B. Gatewood, Jr.*, ed. Randy Finley and Thomas A. DeBlack, with a foreword by James C. Cobb (Fayetteville: University of Arkansas Press, 2002), pp. 164–176.
32. Wolff interview.
33. Ibid.
34. Duncan, "Women Seek to Add New Dimensions," p. 18.
35. Jimmie Covington, "School Board Plans Night Meetings," Memphis *Commercial Appeal*, 15 December 1971, p. 29.
36. Michael Lollar, "U.S. Keeps Hands Off in City's School Case; Hearings Open Today," Memphis *Commercial Appeal*, 28 March 1972, p. 1. See also James Chisum, "Chamber of Commerce Urges Public Education Support" and Michael Lollar, "Attorney Claims Errors in NAACP Busing Plan," 5 April 1972, pp. 1, 12; "Schools in Trouble," 6 April 1972, p. 6; Joseph Kraft, "Busing and the Hush-Hush Lambda Study," 6 April 1972, p. 6, all in Memphis *Commercial Appeal*.
37. Charles Thornton, "Foes of Busing March, Then Ride Buses Home," 29 March 1972, p. 1; Michael Lollar, "Board Witness Points to Enrollment Decline in City School System," 30 March 1972, pp. 1, 16, both in Memphis *Commercial Appeal*.
38. Jimmie Covington, "Plan to Bus 13,789 Students by Fall Is Seen as Feasible," Memphis *Commercial Appeal*, 31 March 1972, pp. 1, 5.
39. For information on the tone of these heated debates, see also Fannie Maxwell, interview by Marjorie Kremer and Selma Lewis, 30 August 1978, Memphis, TN, Box 3, Folder 4, Selma Lewis Papers, History Department, Memphis Public Library, Memphis, TN. Hereafter cited as Lewis Papers.
40. Jimmie Covington, "Judge Orders Busing for 13,789, Says 'Practicalities' Limit Change," Memphis *Commercial Appeal*, 21 April 1972, pp. 1, 13. See also "'Transporting' Called Necessary to End Dual School System," pp. 12, 13; "New Alignment Cuts List of One-Race School to 36," p. 25, both in Memphis *Commercial Appeal*, 21 April 1972; Morris Cunningham, "Measure to Halt Busing Clears Hurdle in House—Awaits Nixon's Signing," Memphis *Commercial Appeal*, 9 June 1972, pp. 1, 5.
41. "Decision Surprises Few, but Fewer Seem Pleased," Memphis *Commercial Appeal*, 21 April 1972, p. 1.
42. Jimmie Covington, "School Officials, Chamber Blast Boycott Plans," Memphis *Commercial Appeal*, 27 April 1972, pp. 1, 7. See also "CAB Calls for Boycott of Schools for Two Days," 26 April 1972, p. 1; "Boycotts: A Mistake," 27 April 1972, p. 6, both in Memphis *Commercial Appeal*.
43. Jimmie Covington, "CAB Asks Widening of School Boycott," 28 April 1972, pp. 1, 4; Jimmie Covington, "City Absenteeism Up; CAB Plans Large Rally," 29 April 1972, p. 1, both in Memphis *Commercial Appeal*. See also "What Did Boycott Achieve?" Memphis *Commercial Appeal*, 29 April 1972, p. 6.

44. James Denley, "Ideas on 'Holiday' Run from Right to Wrong," 28 October 1969, p. 17; "NAACP Says Negotiations Could Ease Protests," 28 October 1969, p. 1, both in Memphis *Commercial Appeal*. See also Louis Hobson, interview by Marjean Kramer, 28 February 1977, Memphis, TN, Box 2, Folder 16, Lewis Papers.
45. Judith Shulz Sullivan, interview with Kimberly K. Little, Memphis, TN, 29 December 1999.
46. Jeanne Dreifus, interview with Kimberly K. Little, Memphis, TN, 21 January 2001.
47. "The Memphis Section of the 'National Council of Jewish Women,'" no author, undated pamphlet, Box 2, Folder 12, Lewis Papers. The Memphis city school board created CLUE in 1970.
48. Claudia Davis, telephone interview with Kimberly K. Little, 15 April 2002. For additional information regarding the exodus of white Memphians to the predominantly white suburbs, see also "Pain of 'White Flight' Shows on Faces," Memphis *Commercial Appeal*, 13 December 1971, p. 21.
49. Linda Allen and Peggy Jemison, interview by Joan Beifuss and Carol Lynn Yellin, 24 February 1969, Box 20, Folder 5, Strike Collection.
50. Jimmie Covington, "Board OKs Contract for Busing after Court Rejects Bid for Delay," Memphis *Commercial Appeal*, 17 October 1972, pp. 1, 4. See also James Denley, "Council Votes to Block Board from Receiving City's Funds for Busing," 18 October 1972, pp. 1, 4; Jimmie Covington, "Stimbert Blames Interference," 7 November 1972, p. 15; James Denley, "Board May Sue City over Busing Funds," 11 November 1972, p. 23, all in Memphis *Commercial Appeal*.
51. Jimmie Covington, "School Board to Appeal McRae's Busing Order," Memphis *Commercial Appeal*, 25 April 1972, p. 13. See also Michael Lollar, "City School Faculty Plan Is Attacked as 'Racist,'" 2 June 1972, p. 1; Jimmie Covington, "Court's Stay Order Casts Doubt on Busing in Fall; NAACP Reacts Quickly," and "Stay Order Unlikely to Cancel Chances," 6 June 1972, pp. 1, 13; "School Ruling Leaves Board Polarized," 30 August 1972, p. 11, all in Memphis *Commercial Appeal*. Frances Coe's personal papers contained a wealth of evidentiary support for her arguments in these heated school board debates. See Irwin Katz, "Review of Evidence Relating to Effects of Desegregation on the Intellectual Performance of Negroes," June 1964, Box 4, Folder 1, Coe Papers; Nancy H. St. John, "Desegregation and Minority Group Performance," *Review of Educational Research* 40 (May 1967): 111–133; Everett Cataldo, Michael Giles, Deborah Athos, and Douglas Gatlin, "Desegregation and White Flight," *Integrated Education* (January/February 1975): 3–5. For additional sources on the debate over the quality of a segregated education, see Ralph Scott, *Education and Ethnicity: The U.S. Experiment in School Integration*, Journal of Social, Political and Economic Studies Monograph Series 17 (Washington: The Council for Social and Economic Studies, 1987); Margaret Anderson, *The Children of the South*, with a foreword by Ralph McGill (New York: Farrar, Straus, and Giroux, 1966); Laurence R. Marcus and Benjamin D. Strickney, *Race and Education: The Unending Controversy* (Springfield, IL: Charles C. Thomas, 1981).
52. Jocelyn Wurzburg, interview by Kimberly K. Little, 2 August 2001, Memphis, TN.
53. Wurzburg interview. See also Panel of American Women, 1971–1972, "Questions," Box 2, Folder 21, Jocelyn Dan Wurzburg Papers, Mississippi Valley Collection, McWherter Library, University of Memphis, Memphis, TN.

54. John Egerton, *Promise of Progress: Memphis School Desegregation, 1972–1973* (Atlanta: Southern Regional Council, 1973), pp. 9–12.
55. Jimmie Covington, "Grade Structure Listed for Paired Schools," Memphis *Commercial Appeal*, 3 January 1973, p. 15.
56. "Symposium Study Puts OK on Integrated Education," Memphis *Commercial Appeal*, 7 April 1972, p. 11.
57. "Absences, Calm Mark Busing," 25 January 1973, p. 1; Jimmie Covington, "Bus Rides Roll Along Smoothly on First Day," 25 January 1973, p. 35, both in Memphis *Commercial Appeal*.
58. Egerton, *Promise of Progress*, p. 35.
59. Roger Biles, "A Bittersweet Victory: Public School Desegregation in Memphis," *The Journal of Negro Education* 55 (Fall 1986): 479.
60. Available from http://www.memphis-schools.k12.tn.us/admin/communications/facts.htm.

Epilogue

1. Jocelyn Wurzburg, interview by Kimberly K. Little, 2 August 2001, Memphis, TN. See also Jocelyn Dan Wurzburg, "Problems of Employment and What the Council Can Do to Take Action," presented to the Tennessee Council on Human Relations Subcommittee on Employment, 4 October 1972, Box 1, Folder 20, Jocelyn Dan Wurzburg Papers, Mississippi Valley Collection, McWherter Library, University of Memphis, Memphis, TN, hereafter cited as Wurzburg Papers; Bill Steinberg, "Divorce: Local Experts Talk About the 'Big D' in Memphis," *The Memphis Flyer*, 2–8 August 2001, pp. 18–21, 62.
2. Dorothy "Happy" Jones, interview with Kimberly K. Little, 3 May 2002, Memphis, TN.
3. Ibid. See also Deborah M. Clubb, comp. and ed., *A Legacy of Achievers: Women of Achievement* (Memphis: Women of Achievement, Inc., 1994), p. 45.
4. Jeanne Varnell, telephone interview with Kimberly K. Little, 9 May 2002; www.memphiswomen.org/membershipInd.html.
5. Flyer of the Women's Resource Center, undated, Box 2, Folder 4, Wurzburg Papers. See also Sara Evans, *Personal Politics: The Roots of Women's Liberation in the Civil Rights Movement and the New Left* (New York: Vintage Books, 1980).
6. Anne Whalen Shafer, *History of the Memphis City Beautiful Commission and Its Impact on Our Lives* (Memphis: Published by the author, 1996), p. 51.
7. Donna Sue Shannon, telephone interview with Kimberly K. Little, 9 April 2002.
8. Ibid.
9. Jeanne Dreifus, interview with Kimberly K. Little, 21 January 2001, Memphis, Tennessee.
10. Bonita Sparrow, "Women Talk Liberation," Memphis *Commercial Appeal*, 18 November 1970, p. 23.
11. Lawrence Buser, "Myra Dreifus, Friend of Needy Children, Dies at 82," Memphis *Commercial Appeal*, 9 January 1987, p. 16. See also Clubb, comp. and ed., *A Legacy of Achievers*, pp. 134–135.

12. "'Woman of Courage' Honor Goes to Mrs. Myra Dreifus," 20 August 1970, p. 13; Buser, "Myra Dreifus," 9 January 1987, p. 16, both in Memphis *Commercial Appeal*.
13. Adrian Marie Hofstetter, *Earth Friendly: Re-Visioning Science and Spirituality through Aristotle, Thomas Aquinas, and Rudolf Steiner* (Herndon, VA: Lindisfarne Books, 2004). For additional published work by Hofstetter, see R. Staub, J. W. Appling, A. M. Hofstetter, I. J. Haas, "The Effects of Industrial Wastes of Memphis and Shelby County on Primary Planktonic Producers," *BioScience*, Vol. 20, No. 16 (Aug. 15, 1970): 905–912.
14. www.teilharddechardin.org/studies.html.
15. Bethany Saltman, "Humbly Sprouting Roses," www.chronogram.com/issue/2005/. See also www.boughtonplace.org.
16. Bert Wolff, interview with Kimberly K. Little, Memphis, TN, 30 April 2002; www.diversitymemphis.org; hadassah.org. For additional information regarding the failure of busing to successfully integrate Memphis area schools, see Jerome Wright, "After the Death Blow in '54—Some Still Try to Keep Jim Crow Alive," Memphis *Commercial Appeal*, 16 June 1974, Section 6, pp. 1, 3; Department of Health, Education, and Welfare, *Minority Education 1960–1978: Grounds, Gains, and Gaps*, prepared by the Office of the Assistant Secretary for Planning and Evaluation, 100-77-104, Box 4, Folder 1, Frances Edgar Coe Papers, Mississippi Valley Collection, McWherter Library, University of Memphis, Memphis, TN.
17. Claudia Davis, telephone interview with Kimberly K. Little, 15 April 2002.
18. James G. Andrews, "Women with Power," *Mid-South Magazine* in Memphis *Commercial Appeal*, 16 June 1974, pp. 24–28, 30, 32.
19. Clark Porteous, "Mayor? No, Says Mrs. Awsumb," *Memphis Press-Scimitar*, 1 January 1971, p. 13.
20. "Mrs. Awsumb Named to Join National Educational Council," *Memphis Press-Scimitar*, 31 January 1973, p. 3; Barney DuBois, "For God, Country, Motherhood—And Some Unexpected Things," *Mid-South Magazine* in Memphis *Commercial Appeal*, 11 May 1969, p. 9.
21. Clubb, comp. and ed., *A Legacy of Achievers*, p. 35. See also curriculum vitae of Joan Turner Beifuss, Box 26, Envelope L, Strike Collection.
22. "Margaret Valiant, Activist, Dies at 81," *Memphis Press-Scimitar*, 13 April 1982, p. 19.
23. Kimberly Springer, Living for the Revolution: Black Feminist Organizations, 1968–1980 (Durham and London: Duke University Press, 2005); Winifred Breines, The Trouble Between Us: An Uneasy History of White and Black Women in the Feminist Movement (Oxford and New York: Oxford University Press, 2006); Lynne Olson, Freedom's Daughters: The Unsung Heroines of the Civil Rights Movement from 1830 to 1970 (New York: Scribner, 2001).

Bibliography

Primary Sources

Books, Articles

Boyle, Sara Patton. "Southerners Will *Like* Integration." *Saturday Evening Post* (19 February 1955): 132–134.

Braden, Anne. "A Continuing Quest." *New South Student* 5 (February 1968): 14–15.

"From Sisterhood to Priesthood: First Women to Be Ordained as Priests in the Episcopal Church." *Newsweek* 84 (12 August 1974): 52.

Garland, Phyllis. "Builders of a New South: Negro Heroines of Dixie Play Major Role in Challenging Racist Tradition." *Ebony* 21 (August 1966): 27–37.

Hayden, Casey. "Thoughts of Young Radicals: Raising the Question of Who Decides." *New Republic* 154 (22 January 1966): 9–11.

Lawson, James. "From a Lunch Counter Stool." *Motive* XXV (February 1965): 42–43.

Newfield, Jack. "SSOC: Bridging the Gap between Bureaucracy and Anarchy." *Motive* XXVI (March 1966): 13–15.

Smith, Lillian. *Our Faces, Our Words*. New York: W. W. Norton and Company, Inc., 1964.

Stembridge, Jane. *I Play Flute and Other Poems*. New York: The Seabury Press, 1966, 1968.

Washington, James Melvin, ed. *A Testament of Hope: The Essential Writings of Martin Luther King, Jr.* San Francisco: Harper and Row Publishers, 1986.

Waskow, Arthur. "Reconstruction of the Cities." *New South Student* 5 (December 1968): 5–7.

Yates, Gayle Graham. "Mississippi's Child." *Motive* XXV (February 1965): 39–40.

Archival Collections

Coe, Frances, Papers. Mississippi Valley Collection, McWherter Library, University of Memphis, Memphis, TN.

Dreifus, Myra, Papers. Mississippi Valley Collection, McWherter Library, University of Memphis, Memphis, TN.

Lewis, Selma, Papers. History Department, Main Library, Memphis Public Library, Memphis, TN.

Loeb, Mayor Henry, Papers. City of Memphis Archives, Cossitt Branch, Memphis Public Library, Memphis, TN.

1968 Sanitation Strike Collection. Mississippi Valley Collection, McWherter Library, University of Memphis, Memphis, TN.
Wurzburg, Jocelyn Dan, Papers. Mississippi Valley Collection, McWherter Library, University of Memphis, Memphis, TN.
Underground Newspaper Collection. University of Cincinnati, Cincinnati, OH. Microfilm.

Oral Histories, Memoirs, Correspondences

Abbott, Shirley. *Womenfolks: Growing Up down South.* New Haven: Ticknor and Fields, 1983.
Abernathy, Ralph David. *And the Walls Came Tumbling Down.* New York: Harper and Row, Publishers, 1989.
Barnett, Ida B. Wells. *Crusade for Justice: The Autobiography of Ida B. Wells.* Edited by Alfreda M. Duster. Negro American Biographies and Autobiographies Series. Chicago and London: University of Chicago Press, 1970.
Bates, Daisy. *The Long Shadow of Little Rock: A Memoir.* With a preface by Willard B. Gatewood, Jr. Fayetteville: University of Arkansas Press, 1987.
Beals, Melba Paltillo. *White Is a State of Mind: A Memoir.* New York: G. P. Putnam's Sons, 1999.
Belfrage, Sally. *Freedom Summer.* With a foreword by Robert P. Moses. Charlottesville and London: University Press of Virginia, 1965.
Bond, Julian. *A Time to Speak, a Time to Act: The Movement in Politics.* New York: Simon and Schuster, 1972.
Boyle, Sara Patton. *The Desegregated Heart: A Virginian's Stand in Time of Transition.* With an introduction by Jennifer Ritterhouse. Charlottesville and London: University Press of Virginia, 2001.
Braden, Anne. *The Wall Between.* New York: Monthly Review Press, 1958.
Brown, Elaine. *A Taste of Power.* New York: Pantheon, 1992.
Campbell, Clarice T. *Civil Rights Chronicle: Letters from the South.* With a foreword by John Dittmer. Jackson: University Press of Mississippi, 1997.
Caplan, Marvin. *Farther Along: A Civil Rights Memoir.* Baton Rouge: Louisiana State University Press, 1999.
Carmichael, Stokely, and Charles V. Hamilton. *Black Power: The Politics of Liberation in America.* New York: Vintage Books, 1967.
Clark, Septima. *Ready from Within: Septima Clark and the Civil Rights Movement.* Edited and with an introduction by Cynthia Stokes Brown. Trenton, NJ: Africa World Press, 1990.
Curry, Constance et al. *Deep in Our Hearts: Nine White Women in the Freedom Movement.* Athens and London: University of Georgia Press, 2000.
Davis, Claudia. Telephone interview with Kimberly K. Little, 15 April 2002.
Davis, Angela Y. *Angela Davis: Autobiography.* New York: Random House, 1974.
Dent, Tom. *Southern Journey: A Return to the Civil Rights Movement.* New York: William Morrow and Company, Inc., 1997.
Dreifus, Jeanne. Interview with Kimberly K. Little, 21 January 2001.
Durr, Virginia Foster. *Outside the Magic Circle: The Autobiography of Virginia Foster Durr.* Edited by Hollinger F. Barnard. With a foreword by Studs Terkel. New York: Simon and Schuster, 1985.

Evans, Eli N. *The Lonely Days Were Sundays: Reflections of a Jewish Southerner*. Jackson: University Press of Mississippi, 1993.

Evers, Myrlie, with William Peters. *For Us, the Living*. Garden City, NY: Doubleday, 1967.

Farmer, James. *Lay Bare the Heart*. New York: Arbor House, 1985.

Forman, James. *The Making of Black Revolutionaries: A Personal Account*. New York: Macmillan, 1972.

Gladney, Margaret Rose, ed. *How Am I To Be Heard? The Letters of Lillian Smith*. Chapel Hill and London: University of North Carolina Press, 1993.

Graetz, Robert S. *Montgomery: A White Preacher's Memoir*. Minneapolis: Fortress Press, 1991.

Hamer, Fannie Lou et al. *To Praise Our Bridges: An Autobiography*. Jackson, MS: KIPCO, 1967.

Hampton, Henry, and Steve Fayer, eds. *Voices of Freedom: An Oral History of the Civil Rights Movement from the 1950s through the 1980s*. New York: Bantam Books, 1990.

Hayden, Tom. *Reunion: A Memoir*. New York: Random House, 1988.

Hemphill, Paul. *Leaving Birmingham: Notes of a Native Son*. New York: Viking Press, 1993.

Holt, Len. *The Summer That Didn't End*. New York: William Morrow, 1965.

Huckaby, Elizabeth. *Crisis at Central High: Little Rock, 1957–1958*. With a foreword by Harry S. Ashmore. Baton Rouge and London: Louisiana State University Press, 1980.

Hudson, Winson, and Constance Curry. *Mississippi Harmony: Memoirs of a Freedom Fighter*. With a foreword by Derrick Bell. New York: Palgrave Macmillan, 2002.

Hunter Gault, Charlayne. *In My Place*. New York: Farrar Straus Giroux, 1992.

Jones, Dorothy "Happy." Interview with Kimberly K. Little, 3 May 2002.

King, Coretta Scott. *My Life with Martin Luther King, Jr*. New York: Holt, Rinehart, and Winston, 1969.

King, Florence. *Confessions of a Failed Southern Lady*. New York: St. Martin's, 1985.

King, Mary. *Freedom Song: A Personal Story of the 1960s Civil Rights Movement*. New York: William Morrow, 1987.

Lumpkin, Katherine DuPre. *The Making of a Southerner*. 1946; reprint, Athens: University of Georgia Press, 1984.

McAdam, Doug. *Freedom Summer*. New York: Oxford University Press, 1988.

Moody, Anne. *Coming of Age in Mississippi*. New York: Dell, 1968.

Ovington, Mary White. *Black and White Sat Down Together: The Reminiscences of an NAACP Founder*. Edited and with a foreword by Ralph E. Luker. New York: The Feminist Press at the City University of New York, 1995.

Parks, Rosa. *Rosa Parks: My Story*. New York: Dial Books, 1992.

Parsons, Sara Mitchell. *From Southern Wrongs to Civil Rights: The Memoir of a White Civil Rights Activist*. With a foreword by David J. Garrow. Tuscaloosa and London: University of Alabama Press, 2000.

Raines, Howell. *My Soul Is Rested: Movement Days in the Deep South Remembered*. New York: Penguin Books, 1977.

Robinson, Jo Ann Gibson. *The Montgomery Bus Boycott and the Women Who Started It: The Memoir of Jo Ann Gibson Robinson*. Edited and with a foreword by David J. Garrow. Knoxville: University of Tennessee Press, 1987.

Rothenberg, Paula. *Invisible Privilege: A Memoir About Race, Class, and Gender*. Lawrence, KS: University Press of Kansas, 2000.

Rowan, Carl T. *Breaking Barriers: A Memoir*. Boston: Little, Brown and Company, 1991.
———. *Go South to Sorrow*. New York: Random House, 1957.
Rustin, Bayard. *Down the Line*. With an introduction by C. Vann Woodward. Chicago: Quadrangle Books, 1971.
Sellers, Cleveland, and Robert Terrell. *The River of No Return: The Autobiography of a Black Militant and the Life and Death of SNCC*. New York: William Morrow, 1973.
Shafer, Anne. Interview with Kimberly K. Little, 12 June 2002.
———. Telephone interview with Kimberly K. Little, 15 April 2002.
Shannon, Donna Sue. Telephone interview with Kimberly K. Little, 9 April 2002.
Smith, Lillian. *Killers of the Dream*. Revised edition. New York: W. W. Norton and Company, Inc., 1949, 1961.
Sugarman, Tracy. *Stranger at the Gates: A Summer in Mississippi*. With a foreword by Fannie Lou Hamer. New York: Hill and Wang, 1966.
Sullivan, Judith Shultz. Interview by Kimberly K. Little, Memphis, TN 29 December 1999.
Sutherland, Elizabeth, ed. *Letters from Mississippi*. New York: McGraw-Hill, 1965.
Tucker, Susan, ed. *Telling Memories among Southern Women: Domestic Workers and Their Employers in the Segregated South*. Baton Rouge: Louisiana State University Press, 1989.
Varnell, Jeanne. Telephone interview with Kimberly K. Little, 9 May 2002.
Wade-Gayles, Gloria. *Pushed Back to Strength: A Black Woman's Journey Home*. Boston: Beacon Press, 1993.
Watters, Pat. *Down to Now: Reflections on the Southern Civil Rights Movement*. New York: Pantheon Books, 1971.
Webb, Sheyann, and Rachel West Nelson, with Frank Sikora. *Selma, Lord, Selma: Girlhood Memories of the Civil-Rights Days*. University: University of Alabama Press, 1980.
Wilkins, Roy. *Standing Fast*. New York: The Viking Press, 1982.
Wolff, Bert. Interview with Kimberly K. Little, 30 April 2002.
Wurzburg, Jocelyn. Interview with Kimberly K. Little, 2 August 2001.
X, Malcolm. *The Autobiography of Malcolm X*. New York: Ballantine, 1964.
Young, Andrew. *An Easy Burden: The Civil Rights Movement and the Transformation of America*. New York: Harper Collins Publisher, 1996.

Newspapers, Periodicals

Memphis *Commercial Appeal*, 1940, 1952, 1954, 1958, 1960, 1962–1974, 1987, 2003.
Memphis *Press-Scimitar*, 1954–1955, 1958, 1960, 1963, 1965, 1968–1971.
New York Times, 1968.
Tri-State Defender, 1953–1954, 1959–1960, 1971.
Wall Street Journal, 1968.

Census Records, Government Documents

U.S. Bureau of the Census. *Age by Color and Sex, for Standard Metropolitan Areas, Urbanized Areas, and Urban Places of 10,000 or More, 1950*, prepared by the Geography Division in cooperation with the Housing Division, Bureau of the Census. Washington, DC, 1955.

———. *Characteristics of the Population for Standard Metropolitan Statistical Areas, Urbanized Areas, and Urban Places of 10,000 or More, 1960,* prepared by the Geography Division in cooperation with the Housing Division, Bureau of the Census. Washington, DC, 1965.

———. *Race by Sex for Areas and Places, 1970,* prepared by the Geography Division in cooperation with the Housing Division, Bureau of the Census. Washington, DC, 1975.

Freedom of Information Act Files, Federal Bureau of Investigation, Parts Three and Five. www.foia.gov.

The National Advisory Commission on Civil Disorders. *Report of the National Advisory Commission on Civil Disorders.* Washington, DC: General Publishing Office, 1968.

Videorecordings

Voices: Women's Reflection of the Memphis Civil Rights Movement. Produced and directed by Facing History and Ourselves. 35 minutes. 1999. Videocassette.

Secondary Sources

Books

Adams, Frank T. *James A. Dombrowski: An American Heretic, 1897–1983.* With a foreword by Arthur Kinoy. Knoxville: University of Tennessee Press, 1992.

Albert, Peter J., and Ronald Hoffman, eds. *We Shall Overcome: Martin Luther King, Jr., and the Black Freedom Struggle.* New York: Pantheon Books, 1990.

Alexander, Maxine, ed. *Speaking for Ourselves: Women of the South.* New York: Pantheon Books, 1977.

Alonso, Harriet Hyman. *Peace as a Women's Issue: A History of the U.S. Movement for World Peace and Women's Rights.* Syracuse: Syracuse University Press, 1993.

Alston, Lee J., and Joseph P. Ferrie. *Southern Paternalism and the Rise of the American Welfare State: Economics, Politics, and Institutions in the South, 1865–1965.* Cambridge and New York: Cambridge University Press, 1999.

Alvis, Joel L., Jr. *Religion and Race: Southern Presbyterians, 1946–1983.* Tuscaloosa and London: University of Alabama Press, 1994.

Anderson, Margaret. *The Children of the South.* With a foreword by Ralph McGill. New York: Farrar, Straus and Giroux, 1958.

Armstrong, Julie Buckner, Susan Hult Edwards, Houston Bryan Roberson, and Rhonda Y. Williams, eds. *Teaching the Civil Rights Movement: Freedom's Bittersweet Song.* New York and London: Routledge, 2002.

Ayers, Edward L. *The Promise of the New South: Life After Reconstruction.* New York and Oxford: Oxford University Press, 1992.

Barlow, William. *Voice Over: The Making of Black Radio.* Philadelphia: Temple University Press, 1999.

Barnouw, Erik. *The Golden Web.* Vol. 2, *A History of Broadcasting in the United States.* New York: Oxford University Press, 1968.

Bartley, Numan V. *The New South, 1945–1980.* Baton Rouge: Louisiana State University Press, 1995.

———. *The Rise of Massive Resistance: Race and Politics in the South during the 1950s*. Baton Rouge: Louisiana State University Press, 1969.

Bartley, Numan, and Hugh Graham. *Southern Politics and the Second Reconstruction*. Baltimore: Johns Hopkins University Press, 1975.

Bass, S. Jonathan. *Blessed Are the Peacemakers: Martin Luther King, Jr., Eight White Religious Leaders and the "Letter From a Birmingham Jail."* Baton Rouge: Louisiana State University Press, 2001.

Bauman, Mark K., and Berkley Kalin, eds. *The Quiet Voices: Southern Rabbis and Black Civil Rights, 1880s to 1990s*. Tuscaloosa and London: University of Alabama Press, 1997.

Beardslee, William R. *The Way Out Must Lead In: Life Histories in the Civil Rights Movement*. Atlanta: Center for Research in Social Change at Emory University, 1977.

Beauchamp, Mary, Ardell Llewellyn, and Vivienne S. Worley. *Building Brotherhood: What Can Elementary Schools Do?* New York: National Conference of Christians and Jews, 1954.

Beifuss, Joan. *At the River I Stand: Memphis, the 1968 Strike, and Martin Luther King*. Memphis: St. Luke's Press, 1990.

Belknap, Michal R. *Federal Law and Southern Order: Racial Violence and Constitutional Conflict in the Post-*Brown *South*. Athens: University of Georgia Press, 1987.

Bell, Derrick, ed. *Shades of* Brown: *New Perspectives on School Desegregation*. New York and London: Teachers College Press, 1980.

———. *Silent Covenants:* Brown v. Board of Education *and the Unfulfilled Hopes for Racial Reform*. Oxford: Oxford University Press, 2004.

Bendroth, Margaret Lamberts, and Virginia Brereton. *Women and Twentieth Century Protestantism*. Urbana and Chicago: University of Illinois Press, 2002.

Bennett, James B. *Religion and the Rise of Jim Crow in New Orleans*. Princeton: Princeton University Press, 2005.

Bercaw, Nancy, ed. *Gender and the Southern Body Politic*. Jackson: University Press of Mississippi, 2000.

Bernard, Virginia et al., eds. *Hidden Histories of Women in the New South*. Columbia: University of Missouri Press, 1994.

Bernard, Virginia, et al., eds. *Southern Women: Histories and Identities*. Columbia and London: University of Missouri Press, 1992.

Biles, Roger. *Memphis in the Great Depression*. Knoxville: University of Tennessee Press, 1986.

Billingsley, K. L. *From Mainline to Sideline: The Social Witness of the National Council of Churches*. Washington, DC: Ethics and Public Policy Center, 1990.

Bishop, Jim. *The Days of Martin Luther King, Jr*. New York: G. P. Putnam's Sons, 1971.

Black, Earl, and Merle Black. *The Rise of Southern Republicans*. Cambridge, MA: Belknap Press of Harvard University Press, 2002.

Blee, Kathleen M., ed. *No Middle Ground: Women and Radical Protest*. New York and London: New York University Press, 1998.

Bloom, Jack M. *Class, Race, and the Civil Rights Movement*. Blacks in the Diaspora Series, ed. Darlene Clark Hine and John McCluskey, Jr. Bloomington and Indianapolis: Indiana University Press, 1987.

Bogle, Donald. *Toms, Coons, Mulattoes, Mammies, and Bucks: An Interpretive History of Blacks in American Films*. New York: Continuum, 1994.

Bond, Beverly G., and Janann Sherman. *Memphis in Black and White*. The Making of America Series. Charleston: Arcadia Publishing, 2003.

Bookman, Ann, and Sandra Morgan, eds. *Women and the Politics of Empowerment*. Philadelphia: Temple University Press, 1988.

Boswell, Angela, and Judith N. McArthur, eds. *Women Shaping the South: Creating and Confronting Change*. Columbia and London: University of Missouri Press, 2006.

Bouvard, Marguerite Guzman. *Women Reshaping Human Rights: How Extraordinary Activists Are Changing the World*. Wilmington, DE: SR Books, 1996.

Bowman, Rob. *Soulsville, U.S.A.: The Story of Stax Records*. New York: Schirmer Books, 1997.

Boyd, Lois A., and R. Douglas Brackenridge. *Presbyterian Women in America: Two Centuries of a Quest for Status*. 2d ed. Westport, CT and London: Greenwood Press, 1996.

Branch, Taylor. *Parting the Waters: America in the King Years, 1954–1963*. New York: Simon and Schuster, Inc., 1988.

———. *Pillar of Fire: America in the King Years, 1963–1965*. New York: Simon and Schuster, 1988.

Brattain, Michelle. *The Politics of Whiteness: Race, Workers, and Culture in the Modern South*. Princeton: Princeton University Press, 2001.

Breines, Winifred. *The Trouble Between Us: An Uneasy History of White and Black Women in the Feminist Movement*. Oxford and New York: Oxford University Press, 2006.

Brinkley, Douglas. *Rosa Parks*. New York: Viking, 2000.

Brisbane, Robert H. *Black Activism: Racial Revolution in the United States, 1954-1970*. Valley Forge: Judson Press, 1974.

Brown, Cynthia Stokes. *Refusing Racism: White Allies and the Struggle for Civil Rights*. The Teaching for Social Justice Series, ed. William Ayers. New York and London: Teachers College Press, 2002.

Bryan, G. McLeod. *These Few Also Paid a Price: Southern Whites Who Fought for Civil Rights*. Macon: Mercer University Press, 2001.

Burner, Eric R. *And Gently He Shall Lead Them: Robert Parris Moses and the Civil Rights Movement in Mississippi*. New York: New York University Press, 1994.

Bynum, Victoria E. *Unruly Women: The Politics of Social and Sexual Control in the Old South*. Chapel Hill: University of North Carolina Press, 1992.

Cantor, Louis. *Wheelin' On Beale: How WDIA-Memphis Became the Nation's First All-Black Radio Station and Created the Sound that Changed America*. New York: Pharos Books, 1992.

Capers, Gerald M., Jr. *The Biography of a River Town, Memphis: Its Heroic Age*. Chapel Hill: University of North Carolina Press, 1939.

Carnes, Mark C., ed. *Past Imperfect*. New York: Henry Holt and Company, 1996.

Carson, Clayborne. *In Struggle: SNCC and the Black Awakening of the 1960s*. Cambridge: Harvard University Press, 1981.

Carson, Clayborne et al., eds. *The Eyes On the Prize Civil Rights Reader: Documents, Speeches, and Firsthand Accounts from the Black Freedom Struggle, 1945–1990*. New York: Penguin Books, 1991.

Carson, Josephine. *Silent Voices: The Southern Negro Woman Today*. New York: Delacorte Press, 1969.

Carter, Dan T. *From George Wallace to Newt Gingrich: Race in the Conservative Counterrevolution, 1963–1994*. Baton Rouge: Louisiana State University Press, 1996.

Cash, Wilbur Joseph. *The Mind of the South*. New York: Knopf, 1941.
Chafe, William Henry. *The American Woman: Her Changing Social, Economic, and Political Roles, 1920–1970*. New York: Oxford University Press, 1972.
———. *Civilities and Civil Rights: Greensboro, North Carolina and the Black Struggle for Freedom*. New York: Oxford University Press, 1980.
Chappell, David. *Inside Agitators: White Southerners in the Civil Rights Movement*. Baltimore and London: Johns Hopkins University Press, 1994.
———. *A Stone of Hope: Prophetic Religion and the Death of Jim Crow*. Chapel Hill: University of North Carolina Press, 2004.
Church, Annette E., and Roberta Church. *The Robert R. Churches of Memphis: A Father and Son Who Achieved in Spite of Race*. Ann Arbor: Edwards Brothers, 1974.
Clark, Roy Peter, and Raymond Arsenault, eds. *The Changing South of Gene Patterson: Journalism and Civil Rights, 1960–1968*. Southern Dissent Series. Gainesville: University of Florida Press, 2002.
Clotfelter, Charles T. *After Brown: The Rise and Retreat of School Desegregation*. Princeton and Oxford: Princeton University Press, 2004.
Clubb, Deborah M., ed. *A Legacy of Achievers: Women of Achievement, 1985-1994*. Memphis: Women of Achievement, Inc., 1994.
Cluster, Dick, ed. *They Should Have Served That Cup of Coffee*. Boston: South End Press, 1979.
Cobb, James C. *The Most Southern Place on Earth: The Mississippi Delta and the Roots of Regional Identity*. New York: Oxford University Press, 1992.
———. *The Selling of the South: The Southern Crusade for Industrial Development*. 2d ed. Urbana: University of Illinois Press, 1993.
Collins, Sheila D. *The Rainbow Challenge: The Jackson Campaign and the Future of U.S. Politics*. New York: Monthly Review Press, 1986.
Coryell, Janet Lee et al., eds. *Beyond Image and Convention: Explorations in Southern Women's History*. Columbia and London: University of Missouri Press, 1998.
Cott, Nancy. *The Grounding of Modern Feminism*. New Haven and London: Yale University Press, 1987.
Cott, Nancy F., Jeanne Boydston, Ann Brande, Lori D. Ginzburg, and Molly Ladd-Taylor, eds. *Root of Bitterness: Documents of the Social History of American Women*. 2d ed. Boston: Northeastern University Press, 1996.
Cott, Nancy F., and Elizabeth H. Pleck, eds. *A Heritage of Her Own: Toward a New Social History of American Women*. New York: Simon and Schuster, 1979.
Cottile, Thomas J. *Busing*. Boston: Beacon Press, 1976.
Couto, Richard A. *Ain't Gonna Let Nobody Turn Me Round: The Pursuit of Racial Justice in the Rural South*. Philadelphia: Temple University Press, 1991.
Crawford, Vicki L., Jacqueline Anne Rouse, and Barbara Woods, eds. *Women in the Civil Rights Movement: Trailblazers and Torchbearers, 1941–1965*. Brooklyn: Carlson Publishers, 1990.
Crespino, Joseph. *In Search of Another Country: Mississippi and the Conservative Counterrevolution*. Princeton and Oxford: Princeton University Press, 2007.
Crosby, Emilye. *A Little Taste of Freedom: The Black Freedom Struggle in Claiborne County, Mississippi*. John Hope Franklin Series in African American History and Culture. Chapel Hill: University of North Carolina Press, 2005.

Curry, Constance. *Silver Rights*. With an introduction by Marian Wright Edelman. Chapel Hill: Algonquin Books, 1995.
Daniel, Pete. *Lost Revolutions: The South in the 1950s*. Chapel Hill: University of North Carolina Press, 2000.
Daniels, Arlene Kaplan. *Invisible Careers: Women Civic Leaders from the Volunteer World*. Chicago: University of Chicago Press, 1988.
Davidson, Chandler. *Biracial Politics: Conflict and Coalition in the Metropolitan South*. Baton Rouge: Louisiana State University Press, 1972.
Davidson, Osha Gray. *The Best of Enemies: Race and Redemption in the New South*. New York: Scribner, 1996.
Davies, David R., ed. *The Press and Race: Mississippi Journalists Confront the Movement*. Jackson: University Press of Mississippi, 2001.
Davis, Angela Y. *Women, Culture, and Politics*. New York: Random House, 1989.
———. *Women, Race, and Class*. New York: Vintage Books, 1983.
Degler, Carl. *At Odds: Women and the Family in America from the Revolution to the Present*. New York: Oxford University Press, 1980.
Demerath, N. J. III, Gerald Marwell, and Michael T. Aiken. *Dynamics of Idealism: White Activists in a Black Movement*. The Jossey-Bass Behavioral Science Series. San Francisco: Jossey-Bass Inc., Publishers, 1971.
Dimond, Paul R. *Beyond Busing: Inside the Challenge to Urban Segregation*. Ann Arbor: University of Michigan Press, 1985.
Dinnerstein, Leonard, and Mary Dale Palsson, eds. *Jews in the South*. Baton Rouge: Louisiana State University Press, 1973.
Dittmer, John. *Local People: The Struggle for Civil Rights in Mississippi*. Urbana and Chicago: University of Illinois Press, 1994.
Dollard, John. *Caste and Class in a Southern Town*. New Haven: Yale University Press, 1937. Reprint, Madison: University of Wisconsin Press, 1988.
Dossett, Kate. *Bridging Race Divides: Black Nationalism, Feminism, and Integration in the United States, 1896–1935*. Gainesville: University Press of Florida.
Douglas, Davison M. *Reading, Writing, and Race: The Desegregation of the Charlotte Schools*. Chapel Hill and London: University of North Carolina Press, 1995.
Draper, Alan. *Conflict of Interests: Organized Labor and the Civil Rights Movement in the South, 1954–1968*. Ithaca: Cornell University Press, 1994.
Dudziak, Mary L. *Cold War Civil Rights: Race and the Image of American Democracy*. Politics and Society in Twentieth-Century America Series, ed. William Chafe, Gary Gerstle, and Linda Gordon. Princeton and Oxford: Princeton University Press, 2000.
Dunbar, Anthony. *Against the Grain: Southern Radicals and Prophets, 1929–1959*. Charlottesville: University Press of Virginia, 1981.
Durr, Kenneth D. *Behind the Backlash: White Working-Class Politics in Baltimore, 1940–1980*. Chapel Hill: University of North Carolina Press, 2003.
Eagles, Charles W., ed. *The Civil Rights Movement in America*. Jackson and London: University Press of Mississippi, 1986.
———. *Outside Agitator: Jon Daniels and the Civil Rights Movement in Alabama*. Tuscaloosa and London: University of Alabama Press, 1993.
Edds, Margaret. *Free At Last: What Really Happened When Civil Rights Came to Southern Politics*. Bethesda: Adler and Adler, Publishers, Inc., 1987.

Egerton, John. *A Mind to Stay Here: Profiles from the South*. London: The Macmillan Company, 1970.

———. *Promise of Progress: Memphis School Desegregation, 1972–1973*. Atlanta: Southern Regional Council, 1973.

———. *Speak Now Against the Day: The Generation Before the Civil Rights Movement in the South*. New York: Alfred A. Knopf, 1994.

Eick, Gretchen Cassel. *Dissent in Wichita: The Civil Rights Movement in the Midwest, 1954–1972*. Urbana and Chicago: University of Illinois Press, 2001.

Escott, Colin, with Martin Hawkins. *Good Rockin' Tonight: Sun Records and the Birth of Rock 'n' Roll*. New York: St. Martin's Press, 1991.

Eskew, Glenn T. *But for Birmingham: The Local and National Movements in the Civil Rights Struggle*. Chapel Hill: University of North Carolina Press, 1997.

———. *The Provincials: A Personal History of Jews in the South*. New York: Atheneum, 1973.

Evans, Sara, ed. *Journeys That Opened Up the World: Women, Student Christian Movements, and Social Justice, 1955–1975*. New Brunswick, NJ and London: Rutgers University Press, 2003.

———. *Personal Politics: The Roots of Women's Liberation in the Civil Rights Movement and the New Left*. New York: Vintage Books, 1979.

———. *Tidal Wave: How Women Changed America at Century's End*. New York: The Free Press, 2003.

Evans, Sara, and Harry C. Boyte. *Free Spaces: The Sources of Democratic Change in America*. New York: Harper and Row, Publishers, 1986.

Fager, Charles E. *White Reflections on Black Power*. Grand Rapids: W. B. Eerdmans Publishing Company, 1967.

Fairclough, Adam. *Race and Democracy: The Civil Rights Struggle in Louisiana, 1915–1972*. Athens: University of Georgia Press, 1995.

———. *To Redeem the Soul of America: The Southern Christian Leadership Conference and Martin Luther King, Jr*. Athens: University of Georgia Press, 1987.

Farnham, Christie Anne, ed. *Women of the American South: A Multicultural Reader*. New York: New York University Press, 1997.

Feldstein, Ruth. *Motherhood in Black and White: Race and Sex in American Liberalism, 1930–1965*. Ithaca and London: Cornell University Press, 2000.

Ferree, Myra Marx, and Patricia Yancey Martin, eds. *Feminist Organizations: Harvest of the New Women's Movement*. Philadelphia: Temple University Press, 1975.

Findlay, James F., Jr. *Church People in the Struggle: The National Council of Churches and the Black Freedom Movement, 1950–1970*. New York and Oxford: Oxford University Press, 1993.

Finley, Randy, and Thomas A. DeBlack, eds. *The Southern Elite and Social Change: Essays in Honor of Willard B. Gatewood, Jr*. With a foreword by James C. Cobb. Fayetteville: University of Arkansas Press, 2002.

Fite, Gilbert C. *Cotton Fields No More: Southern Agriculture, 1865–1980*. Lexington: University Press of Kentucky, 1984.

Fleming, Cynthia Griggs. *Soon We Will Not Cry: The Liberation of Ruby Doris Smith Robinson*. New York and Oxford: Rowman and Littlefield Publishers, Inc., 1998.

Flynt, J. Wayne. *Dixie's Forgotten People: The South's Poor Whites*. Bloomington: Indiana University Press, 1979.

Foner, Eric. *Reconstruction: America's Unfinished Revolution, 1863–1877.* New York: Harper and Row, Publishers, 1988.
Formisano, Ronald P. *Boston Against Busing: Race, Class, and Ethnicity in the 1960s and 1970s.* Chapel Hill and London: University of North Carolina Press, 1991.
Fosl, Catherine. *Subversive Southerner: Anne Braden and the Struggle for Racial Justice in the Cold War South.* With a foreword by Angela Davis. New York: Palgrave Macmillan, 2002.
Frady, Marshall. *Southerners: A Journalist's Odyssey.* New York: New American Library, 1980.
Frank, Gerold. *An American Death: The True Story of the Assassination of Dr. Martin Luther King, Jr., and the Greatest Manhunt of Our Time.* Garden City, NY: Doubleday and Company, Inc., 1972.
Franklin, V. P., Nancy L. Grant, Harold M. Kletnick, and Genna Rae McNeil, eds. *African Americans and Jews in the Twentieth Century: Studies in Convergence and Conflict.* Columbia and London: University of Missouri Press, 1998.
Frazier, E. Franklin. *The Negro Church in America*/C. Eric Lincoln, *The Black Church Since Frazier.* New York: Schocken Books, 1974.
Frederickson, Kari A. *The Dixiecrat Revolt and the End of the Solid South, 1932–1968.* Chapel Hill: University of North Carolina Press, 2001.
Friedland, Michael B. *Lift Up Your Voice Like a Trumpet: White Clergy and the Civil Rights and Antiwar Movements, 1954–1973.* Chapel Hill: University of North Carolina Press, 1998.
Friedman, Jean E. *The Enclosed Garden: Women and Community in the Evangelical South, 1830–1900.* The Fred W. Morrison Series in Southern Studies. Chapel Hill and London: University of North Carolina Press, 1985.
Friedman, Lawrence J., and Mark D. McGarvie, eds. *Charity, Philanthropy, and Civility in American History.* Cambridge: Cambridge University Press, 2003.
Frost, Jennifer. *"An Interracial Movement of the Poor": Community Organizing and the New Left in the 1960s.* New York: New York University Press, 2001.
Fullinwider, Robert K., ed. *Civil Society, Democracy, and Civic Renewal.* Lanham, MD: Rowan and Littlefield Publishers, Inc., 1999.
Gaillard, Frye. *The Dream Long Deferred.* Chapel Hill and London: University of North Carolina Press, 1988.
Gaines, Kevin. *Uplifting the Race: Black Leadership, Politics, and Culture in the Twentieth Century.* Chapel Hill: University of North Carolina Press, 1996.
Garrow, David J., ed. *Atlanta, Georgia, 1960–1961: Sit-Ins and Student Activism.* Brooklyn: Carlson Publishers, 1989.
——— . *Bearing the Cross: Martin Luther King, Jr., and the Southern Christian Leadership Conference.* New York: William Morrow, 1986.
——— . *The FBI and Martin Luther King, Jr.: From "Solo" to Memphis.* New York and London: W. W. Norton, 1981.
Gerster, Patrick, and Nicholas Cords, eds. *Myth and Southern History.* Vol. 2, *The New South.* 2d ed. Urbana and Chicago: University of Illinois Press, 1989.
Giddings, Paula J. *Ida: A Sword Among Lions: Ida B. Wells and the Campaign Against Lynching.* New York: Amistad, 2008.
——— . *When and Where I Enter: The Impact of Black Women on Race and Sex in America.* New York: Morrow, 1984.

Gilbert, Ben W. *Ten Blocks from the White House: Anatomy of the Washington Riots of 1968.* New York: Fredrick A. Praeger, Publishers, 1968.

Gillespie, Michelle, and Catherine Clinton, eds. *Taking Off the White Gloves: Southern Women and Southern Historians.* Columbia and London: University of Missouri Press, 1998.

Gilmore, Glenda Elizabeth. *Gender and Jim Crow: Women and the Politics of White Supremacy in North Carolina, 1896–1920.* Chapel Hill: University of North Carolina Press, 1996.

Gitlin, Todd. *The Sixties: Years of Hope, Days of Rage.* New York: Bantam, 1986.

Glenn, Evelyn Nakano, Grace Chang, and Linda Rennie Forcey. *Mothering: Ideology, Experience, and Agency.* New York: Routledge, 1994.

Goldfield, David R. *Black, White, and Southern: Race Relations and Southern Culture, 1940 to the Present.* Baton Rouge: Louisiana State University Press, 1990.

———. *Cotton Fields and Skyscrapers: Southern City and Region, 1607–1980.* Baton Rouge: Louisiana State University Press, 1982.

———. *Region, Race, and Cities: Interpreting the Urban South.* Baton Rouge: Louisiana State University Press, 1997.

———. *Still Fighting the Civil War: The American South and Southern History.* Baton Rouge: Louisiana State University Press, 2002.

Graham, Hugh Davis. *Crisis in Print: Desegregation and the Press in Tennessee.* Nashville: Vanderbilt University Press, 1967.

Grant, Jacquelyn. *White Women's Christ and Black Women's Jesus: Feminist Christology and Womanist Response.* Atlanta: Scholars Press, 1989.

Grant, Joanne. *Ella Baker: Freedom Bound.* With a foreword by Julian Bond. New York: John Wiley and Sons, Inc., 1998.

Grantham, Dewey W. *Southern Progressivism: The Reconciliation of Progress and Tradition.* Knoxville: University of Tennessee Press, 1983.

Graziani, Bernice. *Where There's A Woman: 75 Years of History as Lived by the National Council of Jewish Women.* With an introduction by Dore Schary. New York: National Council of Jewish Women, Inc., 1967.

Green, Laurie B. *Battling the Plantation Mentality: Memphis and the Black Freedom Struggle.* Chapel Hill: University of North Carolina Press, 2007.

Greenberg, Cheryl Lynn, ed. *A Circle of Trust: Remembering SNCC.* New Brunswick, NJ and London: Rutgers University Press, 1998.

———. *Troubling the Waters: Black-Jewish Relations in the American Century.* Princeton and Oxford: Princeton University Press, 2006.

Greene, Christina. *Our Separate Ways: Women and the Black Freedom Movement in Durham, North Carolina.* Chapel Hill: University of North Carolina Press, 2005.

Grier, William H., and Price M. Cobbs. *Black Rage.* With a foreword by Fred R. Harris. New York: Bantam Books, 1968.

Grubbs, Donald H. *Cry from the Cotton: The Southern Tenant Farmers' Union and the New Deal.* Chapel Hill: University of North Carolina Press, 1971.

Guralnick, Peter. *Last Train to Memphis: The Rise of Elvis Presley.* Boston: Little, Brown and Company, 1994.

———. *Sweet Soul Music: Rhythm and Blues and the Southern Dream of Freedom.* New York: Harper and Row Publishers, 1986.

Guy-Sheftall, Beverly. *Daughters of Sorrow: Attitudes Toward Black Women.* Brooklyn: Carlson Publishers, 1990.

Hale, Grace Elizabeth. *Making Whiteness: The Culture of Segregation in the South, 1890–1940*. New York: Pantheon, 1998.

Hall, Jacquelyn Dowd. *Revolt Against Chivalry: Jessie Daniel Ames and the Women's Campaign Against Lynching*. New York: Columbia University Press, 1979.

Hamburger, Robert. *Our Portion of Hell: Fayette County, Tennessee: An Oral History of the Struggle for Civil Rights*. New York: Links Books, 1973.

Hardy, Gayle J. *American Civil Rights Activists: Biobibliographies of 68 Leaders, 1825–1992*. Jefferson, NC: McFarland, 1993.

Hartmann, Susan M. *From Margin to Mainstream: American Women and Politics Since 1960*. Philadelphia: Temple University Press, 1989.

Hess, Beth B. *Controversy and Coalition: The New Feminist Movement*. Boston: Twayne Publishers, 1985.

Hewitt, Nancy A. *Southern Discomfort: Women's Activism in Tampa, Florida, 1880s–1920s*. Women in American History Series, ed. Anne Firor Scott, Nancy A. Hewitt, and Stephanie Shaw. Urbana and Chicago: University of Illinois Press, 2001.

Hewitt, Nancy A., and Suzanne Lebsock, eds. *Visible Women: New Essays on American Activism*. Urbana and Chicago: University of Illinois Press, 1993.

Hickey, Georgina. *Hope and Danger in the New South City: Working Class Women and Urban Development in Atlanta, 1890–1940*. Athens and London: University of Georgia Press, 2003.

Higham, John, ed. *Civil Rights and Social Wrongs: Black-White Relations Since World War II*. University Park: Pennsylvania State University Press, 1997.

Hill, Samuel S. *Southern Churches in Crisis*. New York: Holt, Rinehart and Winston, 1967.

Hobson, Fred. *But Now I See: The White Southern Racial Conversion Narrative*. Baton Rouge: Louisiana State University Press, 1999.

Hofstetter, Adrian Marie. *Earth Friendly: Re-Visioning Science and Spirituality through Aristotle, Thomas Aquinas, and Rudolf Steiner*. Herndon, VA: Lindisfarne Books, 2004.

Honey, Michael K. *Black Workers Remember: An Oral History of Segregation, Unionism and the Freedom Struggle*. Berkeley: University of California Press, 1999.

———. *Southern Labor and Black Civil Rights: Organizing Memphis Workers*. Urbana and Chicago: University of Illinois Press, 1993.

hooks, bell. *Ain't I a Woman: Black Women and Feminism*. Boston: South End Press, 1981.

Hoppe, Sherry L., and Bruce W. Speck. *Maxine Smith's Unwilling Pupils: Lessons Learned in Memphis's Civil Rights Classroom*. Knoxville: University of Tennessee Press, 2007.

Horne, Gerald. *Communist Front? The Civil Rights Congress, 1946–1956*. Rutherford, NJ: Fairleigh Dickinson University Press, 1988.

Hunter, Tera. *To 'Joy My Freedom: Southern Black Women's Lives and Labors after the Civil War*. Cambridge, MA: Harvard University Press, 1997.

Huntley, Horace, and David Montgomery, eds. *Black Workers' Struggle for Equality in Birmingham*. Afterword by Odessa Woolfolk. The Working Class in American History Series. Urbana and Chicago: University of Illinois Press, 2004.

Hutchison, William R., ed. *Between the Times: The Travail of the Protestant Establishment in America, 1900–1960*. Cambridge Studies in Religion and American Life Series, ed. Robin W. Lovin. Cambridge: Cambridge University Press, 1989.

Hyde, Samuel C., Jr., ed. *Sunbelt Revolution: The Historical Progression of the Civil Rights Struggle in the Gulf South, 1866–2000*. Gainesville: University Press of Florida, 2003.

Irons, Peter H. *Jim Crow's Children: The Broken Promises of the Brown Decision.* New York: Viking, 2002.

Jackson, John P., Jr. *Social Scientists for Social Justice: Making the Case Against Segregation.* New York: New York University Press, 2001.

Jackson, Thomas F. *From Civil Rights to Human Rights: Martin Luther King, Jr., and the Struggle for Economic Justice.* Philadelphia: University of Pennsylvania Press, 2007.

Jacobson, Matthew Frye. *Whiteness of a Different Color: European Immigrants and the Alchemy of Race.* Cambridge, MA: Harvard University Press, 1998.

Jacoway, Elizabeth, and David R. Cothburn, eds. *Southern Businessmen and Desegregation.* Baton Rouge and London: Louisiana State University Press, 1982.

Janiewski, Dolores. *Sisterhood Denied: Race, Gender, and Class in a New South Community.* Philadelphia: Temple University Press, 1985.

Jetter, Alexis, Annelise Orleck, and Diana Taylor, eds. *The Politics of Motherhood: Activist Voices from Left to Right.* Hanover, NH: University Press of New England, 1997.

Jones, Jacqueline. *Labor of Love, Labor of Sorrow: Black Women, Work and the Family, From Slavery to the Present.* New York: Basic Books, Inc., 1985.

Jordan, Winthrop D. *White Over Black: American Attitudes Toward the Negro.* Baltimore: Penguin Books, Inc., 1969.

Kaplan, Temma. *Crazy for Democracy: Women in Grassroots Movements.* New York: Routledge, 1997.

Katagiri, Yasuhiro. *The Mississippi State Sovereignty Commission: Civil Rights and States' Rights.* Jackson: University Press of Mississippi, 2001.

Katz, Michael B. *The Undeserving Poor: From the War on Poverty to the War on Welfare.* New York: Pantheon, 1989.

Kaufman, Jonathan. *Broken Alliance: The Turbulent Times Between Blacks and Jews in America.* New York: Charles Scribner's Sons, 1988.

Kelley, Robin D. G. *Race Rebels: Culture, Politics, and the Black Working Class.* New York: Free Press, 1994.

Kessler-Harris, Alice. *Out to Work: A History of Wage-Earning Women in the United States.* New York: Oxford University Press, 1982.

Keyserling, Mary Dublin. *Windows on Day Care: A Report Based on Findings of the National Council of Jewish Women on Day Care Needs and Services in Their Communities.* New York: National Council of Jewish Women, Inc., 1972.

Killian, Lewis M. *White Southerners.* Revised edition. Amherst: University of Massachusetts Press, 1985.

King, Martin Luther, Jr. *Stride Toward Freedom: The Montgomery Story.* New York: Harper and Brothers, Publishers, 1958.

———. *Where Do We Go from Here? Chaos or Community?* Boston: Beacon Press, 1967.

———. *Why We Can't Wait.* New York: The New American Library, 1964.

King, Richard H. *Civil Rights and the Idea of Freedom.* New York and Oxford: Oxford University Press, 1992.

Klein, Gerda Weissman. *A Passion for Sharing: The Life of Edith Rosenwald Stern.* Chappaqua, NY: Rossel Books, 1984.

Klibaner, Irwin. *Conscience of a Troubled South: The Southern Conference Educational Fund, 1946–1966.* Brooklyn, NY: Carlson Publishing, Inc., 1989.

Kluger, Richard. *Simple Justice: The History of* Brown v. Board of Education *and Black America's Struggle for Equality.* New York: Alfred A. Knopf, 1976.

Kotz, Nick. *Let Them Eat Promises: The Politics of Hunger in America*. With an introduction by Senator George S. McGovern. Englewood Cliffs, NJ: Prentice-Hall, Inc., 1969.

Kotz, Nick, and Mary Lynn Kotz. *A Passion for Equality: George A. Wiley and the Movement*. New York: W. W. Norton, 1977.

Kovin, Seth, and Sonya Michel, eds. *Mothers of a New World: Maternalist Politics and the Origins of Welfare States*. New York and London: Routledge, Inc., 1993.

Kozol, Jonathan. *Savage Inequalities: Children in America's Schools*. New York: Harper Perennial, 1992.

Kruse, Kevin M. *White Flight: Atlanta and the Making of Modern Conservatism*. Princeton and Oxford: Princeton University Press, 2005.

Lamon, Lester C. *Black Tennesseans, 1900–1930*. Knoxville: University of Tennessee Press, 1977.

Lane, Mark, and Dick Gregory. *Murder in Memphis: The FBI and the Assassination of Martin Luther King*. New York: Thunder's Mouth Press, 1993.

Lassiter, Matthew D. *The Silent Majority: Suburban Politics in the Sunbelt South*. Politics and Society in Twentieth-Century America Series. Princeton and Oxford: Princeton University Press, 2006.

Lawson, Steven F. *Black Ballots: Voting Rights in the South, 1944–1969*. New York: Columbia University Press, 1976.

———. *Civil Rights Crossroads: Nation, Community, and the Black Freedom Struggle*. Lexington: University Press of Kentucky, 2003.

———. *Running for Freedom: Civil Rights and Black Politics in America since 1941*. 2d ed. New York: McGraw-Hill, 1991.

Lee, Chana Kai. *For Freedom's Sake: The Life of Fannie Lou Hamer*. Urbana: University of Illinois Press, 1999.

Lee, Janet et al., eds. *Beyond Image and Convention: Explorations in Southern Women's History*. Columbia and London: University of Missouri Press, 1998.

Lerner, Gerda. *The Grimke Sisters from South Carolina: Pioneers for Women's Rights and Abolition*. New York: Schocken Books, 1971.

———, ed. *Black Women in White America: A Documentary History*. New York: Vintage Books, 1972.

Levine, Susan. *Degrees of Equality: The American Association of University Women and the Challenge of Twentieth-Century Feminism*. Philadelphia: Temple University Press, 1995.

Levy, Peter B., ed. *Documentary History of the Modern Civil Rights Movement*. New York: Greenwood Press, 1992.

Lewis, David Levering. *King: A Biography*. 2d ed. Urbana: University of Illinois Press, 1978.

Lincoln, C. Eric, and Lawrence H. Mamiya. *The Black Church in the African American Experience*. Durham: Duke University Press, 1990.

Ling, Peter J., and Sharon Monteith, eds. *Gender in the Civil Rights Movement*. New York: Garland, 1999.

Link, William A. *The Paradox of Southern Progressivism, 1880–1930*. Chapel Hill: University of North Carolina Press, 1992.

Louis, Debbie. *And We Are Not Saved: A History of the Movement As People*. Garden City, NY: Doubleday, 1970.

Lovett, Bobby L. *The Civil Rights Movement in Tennessee: A Narrative History*. Knoxville: University of Tennessee Press, 2005.

Lukas, J. Anthony. *Common Ground: A Turbulent Decade in the Lives of Three American Families*. New York: Alfred A. Knopf, 1985.

Lynn, Susan. *Progressive Women in Conservative Times: Racial Justice, Peace and Feminism, 1945 to the 1960s*. New Brunswick, NJ: Rutgers University Press, 1992.

Macdonald, J. Fred. *Don't Touch That Dial! Radio Programming in American Life from 1920 to 1960*. Chicago: Nelson Hall, 1979.

Manis, Andrew Michael. *Southern Civil Religions in Conflict: Black and White Baptists and Civil Rights, 1947–1957*. Athens and London: University of Georgia Press, 1987.

Mapes, Mary L. *A Public Charity: Religion and Social Welfare in Indianapolis, 1929–2002*. Bloomington: Indiana University Press, 2004.

Marable, Manning. *Black American Politics: From the Washington Marches to Jesse Jackson*. London: Verso, 1985.

———. *Race, Reform and Rebellion: The Second Reconstruction in Black America, 1945–1990*. 2d ed. Jackson: University Press of Mississippi, 1991.

Marcus, Jacob Rader. *The American Jewish Woman, 1654–1980*. Cincinnati: American Jewish Archives, 1981.

Marcus, Laurence R., and Benjamin D. Strickney. *Race and Education: The Unending Controversy*. Springfield, IL: Charles C. Thomas, 1981.

Marsh, Charles. *God's Long Summer: Stories of Faith and Civil Rights*. Princeton: Princeton University Press, 1997.

Massey, Douglas S., and Nancy A. Denton. *American Apartheid: Segregation and the Making of the Underclass*. Cambridge and London: Harvard University Press, 1993.

———. *Political Process and the Development of Black Insurgency, 1930–1970*. Chicago and London: University of Chicago Press, 1982.

May, Gary. *The Informant: The FBI, the Ku Klux Klan, and the Murder of Viola Liuzzo*. New Haven: Yale University Press, 2005.

McDowell, John Patrick. *The Social Gospel in the South: The Woman's Home Mission Movement in the Methodist Episcopal Church, South, 1886–1939*. Baton Rouge and London: Louisiana State University Press, 1982.

McIntosh, Peggy. *White Privilege and Male Privilege: A Personal Account of Coming to See Correspondences Through Work in Women's Studies*. Wellesley, MA: Wellesley College, Center for Research on Women, 1988.

McKee, Margaret, and Fred Chisenhall. *Beale Black & Blue: Life and Music on Black America's Main Street*. Baton Rouge: Louisiana State University Press, 1981.

McKnight, Gerald. *The Last Crusade: Martin Luther King, Jr., the FBI, and the Poor People's Campaign*. Boulder and Oxford: Westview Press, 1998.

McMillen, Neil R. *The Citizens' Council: Organized Resistance in the Second Reconstruction, 1954–1964*. Urbana: University of Illinois Press, 1971.

———. *Dark Journey: Black Mississippians in the Age of Jim Crow*. Urbana: University of Illinois Press, 1989.

———, ed. *Remaking Dixie: The Impact of World War II on the American South*. Jackson: University Press of Mississippi, 1997.

McMurry, Linda O. *To Keep the Waters Troubled: The Life of Ida B. Wells, Agitator*. New York: Oxford University Press, 1998.

McWhorter, Diane. *Carry Me Home: Birmingham, Alabama, the Climactic Battle of the Civil Rights Revolution*. New York: Simon and Schuster, 2001.

Mead, Margaret, and James Baldwin. *A Rap on Race*. Philadelphia and New York: J. B. Lippincott Company, 1971.

Meier, August, and Elliott Rudwick. *CORE: A Study in the Civil Rights Movement, 1942–1968*. Urbana: University of Illinois Press, 1975.

Meier, August, Elliott Rudwick, and Francis L. Broderick, eds. *Black Protest Thought in the Twentieth Century*. 2d ed. Indianapolis: Bobbs-Merrill, 1971.

Meyer, Stephen Grant. *As Long as They Don't Move Next Door: Segregation and Racial Conflict in American Neighborhoods*. Lanham, MD: Rowan and Littlefield, 2000.

Meyerowitz, Joanne, ed. *Not June Cleaver: Women and Gender in Postwar America, 1945–1960*. Philadelphia: Temple University Press, 1994.

Michel, Gregg L. *Struggle for a Better South: The Southern Student Organizing Committee, 1964–1969*. New York: Palgrave, 2004.

Michel, Sonya, and Seth Koven, eds. *Mothers of a New World: Maternalist Politics and the Origins of Welfare States*. New York: Routledge, 1993.

Miles, Margaret. *Seeing and Believing: Religion and Values in the Movies*. Boston: Beacon Press, 1996.

Miller, James. *"Democracy Is in the Streets": From Port Huron to the Siege of Chicago*. New York: Simon and Schuster, 1987.

Miller, William D. *Mr. Crump of Memphis*. Baton Rouge: Louisiana State University Press, 1964.

Mills, Kay. *This Little Light of Mine: The Life of Fannie Lou Hamer*. New York: Dutton, 1993.

Morris, Aldon D. *The Origins of the Civil Rights Movement: Black Communities Organizing for Change*. New York: The Free Press, 1984.

Muncy, Robin. *Creating a Female Dominion in American Reform, 1890–1935*. New York and Oxford: Oxford University Press, 1991.

Murphree, Vanessa. *The Selling of Civil Rights: The Student Nonviolent Coordinating Committee and the Use of Public Relations*. New York and London: Routledge, 2006.

Murphy, Reg, and Hal Gulliver. *The Southern Strategy*. New York: Scribner, 1971.

Murphy, Sara Alderman. *Breaking the Silence: Little Rock's Emergency Committee to Open Our Schools, 1958–1963*. Fayetteville: University of Arkansas Press, 1997.

Murray, Gail S., ed. *Throwing Off the Cloak of Privilege: White Southern Women Activists in the Civil Rights Era*. With a foreword by Stanley Harrold and Randall M. Miller. Gainesville: University Press of Florida, 2004.

Myrdal, Gunnar. *An American Dilemma: The Negro Problem and Modern Democracy*. New York: Harper and Brothers, 1944.

Nager, Larry. *Memphis Beat: The Lives and Times of America's Musical Crossroads*. New York: St. Martin's Press, 1998.

Namorato, Michael V., ed. *Have We Overcome? Race Relations Since* Brown. Jackson: University Press of Mississippi, 1979.

Naples, Nancy. *Grassroots Warriors: Activist Mothering, Community Work, and the War on Poverty*. New York: Routledge, 1998.

Nasstrom, Kathryn L. *Everybody's Grandmother and Nobody's Fool: Frances Freeborn Pauley and the Struggle for Social Justice*. With a foreword by Julian Bond. Ithaca and London: Cornell University Press, 2000.

———. *Women, the Civil Rights Movement, and the Politics of Historical Memory in Atlanta, 1946–1973*. Chapel Hill: University of North Carolina Press, 1993.

Nelson, Adam R. *The Elusive Ideal: Equal Educational Opportunity and the Federal Role in Boston's Public Schools, 1950–1985*. Chicago: University of Chicago Press, 2005.

Newman, Mark. *Entrepreneurs of Profit and Pride: From Black Appeal to Radio Soul*. New York: Praeger, 1988.

———. *Divine Agitators: The Delta Ministry and Civil Rights in Mississippi*. Athens and London: The University of Georgia Press, 2004.

———. *Getting Right with God: Southern Baptists and Desegregation, 1945–1995*. Religion and American Culture Series, ed. David Edwin Harrell, Jr., Wayne Flynt, and Edith L. Blumhoffer. Tuscaloosa and London: University of Alabama Press, 2001.

Novick, Michael. *White Lies, White Power: The Fight Against White Supremacy and Reactionary Violence*. Monroe, ME: Common Courage Press, 1995.

Oates, Stephen B. *Let the Trumpet Sound: The Life of Martin Luther King, Jr*. New York: Harper and Row Publishers, 1982.

O'Connor, Alice. *Poverty Knowledge: Social Science, Social Policy, and the Poor in Twentieth-Century U.S. History*. Princeton: Princeton University Press, 2001.

Olson, Lynne. *Freedom's Daughters: The Unsung Heroines of the Civil Rights Movement from 1830 to 1970*. New York: Scribner Publishers, 2001.

O'Neill, William. *Coming Apart: An Informal History of America in the 1960s*. New York: Quadrangle, 1971.

O'Reilly, Kenneth. *"Racial Matters": The FBI's Secret File on Black America*. New York: The Free Press, 1989.

Orleck, Annelise. *Common Sense and a Little Fire: Women and Working-Class Politics in the United States, 1900–1965*. Chapel Hill: University of North Carolina Press, 1995.

Painter, Nell Irvin. *Southern History Across the Color Line*. Gender and American Culture Series. Chapel Hill: University of North Carolina Press, 2002.

Paris, Peter. *The Social Teaching of the Black Churches*. Philadelphia: Fortress Press, 1985.

Pascoe, Craig S., Karen Trahan Leathem, and Andy Ambrose, eds. *The American South in the Twentieth Century*. Athens and London: University of Georgia Press, 2005.

Pascoe, Peggy. *Relations of Rescue: The Search for Female Moral Authority in the American West, 1874–1939*. New York and Oxford: Oxford University Press, 1990.

Patterson, James T. *America's Struggle Against Poverty, 1900–1994*. Cambridge and London: Harvard University Press, 1994.

———. *Brown v. Board of Education: A Civil Rights Milestone and Its Troubled Legacy*. Oxford: Oxford University Press, 2001.

Payne, Charles M. *I've Got the Light of Freedom: The Organizing Tradition and the Mississippi Freedom Struggle*. Berkeley: University of California Press, 1995.

Phillips, Barbara Y. *How To Use Section 5 of the Voting Rights Act*. 3d ed. Washington, DC: Joint Center for Political Studies, 1983.

Pierce, Richard B. *Polite Protest: The Political Economy of Race in Indianapolis, 1920–1970*. Bloomington: Indiana University Press, 2005.

Pinkney, Alphonso. *The Committed: White Activists in the Civil Rights Movement*. New Haven: College and University Press, 1968.

Piven, Frances Fox, and Richard A. Cloward. *Poor People's Movements: Why They Succeed, How They Fail*. New York: Pantheon Books, 1977.

———. *Regulating the Poor: The Functions of Public Welfare*. Updated edition. New York: Vintage Books, 1993.

Pohlman, Marcus D., and Michael P. Kirby. *Racial Politics at the Crossroads: Memphis Elects Dr. W. W. Herenton.* Knoxville: University of Tennessee Press, 1996.
Pratt, Robert A. *We Shall Not Be Moved: The Desegregation of the University of Georgia.* Athens and London: University of Georgia Press, 2002.
Pride, Richard A. *The Political Use of Racial Narratives: School Desegregation in Mobile, Alabama, 1954–97.* Urbana and Chicago: University of Illinois Press, 2002.
Pride, Richard A., and J. David Woodard. *The Burden of Busing: The Politics of Desegregation in Nashville, Tennessee.* Knoxville: University of Tennessee Press, 1985.
Prowledge, Fred. *Free At Last? The Civil Rights Movement and the People Who Made It.* Boston: Little, Brown, 1991.
Quadagno, Jill. *The Color of Welfare: How Racism Undermined the War on Poverty.* New York: Oxford University Press, 1995.
Raboteau, Albert J. *Slave Religion: The "Invisible Institution" in the Antebellum South.* Oxford: Oxford University Press, 1980.
Ramsey, Sonya. *Reading, Writing, and Segregation: A Century of Black Women Teachers in Nashville.* Urbana and Chicago: University of Illinois Press, 2008.
Ransby, Barbara. *Ella Baker and the Black Freedom Movement: A Radical Democratic Vision.* Chapel Hill and London: University of North Carolina Press, 2003.
Reed, Linda. *Simple Decency & Common Sense: The Southern Conference Movement, 1938–1963.* Blacks in the Diaspora Series, ed. Darlene Clark Hine, John McCluskey, Jr., and David Barry Gaspar. Bloomington and Indianapolis: Indiana University Press, 1991.
Riemers, David M. *White Protestantism and the Negro.* New York: Oxford University Press, 1965.
Robinson, Armstead L., and Patricia Sullivan, eds. *New Directions in Civil Rights Studies.* Charlottesville and London: University Press of Virginia, 1991.
Robinson, Charles F. *Dangerous Liaisons: Sex and Love in the Segregated South.* Fayetteville: University of Arkansas Press, 2003.
Robnett, Belinda. *How Long? How Long? African-American Women and the Struggle for Freedom and Justice.* New York: Oxford University Press, 1997.
Rogers, Kim Lacy. *Righteous Lives: Narratives of the New Orleans Civil Rights Movement.* New York: New York University Press, 1993.
Rogow, Faith. *Gone to Another Meeting: The National Council of Jewish Women, 1893–1993.* With a foreword by Joan Bronk. Tuscaloosa and London: University of Alabama Press, 1993.
Rose, Arnold. *De Facto School Segregation.* New York: National Conference of Christians and Jews, 1964.
Rosenberg, Jonathan. *How Far the Promised Land? World Affairs and the American Civil Rights Movement from the First World War to Vietnam.* Princeton and Oxford: Princeton University Press, 2006.
Rossinow, Doug. *The Politics of Authenticity: Liberalism, Christianity and the New Left in America.* New York: Columbia University Press, 1998.
Rosswurm, Steve, ed. *The CIO's Left-Led Unions.* New Brunswick, NJ: Rutgers University Press, 1992.
Roszak, Betty, and Theodore Roszak, eds. *Masculine/Feminine: Readings in Sexual Mythology and the Liberation of Women.* New York: Harper and Row, Publishers, 1969.

Rothschild, Mary Aicken. *A Case of Black and White: Northern Volunteers and the Southern Freedom Summers, 1964–1965*. Westport, CT: Greenwood Press, 1982.

Roy, Beth. *Bitters in the Honey: Tales of Hope and Disappointment Across Divides of Race and Time*. Fayetteville: University of Arkansas Press, 1999.

Ruiz, Vicki L., and Ellen Carol DuBois, eds. *Unequal Sisters: A Multicultural Reader in U.S. Women's History*. 3d ed. New York and London: Routledge, 2000.

Rupp, Leila. *Survival in the Doldrums: The American Women's Rights Movement, 1945 to the 1960s*. New York: Oxford University Press, 1987.

Salmond, John A. *Conscience of a Lawyer: Clifford Durr and American Civil Liberties*. Tuscaloosa: University of Alabama Press, 1990.

———. *Southern Struggles: The Southern Labor Movement and the Civil Rights Struggle*. Gainesville: University Press of Florida, 2004.

Scharf, Lois, and Joan M. Jensen, eds. *Decades of Discontent: The Women's Movement, 1920–1940*. Westport, CT: Greenwood Press, 1983.

Schechter, Patricia Ann. *Ida B. Wells-Barnett and American Reform, 1880–1930*. Chapel Hill: University of North Carolina Press, 2001.

Schneider. William J., ed. *American Martyr: The Jon Daniels Story*. Harrisburg, PA: Morehouse Publishers, 1992.

Schrecker, Ellen. *Many Are the Crimes: McCarthyism in America*. Boston: Little, Brown, 1998.

Schulman, Bruce. *From Cotton Belt to Sunbelt: Federal Policy, Economic Development, and the Transformation of the South*. New York: Oxford University Press, 1991.

Schultz, Debra L. *Going South: Jewish Women in the Civil Rights Movement*. With a foreword by Blanche Weisen Cook. New York and London: New York University Press, 2001.

Schwartz, Bernard. *Swann's Way: The School Busing Case and the Supreme Court*. New York and Oxford: Oxford University Press, 1986.

Scott, Anne Firor. *The Southern Lady: From Pedestal to Politics, 1830–1930*. Chicago and London: University of Chicago Press, 1970.

———, ed. *Unheard Voices: The First Historians of Southern Women*. Charlottesville and London: University Press of Virginia, 1993.

Scott, Ralph. *Education and Ethnicity: The U.S. Experiment in School Integration*. Journal of Social, Political and Economic Studies Monograph Series 17. Washington: The Council for Social and Economic Studies, 1987.

Seebach, Margaret R. *Man in the Bush*. Baltimore: The Board of Foreign Missions of the United Lutheran Church in America, 1945.

Shafer, Anne Whalen. *History of the Memphis City Beautiful Commission and Its Impact on Our Lives*. Memphis: Published by the author, 1996.

Shannon, Margaret. *Just Because: The Story of the National Movement of Church Women United in the USA, 1941 through 1975*. Corte Madera, CA: Omega Books, 1977.

Shapiro, Herbert. *White Violence and Black Response: From Reconstruction to Montgomery*. Amherst: University of Massachusetts Press, 1988.

Shattuck, Gardiner H., Jr. *Episcopalians and Race: Civil War to Civil Rights*. Lexington: University Press of Kentucky, 2000.

Shaw, Stephanie J. *What a Woman Ought to Be and to Do: Black Professional Women during the Jim Crow Era*. Chicago: University of Chicago Press, 1996.

Siegel, Beatrice. *Murder on the Highway: The Viola Liuzzo Story*. With a foreword by Rosa Parks. New York: Four Winds Press, 1993.

Sigafoos, Robert. *Cotton Row to Beale Street: A Business History of Memphis*. Memphis: University of Memphis Press, 1999.

Silver, Christopher, and John V. Moeser. *The Separate City: Black Communities in the Urban South, 1940–1968*. Lexington: University Press of Kentucky, 1995.

Silverstein, Clara. *White Girl: A Story of School Desegregation*. Athens and London: University of Georgia Press, 2004.

Sitkoff, Harvard. *A New Deal for Blacks: The Emergence of Civil Rights as a National Issue: The Depression Decade*. New York: Oxford University Press, 1978.

———. *The Struggle for Black Equality, 1954–1980*. New York: Hill and Wang, 1981.

Sklar, Kathryn Kish. *Florence Kelley and the Nation's Work: The Rise of Political Culture, 1830–1900*. New Haven: Yale University Press, 1995.

Skocpol, Theda. *Protecting Soldiers and Mothers: The Political Origins of Social Policy in the United States*. Cambridge, MA and London: Harvard University Press, 1992.

Smith, Barbara Ellen, ed. *Neither Separate Nor Equal: Women, Race, and Class in the South*. Women in the Political Economy Series. Philadelphia: Temple University Press, 1999.

Smith, Stephen A. *Myth, Media, and the Southern Mind*. Fayetteville: University of Arkansas Press, 1985.

Sokol, Jason. *There Goes My Everything: White Southerners in the Age of Civil Rights, 1945–1975*. New York: Knopf, 2006.

Sosna, Morton. *In Search of the Silent South: Southern Liberals and the Race Issue*. New York: Columbia University Press, 1977.

Southern, David W. *John LeFarge and the Limits of Catholic Interracialism, 1911–1963*. Baton Rouge and London: Louisiana State University Press, 1996.

Stanton, Mary. *Freedom Walk: Mississippi or Bust*. Jackson: University Press of Mississippi, 2003.

———. *From Selma to Sorrow: The Life and Death of Viola Liuzzo*. Athens and London: University of Georgia Press, 1998.

Stoper, Emily. *The Student Nonviolent Coordinating Committee: The Growth of Radicalism in a Civil Rights Organization*. With a preface by David J. Garrow. Brooklyn: Carlson Publishers, 1989.

Street, Joe. *The Culture War in the Civil Rights Movement*. Gainesville: University Press of Florida, 2007.

Stuhler, Barbara. *For the Public Record: A Documentary History of the League of Women Voters*. Westport, CT and London: Greenwood Press, 2000.

Swerdlow, Amy. *Women Strike for Peace: Traditional Motherhood and Radical Politics in the 1960s*. Chicago and London: University of Chicago Press, 1993.

Thomas, Mary Martha. *Riveting and Rationing in Dixie: Alabama Women and the Second World War*. Tuscaloosa: University of Alabama Press, 1987.

Thompson, Becky. *A Promise and a Way of Life: White Antiracist Activism*. Minneapolis and London: University of Minnesota Press, 2001.

Thompson, Ernest Trice. *Presbyterians in the South, Volume 3: 1890–1972*. Richmond, VA: John Knox Press, 1973.

Thornton, J. Mills III. *Dividing Lines: Municipal Politics and the Struggle for Civil Rights in Montgomery, Birmingham, and Selma*. Tuscaloosa and London: University of Alabama Press, 2002.

Tilley, Louise A., and Patricia Gurin, eds. *Women, Politics, and Change*. New York: Russell Sage Foundation, 1990.

Tucker, David M. *Black Pastors and Leaders: Memphis, 1819–1972*. Memphis: University of Memphis Press, 1975.

———. *Lieutenant Lee of Beale Street*. Nashville: Vanderbilt University Press, 1971.

———. *Memphis Since Crump: Bossism, Blacks, and Civic Reformers, 1948–1968*. Knoxville: University of Tennessee Press, 1980.

Tucker, Susan. *Telling Memories among Southern Women: Domestic Workers and Their Employers in the Segregated South*. Baton Rouge: Louisiana State University Press, 1988.

Tuchnet, Mark V. *The NAACP's Legal Strategy against Segregated Education, 1925–1950*. Chapel Hill: University of North Carolina Press, 1987.

Tyler, Pamela. *Silk Stockings and Ballot Boxes: Women and Politics in New Orleans, 1930–1963*. Athens: University of Georgia Press, 1996.

Umansky, Lauri. *Motherhood Reconceived: Feminism and the Legacies of the 1960s*. New York: New York University Press, 1996.

Van DeBurg, William L. *New Day in Babylon: The Black Power Movement and American Culture, 1965–1975*. Chicago: University of Chicago Press, 1992.

Van West, Carroll, ed. *Trial and Triumph: Essays in Tennessee's African American History*. Knoxville: University of Tennessee Press, 2002.

Vinovskis, Maris A. *The Birth of Head Start: Preschool Education Policies in the Kennedy and Johnson Administrations*. Chicago: University of Chicago Press, 2005.

Viorst, Milton. *Fire in the Streets: America in the 1960s*. New York: Simon and Schuster, 1981.

Wailoo, Keith. *Dying in the City of Blues: Sickle Cell Anemia and the Politics of Race and Health*. Chapel Hill: University of North Carolina Press, 2001.

Wakin, Edward. *Children Without Justice: A Report by the National Council of Jewish Women*. New York: National Council of Jewish Women, Inc., 1975.

Ware, Vron. *Beyond the Pale: White Women, Racism and History*. London and New York: Verso Books, 1992.

Webb, Clive. *Fight Against Fear: Southern Jews and Black Civil Rights*. Athens and London: University of Georgia Press, 2001.

Wedell, Marsha. *Elite Women and the Reform Impulse in Memphis, 1875–1915*. Knoxville: University of Tennessee Press, 1991.

Wedin, Carolyn. *Inheritors of the Spirit: Mary White Ovington and the Founding of the NAACP*. New York: John Wiley and Sons, Inc., 1998.

Weeks, Linton. *Memphis: A Folk History*. Little Rock: Pankhurst, 1982.

Weigand, Kate. *Red Feminism: American Communism and the Making of Women's Liberation*. Baltimore: Johns Hopkins University Press, 2001.

Weisbrot, Robert. *Freedom Bound: A History of America's Civil Rights Movement*. New York: Norton, 1990.

Weiss, Nancy. *Farewell to the Party of Lincoln: Black Politics in the Age of F.D.R.* Princeton, NJ: Princeton University Press, 1983.

West, Guida. *The National Welfare Rights Movement: The Social Protest of Poor Women*. New York: Praeger, 1981.

Whayne, Jeannie, and Willard B. Gatewood, eds. *The Arkansas Delta: Land of Paradox*. Fayetteville: University of Arkansas Press, 1993.

Wheeler, Marjorie Spruill. *New Women of the New South: The Leaders of the Woman Suffrage Movement in the Southern States.* New York and Oxford: Oxford University Press, 1993.

White, Deborah Gray. *Too Heavy a Load: Black Women in Defense of Themselves, 1894–1994.* New York and London: W. W. Norton and Company, 1999.

Wieder, Alan. *Race and Education: Narrative Essays, Oral Histories, and Documentary Photography.* Counterpoints: Studies in the Postmodern Theory of Education Series, ed. Joe L. Kincheloe and Shirley R. Steinberg. New York: Peter Lang Publishing, Inc., 1997.

Wilkerson, Yolanda B. *Interracial Programs of Student YWCA's.* New York: Woman's Press, 1948.

Wilkinson, J. Harvie III. *From Brown to Bakke: The Supreme Court and Integration, 1954–1978.* New York and Oxford: Oxford University Press, 1979.

Williams, Gilbert A. *Legendary Pioneers of Black Radio.* Westport, CT: Praeger, 1998.

Williams, Juan. *Eyes on the Prize: America's Civil Rights Years, 1954–1965.* With an introduction by Julian Bond. New York: Penguin Books, 1987.

Williamson, Joel. *The Crucible of Race: Black-White Relations in the American South Since Emancipation.* New York and Oxford: Oxford University Press, 1984.

Willis, Alan Scot. *All According to God's Plan: Southern Baptist Missions and Race, 1945–1970.* Religion in the South Series. Lexington: University Press of Kentucky, 2005.

Willis, John C. *Forgotten Time: The Yazoo-Mississippi Delta After the Civil War.* The American South Series, ed. Edward L. Ayers. Charlottesville and London: University Press of Virginia, 2000.

Wilson, Jan Doolittle. *The Women's Joint Congressional Committee and the Politics of Maternalism, 1920–1930.* Urbana and Chicago: University of Illinois Press, 2007.

Woodward, C. Vann. *The Burden of Southern History.* Baton Rouge: Louisiana State University Press, 1960.

———. *Origins of the New South, 1877–1913.* A History of the South Series, ed. Wendell Holmes Stephenson and E. Merton Coulter, vol. 9. Baton Rouge: Louisiana State University Press, 1951.

———. *The Strange Career of Jim Crow.* 3d revised edition. New York: Oxford University Press, 1974.

Wright, Sharon D. *Race, Power, and Political Emergence in Memphis.* New York: Garland, 2000.

Wright, William E. *Memphis Politics: A Study in Racial Bloc Voting.* Eagleton Institute of Politics Cases in Practical Politics, Case 27. New York: McGraw-Hill Company, Inc., 1962.

Wuthnow, Robert, Virginia A. Hogkinson and Associates, eds. *Faith and Philanthropy in America: Exploring the Role of Religion in America's Voluntary Sector.* San Francisco: Jossey-Bass Publishers, 1990.

Wyatt-Brown, Bertram. *Honor and Violence in the Old South.* New York: Oxford University Press, 1986.

———. *Southern Honor: Ethics and Behavior in the Old South.* New York: Oxford University Press, 1982.

Wynes, Charles, ed. *Forgotten Voices: Dissenting Southerners in an Age of Conformity.* Baton Rouge: Louisiana State University Press, 1967.

Yellin, Carol Lynn, and Janann Sherman. *The Perfect 36: Tennessee Delivers Woman Suffrage*. Edited by Ilene Jones-Cornwell. With a foreword by Governor Don Sundquist and Martha Sundquist. Oak Ridge, TN: Iris Press, 1998.

Young, Louise M. *In the Public Interest: The League of Women Voters, 1920–1970*. New York and London: Greenwood Press, 1989.

Zinn, Howard. *The Southern Mystique*. New York: Knopf, 1968.

———. *SNCC: The New Abolitionists*. Boston: Beacon Press, 1964.

Articles

Biles, Roger. "A Bittersweet Victory: Public School Desegregation in Memphis." *Journal of Negro Education* 55 (1986): 470–483.

Blumberg, Janice Rothschild. "The Bomb that Healed: A Personal Memoir of the Bombing of the Temple in Atlanta, 1958." *American Jewish History* 78 (September 1983): 20–38.

Bynum, Victoria E. "'White Negroes' in Segregated Mississippi: Miscegenation, Racial Identity, and the Law." *The Journal of Southern History* 64 (May 1998): 247–276.

Cataldo, Everett, Michael Giles, Deborah Athos, and Douglas Gatlin. "Desegregation and White Flight." *Integrated Education* (January/February 1975): 3–5.

Chappell, David. "A Stone of Hope: Prophetic Faith, Liberalism, and the Death of Jim Crow." *Journal of the Historical Society* 3 (March 2003): 129–163.

Eagles, Charles W. "Toward New Histories of the Civil Rights Era." *The Journal of Southern History* 66 (November 2000): 815–848.

Estes, Steve. "'I AM A MAN!': Race, Masculinity, and the 1968 Memphis Sanitation Strike." *Labor History* 41 (May 2000): 153–170.

Goings, Kenneth W., and Gerald L. Smith. "'Unhidden' Transcripts: Memphis and African American Agency, 1862–1920." *Journal of Urban History* 21 (March 1995): 372–394.

Goodstein, Anita Shafer. "A Rare Alliance: African American and White Women in the Tennessee Elections of 1919 and 1920." *The Journal of Southern History* 64 (May 1998): 219–246.

Gordon, Linda. "Black and White Visions of Welfare: Women's Welfare Activism, 1890–1945." *Journal of American History* 78 (September 1991): 559–590.

Hayden, Casey. "The Movement." *Witness: The 1960s* 11 (Summer/Fall 1988): 244–248.

———. "A Nurturing Movement: Nonviolence, SNCC, and Feminism." *Southern Exposure* 16 (Summer 1998): 48–53.

Jabour, Anya. "'Grown Girls, Highly Cultivated': Female Education in an Antebellum Family." *The Journal of Southern History* 64 (February 1989): 23–64.

Katz, Michael B., and Lorrin B. Thomas. "The Invention of 'Welfare' in America." *Journal of Policy History* 10 (4) (1998): 399–418.

King, William M. "The Reemerging Revolutionary Consciousness of the Reverend Dr. Martin Luther King, Jr., 1965–1968." *Journal of Negro History* 71 (Winter 1986): 1–22.

Korstad, Robert, and Nelson Lichtenstein. "Opportunities Found and Lost: Labor, Radicals, and the Early Civil Rights Movement." *Journal of American History* 75 (December 1988): 786–811.

Nasstrom, Kathryn L. "Beginnings and Endings: Life Stories and the Periodization of the Civil Rights Movement." *Journal of American History* 86 (September 1999): 700–711.

Orfield, Gary. "Congress, the President, and Anti-Busing Legislation, 1966–1974." *Journal of Law and Education* 4 (January 1975): 81–139.

Plank, David N. "Contrasting Patterns in Black School Politics: Atlanta and Memphis, 1865–1985." *Journal of Negro Education* 60 (1991): 203–218.

Polonick, Rivka. "Diversity in Women's Liberation Ideology: How a Black and White Group of the 1960's Viewed Motherhood." *Signs* 21 (Spring 1996): 679–706.

St. John, Nancy H. "Desegregation and Minority Group Performance." *Review of Educational Research* 40 (May 1967): 111–133.

Stitzel, Kimberly F. "Child Nutrition Programs Legislation: Past and Present." *Topics in Clinical Nutrition* 19 (January–March 2001): 9–19.

Videorecordings

The Long Walk Home. Directed by Richard Pearce. 98 minutes. Miramax Films, 1990, videocassette.

Unpublished Materials, Speeches

D'Aquila, Suzanne Nicole. "White Southern Women in the Jackson, Mississippi, 1960s Civil Rights Movement: A Case Study." B.A. senior project, Antioch College, Antioch, OH, 1993.

Green, Laurie. "Beyond the Plantation Mentality: Race, Class, and Gender in Memphis, 1945–1968." Ph.D. dissertation, University of Chicago, 1999.

Hayden, Casey. "Race, Feminism, and the New Left: An Artifactual Journey." Lecture presented at the Baker Peace Committee Conference, "1968 Revisited," Athens, OH, 24 April 1998.

Shafer, Anne Whalen, Papers. Private collection, Memphis, TN.

Taylor, Frances Sanders. "'On the Edge of Tomorrow'": Southern Women, the Student YWCA, and Race, 1920–1944." Ph.D. thesis, Stanford, 1984.

INDEX

Alders, Linda, 75
Allen, Linda, 67, 71–72, 80, 97, 107, 131, 141–42
American Federation of State, County, and Municipal Employees (AFSCME), 4, 66, 95, 96, 97, 99, 100, 101, 126
Anti-Defamation League of B'nai B'rith, 70, 88
Awsumb, Gwen Robinson, 65–68, 133, 139, 150–51

Baker, Ella, 30
Beifuss, Joan Turner, 71, 73, 74, 80, 88, 89, 114–15, 124, 151
Bell, Ezekial, 132
Black Panther Party, 75, 119
Boyle, Sarah Patton, 12, 75, 112, 117–18
Braden, Anne, 12, 50, 51, 75, 76, 112–13, 114, 115
Brown, Esther, 92
Brown v. Board of Education, 12, 13, 22, 54, 127
Busing, 107, 108, 128–44, 151

Cade, Cathy, 52
Carver High School, 138
Casey, Bill, 16
Catholic Human Relations Council (CHRC), 46, 58, 70, 88, 114, 151, 155
Chandler, Mayor Wyeth, 46, 129
Cherry, Marjorie, 12, 17, 18, 19, 52, 66, 83, 117
Childress, Lorenzo, 16
Christian Faith and Life Community, 60
Church Women United (CWU), 40, 53, 54, 55, 90, 104, 147, 148, 150, 155.

See also United Council of Church Women
Citizens Against Busing (CAB), 133–34, 139–40, 143–44
Citizens' Committee to Study Poverty, 42
Clark, Septima, 113
Clayborne Temple, 73, 111
Coe, Frances Edgar, 32–36, 37, 39, 62, 107, 131, 132, 133, 135–36, 138–40, 142
Cole, Echol, 3, 72
Collier, Mary, 80, 81, 82
Community on the Move for Equality (COME), 85, 96, 111, 155
Concerned Women of Memphis, 87, 97, 99–101, 103, 107, 108–9, 121–22, 123, 125, 126, 155
Congress of Racial Equality (CORE), 28, 57, 111
Council of Catholic Women (CCW), 114, 155
Creative Learning in a Unique Environment (CLUE), 141
Crump, Mayor William Henry, 25, 32, 47, 65
Curry, Constance, 78, 115

Davis, Claudia, 8, 54–56, 89–90, 91, 94, 141, 150
Davis, Fred, 67
Dickson, Jane, 85
Diversity Memphis, 150
Doughty, Mary, 94
Dreifus, Jeanne, 62–63, 141, 148
Dreifus, Myra, 8, 32, 35–38, 40–41, 43–44, 48–49, 61, 62, 64, 96, 97, 102, 104–5, 107, 126, 131, 138, 148, 149

Durr, Virginia Foster, 12, 30–32, 75, 98, 112–13

Emergency School Assistance Program (ESAP), 137, 142–43
Epps, Jesse, 96, 97, 99
Ewing, Herman, 137

Faculty Wives and Women, 41
Fellowship of Reconciliation, 27, 57
Fisher, Jean, 126
Florida Street School Project, 97–98, 105–7, 123, 131
Food for Fitness, 38–40, 61. *See also* Fund for Needy Schoolchildren
Frich, Marty, 16, 75, 76, 77, 122–23, 124, 125
Fund for Needy Schoolchildren (Fund), 35, 37–39, 40–44, 56, 61, 62, 64, 87, 104–6, 126, 127, 131, 134, 138, 155. *See also* Food for Fitness

Geary, Ann, 76, 118, 124
Gilliam, Pat, 94

Hadassah, 150
Hamilton High School, 73
Hayden, Casey, 11, 60, 115, 116, 127
Hayes, Elton, 128, 130, 146
Hayes, Jim, 77
Highlander Folk School, 31, 57, 113
Hofstetter, Sister Adrian Marie, 72, 85, 97, 101–2, 149
Horton, Odell, 95

Independent Presbyterian Church, 53
Ingram, Mayor William B., Jr., 47
Invaders, 75, 76, 119
Involved Memphis Parents Assisting Children and Teachers (IMPACT), 143

Jemison, Peggy, 6, 68–69, 80, 97, 107, 118
John Gaston Hospital, 33, 37
Johnson, Carrie Parks, 84

Johnston, Ann, 17, 19, 20
Jones, Dorothy "Happy" Snowden, 6, 94, 97–100, 103, 105–7, 109, 123–24, 127, 128–30, 142–43, 146
Jones, Elizabeth, 43
Junior League, 7, 30, 67, 68, 69, 80, 97, 105–6, 107

Kansas Street School, 62
Katz, Nina, 60
Kefauver, Estes, 34
Kerner Report, 103
King, Coretta Scott, 80
King, Dr. Martin Luther, Jr., 4, 5, 6, 7, 9, 30, 64, 66, 72, 73, 74, 76, 79, 80, 81, 82, 83, 85, 86, 87, 88, 93, 94, 95, 99, 102, 103, 105, 107, 108, 109, 111, 112, 116, 118, 119, 120, 121, 124, 126, 130, 141, 150, 151, 153
Korones, Judy, 63
Kyles, Billy, 83
Kyles, Gwen, 83, 84

Lacey, Mary Frances, 13
Lawson, Dorothy, 71
Lawson, James, 59, 71, 102, 106, 111
League of Women Voters, 29, 117, 134, 151; Memphis branch, 34, 46
Lemoyne College, 14, 15, 20, 25–26, 37, 46
Lemoyne Gardens, 24, 26, 27
Lend-A-Hand Club, 40
Lewis, Selma, 9, 38, 40, 41, 107, 148, 149
Liuzzo, Violet, 111, 124–25, 127
Loeb, Mayor Henry, 3, 14, 64, 65–66, 67, 68, 69, 70, 71, 72, 74, 75, 77, 81, 85, 86, 94, 96, 97, 98, 129, 130, 131–32, 133
Loeb, Mary Gregg, 65, 68
Long Walk Home, The, 7–8

March on Washington (1963), 24
Mason Temple, 68, 82
Maternal Welfare League, 108
Memphis Area Project-South (MAP-South), 106–7, 155

Memphis Area Women's Council, 146, 150
Memphis Board of Education, 32, 34, 35, 37–40, 42, 107, 108, 123, 131–36, 138–44
Memphis Cares, 79, 80, 81, 86, 126
Memphis City Beautiful Commission, 44, 46–48, 56, 66, 155
Memphis Commercial Appeal, 26, 33, 69, 117, 122
Memphis Committee on Human Relations, 24, 99, 128–29, 146
Memphis Community Relations Commission (MCCR), 128–30, 146
Memphis Health and Welfare Planning Council, 37
Memphis Interfaith Association, 95, 146
Memphis Jewish Community Center, 37, 88
Memphis Jewish Family Services, 38
Memphis Mental Health Association, 37
"Memphis Plan," 135
Memphis Press-Scimitar, 26
Memphis Railway System, 12
Memphis Search for Meaning Committee, 94, 95, 151, 155
Memphis State College, 13, 16, 33, 34
Memphis State University, 69, 81, 89, 93, 94, 151. *See also* University of Memphis
Memphis World, 61
Methodist Student Movement, 58–60, 155
Mid-South Courier, 61
Moon, Glenda, 74
Moon, Richard, 74
Mother of Young Children, 56
Moton, Leroy, 125

National Association for the Advancement of Colored People (NAACP), 4, 5, 13, 14, 18, 28, 69, 74, 97, 113, 114, 132, 134, 138
National Coalition of American Nuns, 101
National Committee to Abolish the Poll Tax, 31, 112
National Conference for Community and Justice, 146, 148, 150
National Conference of Christians and Jews (NCCJ), 60, 70, 81, 87, 88, 104, 141
National Council of Catholic Women, 54, 57
National Council of Jewish Women (NCJW), 36, 54, 61, 62, 63, 92, 141, 147, 148
National Council of Negro Women, 54
Netters, James, 67, 129
New Attitude-Memphis Encounter (NAME), 87, 102–3, 115, 121, 125, 149, 155

Osborne, Lorene, 20
Outpost Sunday School, 55, 155
Owen College, 14, 15

Palmer, Joyce, 72–73, 111
Panel of American Women (Panel), 55, 56, 82, 87, 92–94, 97, 99, 102, 104, 105, 108, 109, 120, 126, 129, 130, 134, 141, 142–43, 145, 146, 147, 155
Parents Against Clustering (PAC), 133
Parent-Teacher Association (PTA), 134, 137
Parks, Rosa, 30, 32
Patterson, J. O., 67
Phillips, Elizabeth, 81
Plessy v. Ferguson, 19
Poor People's Campaign (PPC), 4, 95, 104, 108
Portman, Kay, 82
Powell, Rachel, 19
Price, Hollis, 37

Queener, Camilla, 85

Rearing Children of Goodwill (RCG), 70–71, 82, 86, 87–92, 94, 109, 121, 127, 130, 155
Reeb, James, 111
Report of the National Advisory Commission on Civil Disorders, 103

Roop, Katharine, 85
Roosevelt, Eleanor, 25, 29, 30, 31
Rozen, Lester A., 99–100

Saed, Ruth, 139–40, 143
Saint Joseph's Hospital, 96, 97, 108, 128, 130
Sanitation Workers' Strike of 1968, 3–9, 13, 16, 27, 48, 59, 63, 64–86, 87, 88, 91, 93, 94, 95, 96, 97, 98, 102, 103, 104, 106, 107, 108, 109, 110, 111, 112, 119, 121, 122, 124, 128, 130, 131, 132, 138, 140, 147
Saturday Luncheon Group (SLG), 12, 17, 20, 21, 22, 23, 24, 43, 46, 52, 67, 68, 69, 71, 72, 76, 80, 82, 83, 84, 86, 95, 97, 118–19, 148, 155
Save Our City, 94, 96, 147
Second Presbyterian Church, 53
Seller, T. J., 118
Sengstacke, Mattie, 69, 80, 118–19
Sengstacke, Whittier, 69
Shafer, Anne Whalen, 32, 44–49, 54, 56–58, 72, 97, 100, 114–15, 121–22
Shannon, Donna Sue, 6, 90–91, 94, 121, 123, 146, 147
Shelby County United Neighbors, 41, 80
Siena College, 85, 101, 121
Smith, Coby, 119
Smith, Lillian, 50, 51, 110–11
Smith, Maxine, 13, 14, 16, 19, 69, 74, 118–19, 132, 138
Sonnenburg, Barbara, 138
Southern Christian Leadership Conference (SCLC), 4, 28, 30, 57, 72, 78, 95, 112, 113
Southern Conference Educational Fund (SCEF), 51, 112
Southern Conference for Human Welfare, 31, 111, 112
Southern Regional Council on Race Relations, 111
Southern Student Organizing Committee (SSOC), 59, 75–79, 116, 155
Southwestern College, 16, 17, 59, 65, 69, 75, 77, 79, 81, 82, 93, 97, 125

Spelman College, 52
"Spread the Misery" Campaign, 99–100
Student Nonviolent Coordinating Committee (SNCC), 28, 30, 52, 77, 78, 79, 106, 111, 113, 115, 116, 152
Students for a Democratic Society, 78
Sugarmon, Laurie, 16
Sullivan, Judith, 6, 20, 21, 22, 23, 140–41
Swanson, Gregory, 118

Temple Israel, 61, 62
Temple Israel Sisterhood, 61–62
Tennessee Fair Employment Practices Commission (TFEPC), 122
Tennessee Human Relations Committee, 108, 145
Thrasher, Sue, 78, 79
Tobey, Mayor Frank, 12
Tolleson, Mary Kay, 19, 118
Tri-State Defender, 27, 69
Tufts, Rutledge, 75

Unitarian Church, 46, 52–53, 84
Unitarian Fellowship, 52
United Black Coalition (UBC), 132–33
United Council of Church Women, 53–54. *See also* Church Women United
University of Memphis, 91, 95. *See also* Memphis State University
Urban League, 137, 146

Valiant, Margaret, 12, 19, 23, 24–27, 52, 68, 119–20, 151
Varnell, Jeanne, 9, 93–94, 120, 123, 126, 146

Wade, Andrew, 113
Walker, Robert, 3, 72
Watkins, Juanita, 138–40
WDIA, 61
Williamson, Juanita, 26
Willis, Ann, 19
Wisconsin Elementary School, 61

Wolf River Society, 19, 23
Wolff, Bert, 92–93, 136–38, 149–50
Women of Achievement, 148
Women of the Church, 114–15
Women's Council of the Commission on Interracial Cooperation, 84
Women's International League for Peace and Freedom, 31
Women's Resource Center, 147
Worsley, Dale, 77
Wurzburg, Jocelyn Maurie Dan, 6, 81–82, 92, 94, 97, 99, 100, 122, 129, 142–43, 145–46, 147

Yates, Gayle Graham, 59–60
Yellin, Carol Lynn, 6, 95, 124
Yellin, David, 95
Young Women's Christian Association (YWCA), 13, 58, 60, 62, 104, 111, 123, 146, 147

www.ingramcontent.com/pod-product-compliance
Lightning Source LLC
Chambersburg PA
CBHW030621230426
43661CB00053B/2098